English as a lingua franca in business negotiations

AF879373

Mehrsprachigkeit/Multilingualism

edited by
Wilhelm Grießhaber
and Jochen Rehbein

Volume 57

Bettina Dresemann

English as a lingua franca in business negotiations

Waxmann 2024
Münster • New York

Bibliographic information published by the Deutsche Nationalbibliothek
The Deutsche Nationalbibliothek lists this publication in the Deutsche Nationalbibliografie; detailed bibliographic data are available in the Internet at http://dnb.dnb.de

Mehrsprachigkeit/Multilingualism, Volume 57

ISSN 1433-0792
Print-ISBN 978-3-8309-4829-2
E-Book-ISBN 978-3-8309-9829-7

© Waxmann Verlag GmbH, 2024
Münster, Germany

www.waxmann.com
info@waxmann.com

Cover Design: Pleßmann Design, Ascheberg
Cover Picture: Ivika Rehbein-Ots
Typesetting: MTS. Satz & Layout, Münster
Print: CPI Books GmbH, Leck

Printed on age-resistant paper, acid-free according to ISO 9706

This book was produced climate-neutrally

MIX
Papier aus verantwortungsvollen Quellen
FSC www.fsc.org FSC® C083411

Klimaschutz-Beitrag
First Climate.com 2024
CO2-Zertifikate

Printed in Germany

All rights reserved. No part of this publication may be reproduced, stored in a retrieval system or transmitted in any form or by any means, electronic, electrostatic, magnetic tape, mechanical, photocopying, recording or otherwise without permission in writing from the copyright holder.

Für Mom und Dad,
Elena und Alexander

Acknowledgements

This dissertation was made possible through the support of various people who offered their help, advice and many motivating words and gestures; most of all through the Language Center (Sprachenzentrum) of the University of Muenster, where it all began and where I spent many happy years studying, learning, teaching and researching. I thank all my colleagues, friends, professors, teachers and co-workers for supporting and encouraging me and for the many joyful moments.

Thank you.

Additionally, I would like to give special thanks to Juliane House, Karlfried Knapp, Christiane Meierkord, Jan ten Thije and Jochen Rehbein for their professional support and encouragement.

Muchas gracias.

Furthermore, I thank Professor Ulrike Gut for taking on the report of this dissertation at short notice and for the motivation and support she offered during those last months.

From the bottom of my heart, I would like to thank Professor Wilhelm Grießhaber, who offered me the chance to do this project and who supported, encouraged and motivated me throughout all these years.

Muito obrigada.

My very special thanks go to my family: My husband Stefan, who is always there for me and who offers me the world; my sister Coco, who supports us in so many ways; my children, Elena and Alexander, who take on the world with me and show me what it means to make a language your own; and my parents, Angelika und Ludwig, who made this all possible.

Danke.

Summary

English has become the most widely used language of international business communication. This dissertation contributes to the description and research of the different forms English takes in different contexts, precisely in oral language use in English as a lingua franca using authentic data from business negotiations. It shows that some of the conditionals that may appear as errors on the surface level really fulfil a communicative function indicating the speaker's commitment to the proposition of the sentence.

In the first part, this dissertation describes structural features of English as a lingua franca, while in the second part, the focus is on the pragmatic function of different forms of conditionals.

In the corpus for this project, on the one hand, forms of English as a lingua franca are used that can be found in other types of discourse as well. On the other hand, speakers also use forms that are not required and therefore not used in other contexts such as different forms of conditionals. However, these forms, especially the conditional sentences in the corpus, are not random, but fulfil communicative functions.

The special focus in the main part of the project is on the diversity of conditional sentences in the corpus. While some conditionals used in the corpus are standard forms, others differ from standard English usage. As the analyses in the dissertation show, different conditionals are used to linguistically mark different degrees of commitment and to differentiate between the realisation of speech acts such as promises and the sheer discussion of different options in a negotiation. And some forms of conditionals are used to avoid commissives such as promises by suspending the illocutionary force of an utterance. This function seems to be characteristic of business negotiations and varies in different discourse phases.

The dissertation project tries to prove that speakers in business negotiations will avoid commissives in order not to come under any legal obligation as long as they are not willing to commit to an aspect of the negotiation and choose linguistic forms such as standard and non-standard conditionals that mark an utterance as a proposal or question rather than a promise. The different conditionals are used to indicate different degrees of commitment.

Contents

1. Introduction

1.1 Scope and overview

In an increasingly globalised world, English has become the most widely used language of communication and serves as the world's first truly global language (cf. Crystal 2003). It has become the most frequently used *lingua franca* (McArthur 2003:1–16), a language that enables communication between speakers of different (first) languages. It is used not only in entertainment, science, education or travel but in many internationally operating businesses, e.g. in negotiations (cf. e.g. Ehrenreich 2010). In general, "global business speaks English" (Neeley 2012). And although communication problems do occur (e.g. House 2002, Firth 1996, Klimpfinger 2007), English is used worldwide as the number one language of business communication.

This dissertation aims to contribute to the study of English as a lingua franca in these settings, precisely in business negotiations. The focus will be on the pragmatic function of grammatical forms of English, such as conditionals, in business negotiations. It reflects a paradigm shift in linguistics: While in former times, English was primarily studied in contexts that were dominated by so-called *native speakers* (NSS), i.e. by speakers who use English as their first language, it is increasingly studied in contexts with speakers from different language backgrounds and proficiency levels. Thus, the study of English in international contexts has gained more attention in the past decades.

Lingua franca is a term that has been in use for centuries, although with different meanings (cf. chapter 3). Halliday et al., for example, used it in the 1960s (Halliday et al. 1964:80). However, the term became popular in the 1990s when research into the actual forms of language use increased. It describes a common phenomenon of human society: the use of a language that is not the first language of its users but enables communication between human beings from different groups. In the past decades, the term and phenomenon experienced a renaissance and have undergone changes in meaning (cf. chapter 3).

Linguistic studies, in general, aim to create an understanding of how communication works. However, the contexts and constellations in lingua franca English studies vary more than in most other research contexts. Aspects like the communicative goals of speakers, their attitude towards the language and their mastery of the language influence language use. These aspects vary to a great degree across lingua franca English settings. Additionally, lingua franca studies aim to help comprehend how understanding is achieved – in the ideal case – between speakers with different levels of proficiency. This dissertation contributes to the description and research of the different forms English takes in different contexts, precisely in business negotiations. It then tries to relate the forms to a communicative function, in this case the differentiation between the realisation of speech acts such as promises and the sheer discussion of different options.

The question as to what makes English so attractive – and successful – for international communication cannot be answered in a small project like this. However, this dissertation project aims to contribute to the on-going description of English in its different usages. The focus is to see if there are features of English in business contexts that are different to the use of English in other contexts. In this thesis, I will therefore focus on analysing linguistic means that speakers use, precisely conditionals, to fulfil communicative functions in business negotiations.

Business negotiations are a form of discourse defined by non-linguistic goals as well as interactive and mental processes (Grießhaber 2000). Its function is different from many other forms of discourse. Language in business negotiations is a language for specific purposes. What makes language use in business contexts stand out are the decision-making processes for which speakers and hearers, i. e. buyers and sellers, for example, need to interact (cf. Grießhaber 2000). These processes shape the use of language in (business) negotiations. Therefore, the question is which language means speakers apply in business negotiations that are different from other lingua franca settings.

I will present the hypothesis that speakers in lingua franca English business negotiations, on the one hand, use forms that can be found in other types of discourse. On the other hand, they will also use forms that are not required and therefore not used in other contexts. Thus, the focus of this dissertation is the analysis of linguistic structures and their functions in English as a lingua franca business negotiations.

In order to see how lingua franca English actually works in business negotiations, I recorded business encounters at an international music trade fair, which turned out to be negotiations of potential or actual cooperations (cf. chapter 7.2).

Conditional sentences turned out to be the decisive linguistic means in my data, the BusinessELF corpus (cf. chapter 7.2). The high number and the diversity of conditional sentences (cf. chapter 9) indicates their relevance. While some conditionals are what might be called 'standard' forms, i. e. educated forms that are used in formal and written language use, others differ from standard English usage. So, in this dissertation project, a special focus will be on the use of the different conditionals in the different phases of business negotiations. The main research questions are if there is a regularity to their use and what functions different forms of conditionals have in lingua franca English business negotiations. For the analysis, I will use a corpus analysis and a qualitative-interpretative approach, i.e. Functional Pragmatics (Ehlich/Rehbein 1972, Grießhaber 2001). I will show that different conditionals are used to indicate different degrees of commitment. Some forms are used to avoid commissives such as promises. This function seems to be characteristic of business negotiations. Speakers make use of these forms to avoid coming under any (legal) obligation as long as they are not ready to commit to the deal 'on the table' (cf. chapter 10).

Former research into *English as a lingua franca (ELF)* or *lingua franca English (LFE)* – which will be used as equivalents in this dissertation – primarily focused on the forms of language and the speakers' (cooperative) behaviour. The aim, in the majority of studies, was to describe how linguistic gaps were overcome and how speakers made communication work despite linguistic difficulties. As a result, lingua franca communication was said to be successful despite deviations.

One of the problems in LFE analysis, however, is often the point of reference. It is often so-called *Standard English*, a debatable notion referring to "the variety of English used as a communicative norm throughout the English-speaking world" (Crystal 2003:431). Despite efforts to emancipate LFE from those native speaker norms (e.g. Seidlhofer 2005; Pölzl/Seidlhofer 2006), the point of reference remains a specific variety of English. It usually was – explicitly or implicitly – and still is the form of English used in the so-called 'inner circle' (Kachru 1985, 1989). The Inner Circle are countries where English is used as the first language by the majority of inhabitants (cf. definition in chapter 3).

Furthermore, most data for research into ELF was recorded in social or academic settings. Communicative success was usually not measured or defined; communication was deemed successful based on the conversation continuing. In high-stakes encounters like business negotiations, however, communication is goal-driven. So the function of a discourse is defined by a non-linguistic aim. The aim can be, for example, to negotiate conditions for contracts or other agreements. Communication in business also needs to be efficient, i.e. it has to be carried out with limited resources such as time. So communicative success needs to be defined by achieving goals within a time frame. Most importantly, communication has to be effective. Negotiators need certainty about the agreement, e.g. the appointment or contract, they have reached. Misunderstandings or vagueness, which might be acceptable in most other contexts, are unacceptable in business negotiations because clarity is paramount when it comes to obligations arising from agreements. So, one crucial function of communication in business encounters such as negotiations is to avoid misunderstandings. Therefore, this dissertation aims to show how misunderstandings are avoided in business negotiations in LFE and communicative means, such as conditionals, are used to avoid misunderstandings and express the speaker's communicative intention.

Most researchers observe that lingua franca communication is less problematic than expected (cf. chapter 4.2). However, sometimes communicative problems do occur yet are not addressed directly. House (1999), for example, found a lack of mutual orientation in lingua franca interactions. She showed that in some ELF interactions, "hearers are not treated as true co-participants. In turn, they often patently do not act as recipients, but only as initiators" (House 1999:82). So, what appears to be communication sometimes is only interaction, and participants do not really exchange ideas or create shared knowledge.

Firth (1996), too, showed that communicative problems such as misunderstandings do occur but are not made explicit until they become problematic. This often happens later in the discourse. So, communication in ELF can be more problematic in high stakes encounters than generally admitted. However, lingua franca communication is a widespread phenomenon. Thus, the question is how speakers reach an understanding and – ideally – agreement if language use is problematic or goals divert.

Therefore, in this dissertation, I will investigate how lingua franca speakers use linguistic forms such as conditionals to facilitate communication and avoid misunderstandings. Whether or not these are merely strategic or used due to a lack of other communicative means might need to be discussed in further studies. However, it will not be in the scope of this dissertation.

It is also not the aim of this dissertation to determine whether linguistic features exist that justify defining the forms of language used in these specific contexts as a variety in its own right. I will also not consider other specific forms of LFE such as *Seaspeak* or *Aviation English*. Both are, by definition, forms of ELF and languages for specific purposes. However, they are different from other forms of professional language uses. They have a defined area of usage and strict regulations that make their use way more restricted – even though no less problematic (cf. Intemann 2005).

I will instead contribute to the research of how speakers of English shape the language. I will show how they vary linguistic forms such as conditionals to ensure understanding. I will approach the question in two steps: First, I will compare linguistic forms in my data, the BusinessELF corpus, to former studies. Then I will analyse the use of conditionals. I will show that the conditionals in the recorded data have different forms. Since these forms differ across the phases of discourse, I will match the different forms with the functions in the different phases of discourse. Then I will discuss the underlying communicative intentions of different forms of conditionals in different phases of the negotiation.

1.2 Research aim

In this dissertation project, I analyse ELF from an applied linguistic perspective. The aim is to see which linguistic forms are used in oral (business) communication. In oral communication, tools like dictionaries or apps that help facilitate communication are usually not available. Yet, the pressure on participants is higher than in written language use because it is a face-to-face situation.

In general, some of the features of oral language use can be found in the BusinessELF corpus, e. g. interrupted or incomplete utterances, mixing of forms, change of plans, hesitations and pauses, self-corrections. However, they are not necessarily typical features of LFE use, but more of oral communication. They will therefore not be discussed unless they give insight into communicative or mental processes that enable understanding.

Achieving understanding is a crucial aspect of all communication. It is especially important in professional lingua franca communication. Not only because business and economic goals are at stake, but because speakers and hearers bring different language backgrounds to the situation. So they need more linguistic work to convey their communicative intention and ensure understanding.

In business negotiation, which is guided by non-linguistic goals, understanding is paramount and resources are scarce. Together with potential legal consequences, the limited resources create the need for efficiency and precision. And since these factors determine the communicative intentions, the question is how far business communication equals lingua franca communication in other contexts. The further question is what forms of language might indicate a difference to these contexts.

In order to define differences and similarities, I need to establish that the recorded data qualifies as 'typical' LFE. I will show that linguistic forms and the communicative behaviour that have been described as LFE features can be found in the BusinessELF corpus. First, I will compare the data for this dissertation project to research findings on a structural level. Then I will describe language forms that stand out in my data, especially forms of conditionals. I will relate them to the form of discourse and explain their communicative function on this basis because it is the type of discourse that determines the communicative function.

One of the characteristics of business discourse is that decisions are taken during the discourse (cf. Grießhaber 2000). These decisions are based on shared knowledge that participants interactively create during the discourse. Participants, therefore, need to rely on their understanding of the on-going discourse. So, the pressure on participants to communicate successfully is higher than in many other contexts. This makes communication in business negotiations a valuable source for linguistic studies. However, linguistic data of business negotiations is hard to come by (cf. Ehlich/Wagner 1995:2). Few businesses allow for their negotiation processes to be observed or even recorded.

In business negotiations, participants need to ensure they receive the required information. At the same time, they need to avoid misunderstandings concerning their communicative intention. On the discourse level, they need to communicate if they are exchanging information or completing other actions such as making or accepting offers. Accepting offers is a form of a *commissive*, i. e. a speech act. Speech acts are utterances by which speakers change an aspect of the world (Austin 1962).

According to Austin (1962), a speech act consists of the *proposition*, i. e. the part that is 'said' or 'uttered', and what he calls the 'illocutionary force'. The illocutionary force is what has an influence on the 'world'. It changes the situation outside the communicative situation. Through the 'illocutionary force' of an utterance, speakers can come under the obligation, e. g. to make what they have uttered true, e. g. by fulfilling a promise. In the case of commissives such as promises, speakers come under the obligation to fulfil a future action. In the case of business negotiations, they come under the obligation e. g. to sell or buy a commodity or perform an action that is part of a business deal (cf. chapter 5.4). This could be paying money for goods or services or providing goods, services or rights. Therefore, it is vital for speakers in business negotiations to mark their communicative intention. They need to indicate, e. g. if they want a certain utterances to be seen as binding or unbinding. So, the second research question is how participants in a lingua franca business negotiation mark the communicative functions of their utterances. I will analyse how they linguistically mark commissives and non-commissives and how they can be told apart. The hypotheses (cf. chapter 6.2), therefore, are that

- speakers in business negotiations will avoid commissives in order not to come under any legal obligation as long as they are not willing to commit to an aspect of the negotiation
- speakers choose linguistic forms that mark an utterance as a proposal, question, comment etc. rather than a promise
- different conditionals as well as matrix-constructions or neutral pronouns etc. are used to indicate different degrees of commitment and therefore fulfil a communicative function.

1.3 Method

In order to discuss the different functions and prove the hypotheses, I recorded business negotiations between representatives of record companies and record distribution companies from different European countries at an international music trade fair. I recorded three business negotiations (cf. chapter 7.2), transcribed them in a relation of approximately 1:20 using the conventions of HIAT (Halbinterpreative Arbeitstranskription (Ehlich/Rehbein 1976)). The transcripts were then transferred into an utterance list with the help of BBedit® and then into a Microsoft Word® document.

In the first part of the analysis, I will compare my language data, the Business-ELF corpus, to other research results (chapter 4) from a structural point of view (chapter 8). I will use the same descriptive categories that were used by other researchers to facilitate comparisons. I will show to what extent my data have the same linguistic features as the data used for other LFE studies.

I will then add a comparison of the quantitative use of some verbs based on Seidlhofer's (2004:38) finding of an "intensive use of semantically wide, general verbs" in ELF. I used a log-likelihood comparison of verbs in the BusinessELF corpus with the spoken part of the British National Corpus (BNC). I will show that not only the 'general verbs' (Seidlhofer 2004) are 'overused' in comparison to the BNC, but also some of the specific verbs. I will discuss if it is the context in which the data were gained that influenced their use. I will also compare the communicative behaviour of participants in the BusinessELF corpus to the existing literature. I will show that many of the aspects that were defined as LFE are also used in the BusinessELF corpus. This indicates that the way English is used in the BusinessELF corpus qualifies as LFE.

In the second part of my analysis, I will focus on different forms of conditionals in the corpus. I will first analyse them on a grammatical-descriptive level and provide a quantitative analysis of the forms of usage (cf. chapter 9). Then I will offer a qualitative-interpretative analysis of conditionals in different phases of discourse. I will use the approach of Functional Pragmatics (Ehlich/Rehbein 1972, Grießhaber 2001) to do so (chapter 10).

Functional Pragmatics is a qualitative-analytical approach to discourse analysis that is based on the works of John L. Austin and Karl Bühler. Austin (1962) sees language as a means to perform 'actions'. And the organon model by Bühler (1934) describes the function of language as threefold: It can be a *representation*, an *expression* or an *appeal*. So speakers, according to the model, use language to either represent the world, to express a feeling or attitude or to influence the hearer. Based on these three functions of utterances, Functional Pragmatics analyses language in institutionalised contexts as actions and mental processes that people ('actants') use to solve societal problems.

I will analyse speakers' intentions and the communicative effects with the help Functional Pragmatics and Austin's definition of speech acts. And I will show how far the use of certain language forms such as conditionals, even if their form is not in line with 'grammars', is intentional. I will discuss to what extent speakers choose these forms to indicate their intention, such as representing rather than promising the content of their utterance. I will argue that so-called 'deviant' forms of conditionals, such as the use of *would* in the protasis, fulfil a communicative function (chapter 10, 11).

Even though I use Functional Pragmatics for the analysis, the focus of my analysis will not be on patterns of action (e.g. Ehlich/Rehbein 1972). It will rather be on the mental actions of the speakers and on the linguistic functions like the avoidance of speech acts such as commissives.

The analysis in chapter 10 will show to what extent speakers commit to these speech acts or use forms such as conditionals to 'suspend' the illocutionary force (Ehlich 1979). I will show that speakers use conditionals in the negotiation, i.e. the discussion of a business cooperation, to utter the *proposition* (the 'content' of the utterance) that they want to discuss, but not the *illocution*, i.e. the force which would oblige them to future deeds if the promises were uttered as such. I will show that speakers create the effect with the help of certain verb forms and forms of conditional sentences.

I will show that the linguistic behaviour differs in different phases of discourse depending on what is at stake and will relate conditionals to the use in the phases of discourse (chapter 10).

1.4 Data

For this dissertation project, I recorded business meetings at an international music trade fair. Since business representatives from many different countries met, the main working language was English. In the recordings, speakers from three different national and linguistic backgrounds, i.e. French, Norwegian and German, meet. They discuss business cooperations for the distribution of musical productions. They all use English as their medium of communication in this particular context. However, it is not the first language (L1) of any one of them. So the constellations constitute a lingua franca situation par excellence.

The three encounters I transcribed and analysed were business negotiations of two different kinds: They all involve a German label manager who discussed forms of cooperation with a Norwegian distribution manager in two recordings.

In the third recording, the same label manager discusses a potential business cooperation with the Head of Distribution of a French record company. The French representative offered him her products for distribution in Germany. However, he did not accept the offer, and no contract was formed. The encounter with the Norwegian manager was interrupted and continued the following date, hence the two recordings. With the Norwegian company, a contract had been established beforehand, but the two representatives needed to negotiate the details of the cooperation. For example, they needed to work out which products to sell in Germany, when to publish them, how to organise for transport etc.

In all of the recordings, speakers use ELF and discuss details of a potential (in case of the French record company) and actual (in case of the Norwegian record company) cooperation. The recordings were mostly in English. The exception is two passages of discourse that were carried out in German. A co-worker of the German distribution manager joined the encounter, and although the Norwegian speaker did not speak German, the German co-worker used German for side-discourses with his German colleague. So the Norwegian speaker used receptive multilingualism, i.e. a "language constellation in which interlocutors use their respective mother tongue while speaking to each other" (Zeevaert/ten Thije 2007:3). Details and research results of the German part of the encounter were published elsewhere (Dresemann 2007).

1.5 Analysis and treatment of examples, excerpts and names

The actual corpus used for the dissertation is called *BusinessELF;* it contains recordings with four active speakers. Participants in the study will either be referred to by their function, e.g. 'distribution manager' or, in the discussion of their contributions discussed in the text, by their abbreviation. The abbreviation contains an "S" for 'speaker', a number by which they are ordered, the letter "f" or "m" for "female" or "male"[1], and a two letters indicating their first language. So "S2fFr", for example, stands for "Speaker 2, female, French".

In the running text, they are also referred to as 'speaker' and 'hearer', based on the classification of actants in Functional Pragmatics. When writing about the person, I will use their natural sex. All other general nouns are gender-neutral. Tables and graphs in the text are numerically ordered and will be referred to by their number in the order of usage.

Different forms of linguistic behaviour will be discussed using different forms of citing examples. Examples can be cited as a single utterance or a sequence of connected utterances. In the first part of the analysis, examples and excerpts will

1 None of the speakers identified as non-binary.

be quoted as segments *(se)* plus their number from the utterance list, e.g. se (13). So the numbers indicate the actual sequence of appearance in the respective recording.

In the second part of the analysis, conditional sentences will be discussed. These conditional sentences were taken from utterances and listed in Table 6. I split the conditional sentences into their two syntactical parts: the subordinate clause with the condition, i.e. the *protasis*, and the main clause, the *apodosis*, with the situation appearing as the consequence of the condition. Then I put them into the order *protasis – apodosis*. It is the order used in classification in grammars. Table 6 is the central list of examples for references in chapters 9 and 10 and offers an overview of all conditional sentences used in the corpus. Conditionals are ordered and classified in categories C1 to C5, depending on the combination of tenses in the corpus (cf. chapter 9).

Table 6 uses continuous numbering for conditionals according to the category to which they are ascribed. As opposed to the numbers of the utterances, which indicate the chronological order of their appearance in the recording, conditional numbers are sorted by categories, i.e. by the sequence of tenses. Each conditional sentence is given a number by which it is cited in the remains of the thesis.

In the last column in Table 6, the source is given, i.e. the reference to the recording. The 'source' gives the abbreviation of the respective recording. It contains the 'name' of the recording, i.e. the title I gave to each recording based on its main topic: DIS for *Distribution agreement*, MARK for *Marketingcooperation*, and BACK for *Backcatalogue*. After that, the speaker's abbreviation is given (e.g. S1mGr = Speaker + Number (1) + sex (male) + first language (German)) and finally the number of the segment in the list of utterances (1084) for cross-references.

In cases where the single utterance is sufficient, I will use the line from Table 6 as in the example below:

12	if Portugal releases it three months after us	that's fine with me	BACK S1mGr 1084

I will then discuss the forms of the predicates in the subordinate clause, i.e. the *protasis*, and in main clause, i.e. the *apodosis*, and their function.

For discussions of the communicative effect, I will use longer excerpts from the utterance list. These excerpts show the segment number in the first column, i.e. the utterance in its chronological position in the list of utterances. The second column shows the abbreviation of the speaker, and the third column quotes the utterance. In HIAT (Ehlich/Rehbein 1976), utterances usually equal a sentence, augment or sometimes single sound. Pauses are seen as part of the following utterance and are given at the beginning of the following utterance and are thus ascribed to the next speaker.

The example below was taken from the recording *Marketingcooperation* (MARK) and encompasses segments (522) to (525). Examples are labeled by the decisive term or topic, given in italics, and the abbreviation of the recording, indicated in capital letters in brackets. Before the excerpt below, the second speaker, S2fFr, offered S1mGr first a record label her company owns for distribution in Germany, which he declined. Her second offer was the rights to distribute musical publications, referred to as *titles,* from her range of products. In the following excerpt, the first speaker, S1mGr, raises the issue of competition. The numbers in the first column indicate the number of the utterance in the utterance list:

(522)	S1mGr	I mean, the thing is if, if we only take certain titles, then it probably would make sense for you to deal with other territories.
(523)	S1mGr	((1s)) Uh, not territories, with other companies in Germany.
(524)	S1mGr	Maybe they think uhm • that other titles could do ((1s)) good as well.
(525)	S1mGr	Know what I mean?

Example: Potential competition (MARK)

S1mGr points out the issue of her potentially doing business with other distribution companies in Germany, i. e. with his competitors. He points out that if his company only distributes some of the records (*titles*), other German companies might want to distribute the same records in Germany (se (522)). He says 'territories', and se (523) is a self-correction of the term *territories* into *countries.* In se (524), he elaborates his concerns. He explains that 'other companies in Germany' (*they;* se (523)), assume potential for the products. He expresses that as *they think [...] other titles could do good as well.* In se (525) he asks the hearer, S2fFr, a question about her understanding. The question is a request for her to communicate if she sees the problem. So he is checking if they both have the same understanding of the situation. She shares his view of the issue. It is one of the examples where the joint creation of discourse knowledge becomes explicit.

1.6 Structure of the dissertation

English has numerous domains of use. They have made the phenomenon of ELF rather complex. In order to set the frame for the dissertation project, chapter 2 provides an overview of the relevant terms that are used when discussing domains of English usage and their different political and linguistic notions such *World English, International English* etc. I will give a short overview and explain similarities, differences and accordances between different terms. Chapter 3 gives an overview of the definitions of the term *lingua franca,* its (assumed) origin and how its meaning has changed over time. It also discusses the differences between *English as a lingua franca* (ELF) and *English as a Foreign Language* (EFL), as well as between *Second Language Acquisition* (SLA) and *Second Language Use* (SLU). I will use these differences as a basis to define the term *lingua franca English* (LFE) in this dissertation.

In chapter 4, I will summarise findings from the field of LFE. I sorted the results by descriptive linguistic categories and by pragmatic aspects reflecting the different foci of research. Chapter 5 gives definitions of the term *business negotiation* as well as *contract. Business negotiation* is the central concept which influences the situation in question. So is *contract.* Both define the situation and its potential outcome and thereby influence the linguistic behaviour of negotiators. On the basis of this definition, I will explain why *commissives,* i.e. speech acts such as promises, – or rather their avoidance – play an important role in business negotiations. These definitions will form the basis for differentiating between LFE encounters in general and LFE business negotiations. It further explains the use of Functional Pragmatics for the qualitative-interpretative analysis of the communicative function of conditionals in business negotiation in chapters 9 and 10.

Chapter 6 defines the research aims and the hypotheses, while the method used for my dissertation is given in chapter 7, and classifies the data, i.e. mainly the roles fo the participants. Chapter 8 gives an overview of the structural aspects of the data found in the corpus. It shows the comparison of categories such as *lexicon, grammar* etc. to other research findings. In order to allow for a comparison of the BusinessELF data to other research findings, it uses the same categories as chapter 4. I will show that most of the features described in the literature can be found in the BusinessELF corpus too, and thereby prove that the language use in the corpus of this dissertation project can be considered 'typical' of LFE in most aspects.

Chapter 9 and 10 focus on conditional sentences. Conditionals are a language aspect that fulfils an important function in LFE in business negotiations in that it enables the marking of different discourse functions. In chapter 9, I define the term *conditional,* compare it to other moods and explain its function in English. I give a short overview of the forms of conditionals in English. Then I compare the forms of conditionals in the BusinessELFcorpus and the different categories and explain similarities and differences to the inner circle use of conditionals. In chapter 10, I explain the use of these categories and their reference to time, likelihood and attitude and their function in different discourse phases. In chapter 11,

I summarise the results and discuss some potential explanations or criticism of the results before the concluding remarks and an outlook in chapter 12.

2. Englishes in different contexts: Definitions, distribution, distinctions

The term *lingua franca* has a long history, which has led to different uses in the past as well as today. It was, for example, used with reference to different languages or varieties. Today, it still lacks agreement and thus refers to different speaking situations. Similarly, different terms are used when talking about English in its different international uses. In order to define the use of the terms *lingua franca English (LFE)* and *English as a lingua franca (ELF)* in this thesis and to differentiate between different phenomena in the context of English in its international use, I will first give an overview of the terms used to refer to English in different international contexts and then define the origin and history of the term *lingua franca* and its meaning(s) today. It is sometimes used in a similar function, sometimes in contrast to terms like *World English* or *World Englishes, English as a global language, English as an international language, English as a world language* and *Euro English* (see below). Other, less politically motivated labels, are e.g. *English as a medium of intercultural communication* (Meierkord 1996) or *English as an international and international language* (Smith 1983). These notions are quite clear in their reference and will not be discussed further.

2.1 English as an international language (EIL)

One notion closely linked to LFE is *English as an international language* (EIL). It can have different meanings: In the more restricted sense, it refers to the use of English in international contexts and can be used as an equivalent to *LFE* or *ELF* (cf. chapter 3). In the second sense it is restricted to the use of English in countries where English has an official status, i.e. the inner and outer circle countries (Kachru 1989; see 2.2 below). In the second sense, it is used, e.g., for the ICE (International Corpus of English), a collection of data "for comparative studies of English worldwide" (ICE homepage; http://ice-corpora.net/ice/index.html). Thus *international English* in this sense excludes countries where English is used but does not have an official status (cf. Greenbaum/Nelson 1996; cf. also Seidlhofer 2004).

In the broadest sense of EIL, English is used either for communication with and among speakers from outer or expanding circle countries – second or foreign language speakers – or even among first language speakers, e.g. Americans or Australians communicating with Britons. These international encounters can bear linguistic problems, although theoretically the interlocutors use the same language (cf. McArthur 1992:605). These speakers, it is assumed in Teaching English as an International Language (TEIL), need to prepare for intercultural communication because

> [they] are also seen as needing help in cross-national and cross-cultural communication rather than as representing the norm at which non-natives should aim. It is assumed in TEIL that English belongs to all of its users (whether in its standard or any other form), and that ways of speaking and patterns of discourse are different across nations (McArthur 1992:605).

In this sense, EIL is not a specific form or variety of English, but a mode of usage between speakers of different languages. In this mode, the broadest interpretation of EIL, almost all constellations of speakers and forms of usage are included (cf. McArthur 1992).

In the stricter interpretation, as e.g. in Greenbaum/Nelson's (1996) definition, expanding circle uses are excluded. In this sense, EIL is in complementary distribution with ELF (Seidlhofer 2004:210): It covers the use between speakers who use it as a first or second language (inner and outer circle countries). ELF, on the other hand, in its conservative interpretation, refers to the use of English among speakers from the expanding circle (Kachru 1989; see below). And although the term *EIL* is quite frequently used in applied linguistics, scholars do not agree on its definition.

To complicate the matter even further, some scholars assume that EIL refers to the same as WS(S)E (=World Standard (Spoken) English) (Jenkins 2006:160), which is not the case. WSSE refers to a standardised form for (oral) international communication some scholars see arising (e.g. Crystal 1997). However, scholars working with empirical data for a great part deny the development of such a monolithic form of English for international communication (e.g. Jenkins 2006).

Although both terms, ELF (or LFE) and EIL, are sometimes applied for the same situations, EIL can be used as a kind of superordinate term including native speakers, while ELF or LFE are mostly used as the more specific term for communication in English among speakers from the outer and expanding circle, aka second and foreign language speakers (cf. Seidlhofer 2004, House 2002, Jenkins 2003; 2006). Some of these notions also come up in the differentiation between *World English* and *World Englishes*, two other labels that are used in this context.

2.2 World English and World Englishes

The terms *World English* and *World Englishes* look like the singular and plural forms of the same lexeme, but have different meanings.

The singular form, *World English,* is used to describe English for international communication. For some scholars, it is characterised by linguistic change resulting from the globalisation process (cf. Brutt-Griffler 2002). Some assume that one international standard form of English is developing out of American Standard English and British Standard English. They regard this form as the solution to communication problems in global communication through a learned, intelligible variety. So does e. g. Crystal (1995; 1997), who labels the variety *global English* or *World English*. Other scholars try to avoid the term for reasons of cautiousness because "for them it suggests global dominance by English and English-speaking countries" (McArthur 2002:660).

The plural form *World Englishes* is used more frequently although not with a clear-cut reference either. The term itself was only established in the 1980s to describe different varieties of English that were and are developing in some countries outside Great Britain or the United States, especially in the former British territories.

A well-known model to describe the different functions of English is Kachru's model of the three concentric circles (Kachru 1985; 1989):

> The INNER CIRCLE refers to the traditional cultural and linguistic bases of English. The OUTER CIRCLE represents the institutionalized non-native varieties (ESL) in the regions which have passed through extended periods of colonization. [...] The EXPANDING CIRCLE includes regions where the performance varieties of the language are used essentially in EFL contexts (i.e. varieties that do not have official status and are typically restricted in their uses) (Kachru 1989:87).

Kachru's division, even in the extended version (Kachru 1985), can only be rough. However, it is frequently used in the field of World Englishes and LFE to illustrate the main functions of English today. Svartvik/Leech (2006), for example, use it to sum up the debate and to define ELF as follows:

> When linguists these days talk about English as a lingua franca (or ELF for short) they are typically focusing on the use of English as an intermediary between people with different native languages, none of them English. The claim is that this type of English is developing its own systematic codes of usage, independent of the Inner Circle countries whose norms of usage have been so far regarded as the target for non-native speakers (Svartvik/Leech 2006:234).

Although other models are used these days in the study of New Englishes – e. g. Schneider's (2007) *Dynamic Model,* Mair's (2013) *World System of Standard and*

Non-standard Englishes – Kachru's model serves as a classification in this thesis because linguistic developments of Englishes within Europe are by far not as fertile and diverse as in World Englishes, e.g. in the African Englishes (cf. Meierkord 2019).

Although the discussion of the status of these new varieties has been going on for more than three decades, no consensus has been reached about their linguistic, social and political status. It is not even accepted by all scholars in applied linguistics (cf. Jenkins 2006). So this quite young term – compared to most terminology in linguistics – lacks an agreed definition. Bolton (2004), e.g., lists three interpretations of *World Englishes* (cf. also Jenkins 2006):

- all varieties of English worldwide plus the different approaches used to describe and analyse them
- the so-called new Englishes in Africa, Asia, and the Caribbean (Kachru's Outer Circle)
- the pluricentric approach to the study of English associated with Kachru and others.

So here is – so far – no clear-cut distinction between *World English* or *World Englishes* and *international English* or *ELF*. Kachru (1996), for example, uses the terms *lingua franca* and *world Englishes* interchangeably in his article "English as a lingua franca" (Kachru 1996), in which he actually focuses on institutionalised varieties in the outer circle. He defines the new meaning of lingua franca by using the example of English in two different functions: "English continues to be referred to as a lingua franca of a particular country (e.g. India, Nigeria), or as an international lingua franca" (Kachru 1996:907). By that he points to the problem that English is not only used in international communication but also in multilingual countries where inhabitants do not share the indigenous languages.

Until recently, most linguists have argued from a Western or European perspective and regarded monolingualism as a rather typical condition. In many European countries, the national language is at the same time the first language (L1) of the majority of the inhabitants. However, in numerous countries the situation is quite different, and inhabitants do not necessarily share a language. Thus a solution had to be found, and in many cases, English was taken on as a means of communication not only with people from 'outside', but also 'inside' a national community. Thus it serves as an international as well as a national lingua franca. These communities developed a form of English adapted to their own needs, which leads to a phenomenon labelled "interactions across Englishes" by Meierkord (2012).

Thus *World English* can be regarded as the overall term for all forms English can take on when it is used in communication within or across national boundaries, while *World Englishes* ought to be reserved for the indigenised forms of English worldwide.

2.3 World English, International English, Global English

When it comes to the difference between *World, international* or *global English*, the focus is not so much on linguistic differences. Rather, the terms differ with regard to their socio-economic and political implications. McArthur (2002) investigated the use of the terms in the literature as well as in dictionaries. Although they are sometimes used synonymously, slight differences in their usage exist:

World English is the oldest of the three terms. It is shorthand for *English as a world language* and a superordinate term for different local varieties. *International English* has been in use since the 1930s. It is in its connotations similar to *World English*, but is mainly used in the field of teaching. And it is the more all-embracing term: "[I]ts essence seems to be three-fold: distribution across nations; standardness; and lingua-franca-hood" (McArthur 2004:9). *Global English* has been a vogue term since the mid-1990s and implies a vast use of English, but also "links the language (often negatively) with socio-economic globalization" (McArthur 2004:3). The three terms can thus be used to refer to the same phenomenon with different implications. However, most differentiations are based on political and socio-economic rather than linguistic criteria. So is the term *Euro English* that, as its name indicates, is supposed to be a local variety developing in the European Union (see below).

2.4 Euro English

Euro English is a relatively new term in the discussion of LFE; sometimes it is also used as a short form for *English as a European lingua franca (EELF)*. It refers to English in continental Europe with reference to "its role as the working language of major transnational companies" (McArthur 2002:157) and within the European Union. There it serves, besides French, as one of the official working languages. Despite the European Union's as well as its sub-organisations' multilingual policies, English is used in all comities and institutions and can be regarded as the "first language" of the EU (for more details about language choice and language policy see e.g. Loos 2000). According to McArthur (2003:158) "for most member countries English represents neutral ground, and might have been the EU lingua franca even if the UK and Ireland had not been members."

Some scholars have discussed the development of a separate variety of English within Europe (e.g. Breiteneder 2005, Jenkins/Modiano/Seidlhofer 2001, Modiano 2006, Mollin 2005; 2007), most of them assuming the emergence of this variety on the grounds that the European Union as an international organisation and as the home of millions of people who do not share an L1 needs to develop its own medium of communication. There are indicators of a linguistic development in Europe like the evolution of specific EU vocabulary which brought about expressions like 'Eurocrats', 'Schengen land' or 'member state' (Modiano 2006:233). However, most studies with the focus describe features of English that can be assigned to learner English or that can be found in other varieties, e.g. *New Englishes*, as well (e.g. Breiteneder 2005).

Mollin (2007) set up criteria to be fulfilled in order to talk of the evolution of a language variety. These are expansion, nativisation and institutionalisation. She investigated the occurrence and acceptance of a limited range of grammatical and lexical features with a corpus and a questionnaire. Although her work was exonormative and thus not in line with the objective of most lingua franca researchers to describe LFE independently of inner circle norms, the results are interesting. They did not indicate any tendency of a development of a specific European variety of LFE. So we can, at least for now, exclude the existence of a specific European variety of ELF. This variety would have been likely to be used by the participants in the study, since they were all from European countries.

Seidlhofer et al. (2006) list some more empirical work on ELF, some with a focus on ELF in Europe. They indicate that ELF as such takes on linguistic forms different to English as a native language (ENL). However, they come to the conclusion that

> [i]t would be premature to ask questions about the degree to which ELF in Europe can be regarded as an actual variety (Euro-English) in any meaningful sense before a better understanding has been achieved of the general processes at work in such an unprecedented situation of language spread. As more descriptive findings become available, it will be interesting to see how they relate to issues of standardization versus self-regulation (Seidlhofer et al. 2006:21).

Thus EELF is one of the labels applied to English with a quite specific definition. However, it is the one that lacks acceptance perhaps more than the other terms discussed. For this thesis, it will be assumed, in accordance with Seidlhofer et al. (2006), that the use of English in international communication in Europe is a form of usage of ELF or LFE.

So the forms of English in this dissertation are forms of LFE in line with Seidlhofer et al.'s (2006) definition. And although they were used by European speakers in a European context, they will be compared to other international research data from other contexts.

3. Lingua Franca

3.1 History of the term

Different hypotheses exist about the origin of the term *lingua franca* and about its reference and definition (cf. e. g. Kahane/Kahane 1976, Gnutzmann 2004, Noll 1999). One hypothesis is that it originated in the West, and is interpreted as "free language" (cf. Gnutzmann 2004, Svartvik/Leech 2006). Other scholars support the hypothesis that the term originated in the oriental, i. e. Arabic, world (e.g. House 2002, Kachru 1986). Another hypothesis, put forward by etymologists, is the so-called "Eastern hypothesis", according to which the term originated in the Byzantine Empire. There, it referred to different forms of Romance vernaculars used in the Western part of the Mediterranean. The exact meaning changed in the course of the centuries. And, in the course of time as well as back then, the same term was used to refer to different linguistic phenomena.

Kahane and Kahane (1976) provide a detailed discussion of the last hypothesis and the development of the term. They cite Byzantine and the Eastern part of the Roman Empire as its cradle, where the Greek term *Phrángoi, Franks*, was used to refer to people from the West in general. So different languages as well as different varieties were used in different constellations and were all referred to by the collective noun. As Kahane and Kahane (1976) explain:

> Phrángoi was, in the period of the Crusades and at the time of the conquest of Constantinople (1204), the Byzantine collective name for the Occidentals, specifically for the Romance groups with whom the Byzantines came into contact in the Mediterranean (Kahane/Kahane 1976:27).

Contacts between Easterners and Westerners in the Byzantine Empire "were carried out […] in formal medieval Latin and its counterpart, formal medieval Greek" (Kahane/Kahane 1976:28). However, the Latin used for written and official discourse existed "side by side with the spoken Romance vernaculars. This official Latin, the *latinum* […] was also called *francum*" (Kahane/Kahane 1976:28).

In the following centuries, a new "Frankish world" (Kahane/Kahane 1976:28) developed in the Levant (and beyond) in which the Lingua Franca, characterised by linguistic merging of the different vernaculars, developed:

> In the centuries following the conquest of Constantinople (1204), in the period known as the Francocracy, the vernaculars increasingly superseded Latin as the means of com-

> munication between Byzantines and Westerners. The different vernaculars received the collective Byzantine designation *phrangiká* or *phrángika* "Frankish", i. e., Romance (Kahane/Kahane 1976:30 f.).

So the specific meaning of the term was dependent on the respective language situation.

Later, the Greek term was borrowed by the Italians and became *franco* or *lingua franca*. In the 13th to 15th century, two different meanings of the term developed. First, it referred to the Romance spoken in the numerous Venetian trading centres between Dalmatia and the Levant. Here, *Lingua Franca* was a language mixture that developed in the colonies as the result of linguistic adaptation by the better-educated class.

At the same time, another linguistic form, a contact vernacular, developed. This vernacular was also referred to as *Lingua Franca*, but which originated with the Westerners themselves: "It was transmitted from generation to generation, not as anyone's native tongue but as a kind of travellers', or traders', or seamen's, jargon" (Kahane/Kahane 1976:35).

Thus, *Lingua Franca* had two meanings: a relatively stable variety spoken in the colonies in the Mediterranean and, at the same time and in the centuries after, a vernacular used for specific purposes. The latter was characterised by linguistic reduction and simplification.

A third meaning of the term developed in the Arabic world: the Arabic form *al-farangi*, which e.g. Noll (1999:219) regards as the origin of the term *lingua franca*. Other researchers, e.g. House (2002:243) and Kachru (1996:906), agree and cite *lisan-al-farang* (*farang* refers to the 'Franks' in the Arabic context) as the origin of the term, which describes an intermediary language (House 2003).

According to Kahane and Kahane (1976:39), however, the term was borrowed from the Byzantine form *phrang-iká* with suffixal adaptation and describes the linguistic relationship between the West and the Arabic world. This relationship was characterised by the use of Romance forms, too, and paralleled that in the Levant. Its specific meaning varied over time, too, and in different situations, i.e. it referred to different registers, different European languages and peoples, e.g. excluding or including the Spanish (cf. Kahane/Kahane 1976:39 f.; Noll 1999:219 f.). Later, it was also used by Westerners themselves to refer to vernaculars based on Italian in the Levant or on Spanish in North Africa, which were also characterised by reduced linguistic forms.

Thus, the meaning of the term *lingua franca* (used by Kahane/Kahane with capital letters to refer to all its different meanings) developed from a contact vernacular in the Mediterranean "to a generic term for any contact vernacular" (Kahane/Kahane 1976:41), a meaning it still holds today.

3.2 Definition

Besides its being called *vernacular*, the term *lingua franca* is often referred to or translated as 'intermediary' or 'contact' language or as 'Verkehrsprache' (cf. Bußmann 1990, Meierkord/Knapp 2002:9, Gnutzmann 2004). In its most neutral definition, it describes a language used among speakers who do not share a first language.[2] Others, however, bring in more critical notions, such as McArthur (2002:2). He calls it a "rough-and-ready socially low kind of medium between people who (for the most part) do not have it as a mother tongue" (ibid.), referring to the linguistic simplifications that may characterise a lingua franca situation. Simplifications can be a feature of lingua francas but are not necessarily so (e.g. Knapp 2002). Instead, the term can refer to different language situations, i.e. spontaneous contacts as well as established, even institutionalised forms of communication. And it can refer to different degrees of proficiency.

Its main characteristic was and still is its function to enable communication between speakers of different first languages, although the use with people who use it as their first language is not necessarily excluded. However, "there seems to be a general consensus in the literature that lingua-franca communication typically is non-native/non-native speaker communication and that a lingua franca is a second or foreign language to its speakers" (Knapp 2002:220). So, too, argues Gnutzmann (1999):

> A *lingua franca* can be defined as an auxiliary language used by people whose mother tongues are different in order to enable communication between them; and by auxiliary language we mean a third, "neutral" language, ie a language which is different from the native languages of the communicators" Gnutzmann (1999:162).

Seidlhofer (2001) also focuses on the function of enabling communication and defines a lingua franca as

> [a] language system that serves as a means of communication between speakers of different first languages, or a language by means of which the members of different speech communities can communicate with each other but which is not the native language of either – a language which has no native speakers (Seidlhofer 2001:146).

Seidlhofer thus implicitly excludes L1 speakers from lingua franca constellations, a definition used explicitly or implicitly by many linguists. And although lingua francas may be used for institutionalised forms of communication in countries

2 All but one definition I found explicitly or implicitly agree on this aspect. The exception is Davies/Elder (2004), who define four ways of understanding ELF, one being: "The use of English in an interaction where all the participants are NNSs and all share the same (or similar) first language" (=ELF 3) (Davies/Elder 2004:282).

where they serve as an official language (e.g. English or French in some former British or French territories) as well as in international communication, they are, to most researchers, by definition second languages (Meierkord/Knapp 2002:10). They are learned after the first language and often do not have all the functions an L1 has or can have in a person's life. This definition leads to the research focus on so-called non-natives speakers (NNS), or L2 speakers, as users of a lingua franca, i.e. outer or expanding circle speakers.

In the field of ELF, usually "researchers specifically exclude mother tongue speakers from their data collection. Indeed, in its purest form, ELF is defined as a contact language used only among non-mother tongue speakers" (Jenkins 2006:160). But it is not a definition shared by all researchers in the field. And Knapp (2002:220) points out that "in real life, there is a considerable degree of variation in what could be termed 'situations of lingua franca use' with respect to these defining criteria".

Another problem that is closely linked to the definition is the determination of speakers' proficiency. Knapp criticises that so-called 'non-native speakers' are usually regarded as less competent than L1 speakers, and the fact that specific features of lingua franca communication are regarded as pragmatic deficits of its users. In contrast, he found that lingua franca speakers can be highly competent in the language (Knapp 2002:220 f.).

Thus, speakers can have different levels of competence in the respective language or in their communicative abilities in general. Besides, lingua francas are used for various purposes so that speakers do not only need to be proficient in the general language, but sometimes in a specific register or a language for specific purposes.

According to House (2002), who also focuses on the attitude speakers have towards the language they use, "English as a lingua franca is a language for communication, i.e., a medium that can be given substance with different national, regional, local, and individual cultural identities" (House 2002:244, original emphasis). It is not a so-called *language of identification*, i.e. one that speakers use to present their personality, background or attitude (cf. Hüllen 1992). According to House, it mainly serves communicative functions as opposed to psycholinguistic functions.

Although English is the most widely spread lingua franca in the world (cf. e.g. Ammon 1994, Crystal 1997, Graddol 2003, Knapp 1998, McArthur 2002), different languages can serve as lingua francas. They can be natural languages like Arabic or French, for example, or artificial languages like Esperanto, which was explicitly developed for that purpose. However, Esperanto never gained the acceptance English and other lingua francas like Arabic, French, Spanish or Swahili have.

Different settings evoke different forms of usage of the language. And these linguistic choices form a pool of forms that speakers show in what Meierkord (2012) refers to as 'interactions across Englishes'. By this term, she refers to different constellations, involving speakers of different varieties of the three circles, including of different varieties within one of the three circles. Her basic assumption is that "the different Englishes potentially merge in these interactions and that this, also potentially, result in the development of new emergent varieties" (Meierkord 2012:2). Due to the different forms English takes in the various settings in which it is used and the "heterogeneity of the functions which English performs as a lingua franca and the diversity of the possible constellations" (Meierkord 2012:2), this will, according to her assumption, not result in one stable variety, "but rather a heterogeneous array of new linguistic systems" (ibid).

So far, research into LFE has proved her right. And despite some attempts to find forms that would justify referring to ELF or *Euroenglish* as a variety of English (cf. e.g. Jenkins et al. 2001, Seidlhofer et al. 2006), researchers have so far only been able to describe forms English takes in different contexts. They have not yet found linguistic features that set them apart from other 'interactions across Englishes' or 'interactions in English(es)'. So no one has yet defined a separate variety that could be referred to as *ELF* or *LFE*. However, what they have been able to show so far is that different 'linguistic systems' develop or emerge in lingua franca situations that enable communication.

Regardless of the question of whether native speakers are involved in the communicative situation or whether lingua francas are used exclusively among L2 speakers, lingua francas are defined by their main function: to enable communication between speakers of different languages. And regardless of the language chosen as the medium of communication, lingua francas have a lot in common. Meierkord/Knapp (2002:10) sum up the characteristics of today's lingua francas as follows:

They
- serve a number of varied purposes
- are employed by a heterogeneous group of speakers for whom the language does not always have the same status of a second or foreign language
- share a number of common characteristics
- may prove difficult to be taught as such due to their heterogeneous character.

From a linguistic point of view, any language may serve as a lingua franca as long as it enables communication between individuals, groups or organisations that do not share a primary language. And it may be adapted to the purpose it has to fulfil and to the linguistic needs as well as the capability of the speakers and hearers in the respective situation. And the language which has been adopted worldwide as the most common and successful lingua franca in today's globalised world seems to be, for different historical and political as well as perhaps linguistic reasons, English.

3.3 English as a lingua franca

Researchers – and most laypeople – agree that today's most widely used lingua franca is English (cf. Meierkord/Knapp 2002; for a more detailed discussion see Knapp 1998; also e. g. Ammon 1994, Crystal 1997, Graddol 2003; 2006, Jenkins 2003, McArthur 2002).

Reasons for its enormous spread in the past are researched and discussed (e.g. by Crystal 1997, Graddol 2003; critically e. g. Phillipson 1992, Pennycook 2000). One reason for its current spread lies in the economic and technical development of the world in the past and current century. As Seidlhofer (2004:211) points out: "For the first time in history, a language has reached truly global dimensions, and as a consequence, is being shaped, in its international uses, at least as much by its nonnative speakers as its native speakers." The special aspect pointed out here is that it is also the 'non-native' speakers who shape the language. They influence its form and development, a phenomenon that is not a natural occurrence in languages. And they are usually considered to 'belong' to their primary speakers, who, over time, change its forms and adapt it to new uses.

However, the reasons for the spread of English go way back to the first 'diaspora' on the British Isles and mainly to the period of colonisation (cf. e. g. Crystal 1997:30 ff.). Some researchers discuss this development critically.

One of the most widely cited theses why English is today's most commonly used language is Phillipson's (1992) claim that it is the result of language policy by the colonial powers. He sees it as the result of Britain's and the US' political and linguistic hegemony. Brutt-Griffler (2002) contradicts his thesis and discusses reasons how and why English became one of the languages of the former colonies *despite* the British educational policy.

According to her findings, it was the active decision of the inhabitants of the colonies to learn the language in order to participate in the economic welfare or for their children to learn it in order to improve their career perspectives. Sometimes, according to Brutt-Griffler (2002), these decisions went against the actual policy of the colonial powers, and so the active language use and acquisition by inhabitants was more decisive than colonial policy.

Scholars do not agree on the reasons why English is the most widely used language today. However, they widely agree that its use as a lingua franca is the most frequent use of English today (see e.g. Graddol 2003, McArthur 2002:3) and that the 'non-native speakers' outnumber the so-called native-speakers (cf. McArthur 2002:3), although actual numbers of users are very difficult to estimate, as Graddol (2003) explains.

Despite the fact that its function as a means of international and intra-national communication is one of the main characteristics of English, LFE was not given much attention by researchers and language scholars until the early 1990s (Jenkins 2006:165). Since then, scholars from different fields like language politics, sociolinguistics, applied linguistics, language pedagogy, and historical linguistics have described and explained different aspects of the phenomenon of English spreading around the world. A lot of progress has been made in understanding and accepting the phenomenon of English used by speakers who are not used to using it in their habitat. And the use of ELF has been an aspect in the German language learning curricula for some years (cf. e.g. *Kernlehrplan Englisch* (Ministerium für Schule und Weiterbildung des Landes Nordrhein-Westfalen 2007)).

3.4 The language teaching paradigm

Even though for more than the past twenty years the interest in the linguistic aspects of LFE has spread, the change in the language teaching paradigm so far seems to be based on political considerations more than on actual linguistic findings. What is still lacking in curricula and teaching materials are usually descriptions and examples of the concrete use of English in lingua franca contexts.

One of the main issues is the concept of the so-called 'native speaker' of English. In theory, the 'native speaker' – at least the model explicitly or implicitly used in teaching – uses 'Standard English', an educated, institutionalised and monolithic variety. This theoretical persona serves as the role model for language use, however vague the concept may be. This fact is not only criticised by educators but by many researchers as well (cf. e.g. Seidlhofer 2001, Jenkins 2006, Kachru 1989, Widdowson 1997, Knapp 2002:220 f.).

There are other voices, though, that argue in favour of a model of usage derived from the speaker's reasons of motivation or as a reference for learners and educators (e.g. Beneke 1991, Crystal 1997, Gnutzmann 1999, Prodromou 2007). However, in the field of lingua franca research – as well as in applied linguistics in general – the question remains what is to be regarded as 'standard' when it comes to language use and what is not.

'Standard English' is a form of English that is well described in the field of linguistics, mainly in grammars, and seen as the variety that would be used written and formal settings such as in the media or in school (cf. Cambridge English Dictionary)[3]. However, it is used only by a minority of speakers and in restricted contexts. Yet it is used as a model for teaching. However, in the context of English as a language used worldwide, the concept has caused ongoing debates. One of the most telling examples is the so-called 'English Today Debate' (see below), in which the late linguist and grammarian Randolph Quirk argued in favour of a standard form as the model for native or inner circle speakers as well as for users (and learners) who use it as an additional language. He was contradicted by other linguists, mainly by Braj Kachru, who argued in favour of more tolerance regarding different forms of usage of English. They discussed their positions in various papers published in the journal *English Today.* The debate therefore became known as the *English Today Debate.* Their discussion demonstrated a paradigm shift in applied linguistics and is briefly outlined below.

3.4.1 *The English Today Debate*

Quirk (1990) regarded formally established standard forms, Standard British English and American English, and one informally established standard form, Australian English, as the models for users. According to him, they were meant to be the yardsticks for measuring a speaker's competence in the language. Other existing forms of language use were labelled 'performance varieties'.

Kachru, who labelled Quirk's position 'deficit linguistics' (Kachru 1991), contradicted Quirk and argued that new varieties of English used for many different purposes are developing, e.g. in former colonies, the so-called *outer circle countries* (Kachru 1985). To him, these are varieties of English in their own right. Quirk called this position 'liberation linguistics'.[4]

All in all, the debate about the usefulness of standards seems not over as can be seen in publications like Seidlhofer (2005b). She, like e.g. Jenkins (2006), argues against the proclamation of Standard English as the only model for teaching. She even regards the notion of 'native-speaker' as "outdated" (Seidlhofer 2005b:160) in times of a worldwide use of English.

---

3 Cambridge University Press 2023: Cambridge English Dictionary; https:dictionary.cambridge.org (accessed 19/05/23)

4 The debate was first published in the journal *English Today* and was reprinted in Seidlhofer 2006. For comments see e.g. Jenkins 2006, Seidlhofer 2005b.

'Standard' and 'native speaker' are laden concepts when it comes to the emancipated use of a language. They are also linguistically debatable, and a clear definition is missing for both (cf. e.g. McArthur 2002, Lesznyák 2004).

However, the notion, as well as the function of the so-called 'native speaker' as a role model for users and learners worldwide, is not easy to overcome because it is established and frequently used in linguistics as well as language teaching. And both notions, as well as the consequences they have for the language teaching industry, are defended by a powerful lobby because national and economic interests come in here. English language teaching and teaching materials are commodities, promoted and defended by national industries of the 'inner circle'. Still, one must not forget that it is also a well-known and prestigious model that a lot of learners around the world choose to strive after and that cannot easily be replaced.

And when it comes to the question of what to teach, it remains difficult to actually teach the use of ELF (or LFE) as long as its forms of usage and underlying strategies have not been described in detail; and they might never be described completely due to the variety of contexts and forms of use. So far, the question of what to teach remains open to debate despite curricular attempts. However, it seems more important to teach about the phenomenon and make students of the language aware of the different forms as well as of the related issues than to focus on the actual variety or forms to be taught in classrooms. The overall aim ought to be to make students conscious and enlightened *users* of the language. And as users, they ought to be able to choose their own objectives and model(s) of reference.

3.5 *English as a lingua franca* vs. *English as a foreign language* (ELF vs. EFL)

Not only is an overall description of the forms of ELF missing. There is not even a consensus yet if a variety of English exists that can be labelled *ELF* (see e.g. Meierkord/Knapp 2002, House 1999, Jenkins/Modiano/Seidlhofer 2001, Prodromou 2007). It is clear, however, that different varieties of English are used in international communication. It is also clear from research into LFE that lingua franca speakers use linguistic forms that are not used by native speakers (cf. e.g. Firth 1990, House 2002, Jenkins 2002, Meierkord 1998, Seidlhofer 2001; 2004).

We do know today that the forms of LFE vary depending on speakers and contexts. It is, however, not clear what, besides the context in which it is used, determines ELF. According to Seidlhofer, though, ELF is "a language", but one that has no native speaker. She explicitly states it is not a pidgin, however, as it is not necessarily restricted in social role and linguistic resources (Seildhofer 2001:146). Thus, it has parallels to the original sense of *lingua franca* in so far as it can fulfil different functions and take on different forms.

When it comes to the functions of the language, English can, roughly speaking, be said to fulfil at least two different functions: that of an international lingua franca used in contexts where it does not necessarily have an official status and that of an *intra*-national lingua franca. As an intra-national lingua franca it is used in some countries where it serves as one of the official or co-official languages but where it is not necessarily the L1 of the majority of speakers. However, most scholars tend to differentiate between *ELF* or *LFE*, which is used for the former definition, and the term *New Englishes* for the latter.

The discussion about the development of a variety of ELF or LFE might go on into the future. And although the forms used in actual communication still need to be described, some overall characteristics and aims of ELF (or LFE) vs. other forms of English usage, mainly English as a Foreign Language (EFL), can be described.

Coming from a teaching background, Gnutzmann (1999) does so by contrasting EFL and ELF with regard to teaching and learning objectives:

ELF prepares learners to communicate with non-native speakers of English from all over the world.

EFL prepares learners to communicate with native speakers of English in English-speaking countries.

ELF is neutral with regard to the different cultural backgrounds of the interlocutors. Depending on how long the communication lasts, the interlocutors will 'negotiate' and establish some kind of common intercultural basis.

EFL is based on the linguistic and sociocultural norms of native speakers of English and their respective cultures.

ELF communication is not based on any particular national linguistic standard of English. Relying on native speaker norms (or near native norms) cannot guarantee that the communication will be successful. On the contrary, using elaborate linguistic structures or vocabulary may even be harmful to the success of the communication, if the interlocutor does not share a similar linguistic repertoire.

EFL communication is based on standard English, generally British or American English. The better the learners are able to handle the grammatical rules and lexis of the standard language, the more successful they tend to be in their communication with native speakers (Gnutzmann 1999:162 f.).

It is very important for the distinction that ELF is not based on "any particular national linguistic standard of English", especially not on assumed forms of English like World Standard (Spoken) English, a variety which is assumed to be developing for communication in international contexts (cf. Crystal 1995). And as Jenkins points out:

> Unfortunately, some WEs [World Englishes] scholars assume that ELF (EIL) refers to the same phenomenon as WS(S)E and then criticise ELF (EIL) for promoting a monocentric view of English based on American or British norms rather than a pluricentric view based on local norms. However, nothing could be further from the truth (Jenkins 2006:160).

Despite some earlier attempts to describe a certain variety in the 1990s – although from a descriptive rather than prescriptive perspective – the main aim of ELF research today is not to describe a form of standard, i. e. a specific model of usage, be it national or international, or to proclaim a certain model of usage. The aim of most researchers is to describe how English can and does work successfully amongst NNSs. And, in the long run, they want to raise awareness of the phenomenon as well as increase the acceptability of different forms of language use. Jenkins (2006:161) describes this objective as follows:

> Although ELF researchers seek to identify frequently and systematically used forms that differ from inner circle forms without causing communication problems and override first language groupings, their purpose is not to describe and codify a single ELF variety. The existence of ELF is not intended to imply that learners should aim for an English that is identical in all respects. ELF researchers do not believe any such monolithic variety of English does or ever will exist.

And although no complete overview of the forms users invent, use, decode or sometimes struggle with is available yet and may never be, and research into its forms is still needed, the target for learning English for communication with speakers from other language backgrounds seems already to be set. As Graddol sums up:

> The target model of English, within the ELF framework, is not a native speaker but a fluent bilingual speaker, who retains a national identity in terms of accent, and who also has the special skills required to negotiate understanding with another non-native speaker (Graddol 2006:87).

So far, no agreed-upon definition has been established, and *ELF* and *LFE* seem to be the most widely used labels in the discussion of English in contexts where the language does not have official status. Both terms usually are employed in the framework of a certain paradigm that seeks to emancipate the speakers from the expanding circle and put them on foot with the inner circle users. *ELF* is mostly used in the field that tries to describe a specific variety; *LFE* mostly in a more neutral form describing its linguistic role.

3.6 *Second language acquisition* vs. *second language use* (SLA vs. SLU)

Two closely related concept in the discussion of English used as a lingua franca are the concepts of *user* vs. *learner*. The concept of 'learner' is a critical one even though frequently used. One issue is that 'learner' usually is implicitly linked to the 'native speaker' reference point (see discussion above) in that learners are regarded as participants in an ongoing process of learning or acquisition of a (foreign) language[5]. 'Language learners' are expected to strive for 'native-like' proficiency, i.e. a level of language use that – as the theoretical concept goes – is characterised by an all-including vocabulary and the lack of so-called 'errors'. It is assumed that they will stay learners until they have reached this goal; a critical notion in lingua franca research as pointed out above.

Lingua franca situations, on the other hand, are regarded as situations where so-called 'native speakers', too, must adapt their ways of communicating to suit a given international situation, as e.g. Ranta (2013:21) argues. Ranta bases her argumentation on Mauranen (2012), who comments that second language acquisition needs to be separated from second language usage; not only are the goals different between learning and using, but the linguistic means in a learning context often differ from those in authentic contexts. In the classroom, educational goals determine the use of language, and ever so often, these goals differ from the users' objectives (cf. Gnutzmann 1999 (above)).

Seidlhofer argues that not only is 'Standard English' "very difficult to define" (Seidlhofer 2005:159). The insistence on it in the context of teaching is also "difficult to justify" (ibid.) since today's reality of a globalised world leads to a much greater variety of forms of English that users, learners and teachers are exposed to. It leads to a "'controversial linguistic matrix' that lingua franca users of English inhabit" (Seidlhofer 2005:161). She argues that "old measures" and authorities might be overcome and need to be replaced by a new description of English as well as a new pedagogy (ibid.).

5 Although language pedagogy and applied linguistics make a difference between *learning* and *acquisition* (cf. Krashen 1981; see also Ellis 1994:14f.), I will use the terms interchangeably in this thesis not only because it is not always possible to define the exact difference in an individual's learning process, but mainly because the focus of this thesis lies on the communicative processes.

Another aspect of the concept of *learner* is the objective. In language learning, it is assumed that a person's aim is to continue the process of learning and probably seek more input or opportunities to enlarge their knowledge of the language. Lingua franca *speakers* (or *users*), however, do not use the language in order to improve their language skills. They, by definition, use the language to reach a goal that lies outside their language. So, by definition, lingua franca speakers use language as a means to an end rather than an object of study.

The cutting edge between both may be thin and blurry. And it is not the focus of this thesis to discuss learning objectives, but rather features of LFE and how they facilitate understanding in business negotiations. I will therefore make a difference between *learners* and *users* of a language and consider the speakers in my data *users* of the language. They do not interact to enlarge their knowledge of the language, but of the non-linguistic aspects of the discourses, such as offers their potential partners are willing to make. Their aim is not to practise their language skills, but to work out conditions of agreements. And in this dissertation, I will focus on the communicative functions of language rather than on questions of acquisition (or learning). I will show in the analysis of my data that some of the forms – of conditionals as well as other language structures – that the speakers use might be marked as 'errors' in a learning context, but actually serve communicative functions and need to be considered as LFE features (cf. chapters 9 ff.).

3.7 Terminology in this study

As the discussion above has shown, so far, no clear-cut definition of the specific terms referring to English used in international communication exists. However, some of the terms, such as *LFE*, are specific enough since they focus on a specific aspect of the use of English: English is used to enable communication between speakers of different languages and speakers of different levels of language proficiency.

In this dissertation, I will use the term *international English* to refer to any form of English in international communication, including or excluding users from inner circle countries. *LFE* as well as *ELF* will be used in the conservative sense, i. e. for English used by and among people whose primary or secondary education did not take place primarily in English and who only use it for restricted purposes. This definition, however, does not determine their mastery of the language. So it is close to Halliday et al.'s (1964) definition of *lingua franca* as a long-term solution in situations of institutionalised bilingualism:

> One language comes to be adopted as the medium of some activity or activities which the different language communities perform in common. It may be a common language

> for commerce, learning, administration, religion or any or all of a variety of purposes: the use determines which members of each language community are the ones who learn it (Halliday et al. 1964:80).

In the context of this dissertation, it is the language, in this case English, adopted for business and commerce to enable communication between speakers of different first languages. I will apply the concept with reference to individuals and will not discuss their language use with a special focus on lexical aspects, as much of the literature on language for specific purposes does, but apply Grießhaber's (2001) definition of *Wirtschaftssprache* (language of business). Grießhaber takes a discourse-based approach to defining business language. Using the approach of Functional Pragmatics, he defines the language of business not only as goal-driven, but as determined by the fact that parts of business, especially negotiations, are characterised by interactional and mental processes, mainly decision-making processes. He defines the language of business by these interactional and goal-oriented forms of language.

Especially in the second part of this dissertation, the focus will be on successful communication guided by economic goals. These economic goals which guide the forms of interaction will be shown to be more important than correspondence with what grammars describe.

And even though L1 speakers were not excluded from this dissertation project, the most conservative definition of lingua franca applies: *LFE* as well as *ELF*, in this dissertation, refer to the language used between speakers from the so-called 'expanding circle' (Kachru 1985). None of the speakers was raised in surroundings where English was the medium of communication. They learned it in institutionalised settings and apply English as a medium of communication in order to fulfil their professional communicative needs. And these needs are defined by their professional, i.e. non-linguistic, goals: to discuss and negotiate forms of business cooperations.

And although there used to be a difference – however vague – between the terms LFE and ELF and the underlying assumptions and aims, I will use the terms interchangeably in this dissertation to reflect the aim that underlies both terms: the emancipation of the use of English in international contexts.

4. Features of lingua franca English

4.1 Comparability of language data

Despite some earlier considerations about the functions of LFE (e.g. Halliday et al. 1964:80), research into its forms only started off in the 1990s (e.g. Firth 1990, 1996; Meierkord 1996, Wagner/Firth 1997).

This dissertation does not focus on political or pedagogical aspects of lingua franca use. It focuses instead on the forms English takes when used as an oral lingua franca. In this overview, I will focus on the language description. But since the literature in the field is too vast to discuss it all in a project like this, I have selected studies from the field hoping to give an overview of findings concerning the forms of language as well as aspects of discourse and communication strategies and of findings about attitudes towards LFE use.

Since the interest in LFE boomed in the 1990s and early 2000s, studies are numerous and diverse and, in some parts, even contradictory. Researchers from different backgrounds have collected and analysed a wide variety of data. In the overview, I will only focus on findings concerning the oral use of ELF. The outline of the tendencies in research gives a rough overview of research interests and results.

Research into LFE comes from different societal and institutional backgrounds. Discourse data from academia, science, business, politics etc. has been used, and researchers concentrated on different levels of language description. One aspect the studies I will consider in this thesis have in common is the fact that they focus on the empirical research of oral language use. So they use interactional data, most of which is authentic rather than elicited data, i. e. gained from interactions that were not carried out for the purpose of the study. The focus of this study is authentic language use, i. e. language that is used in order to pursue aims and purposes that lie outside the interaction. Therefore, I will primarily focus on the results of studies using authentic material. Some of the early studies, however, used elicited data (e.g. House 1999; 2002). And since the findings were groundbreaking and started off research into the phenomena, I have included them in the overview.

After a short overview of more general findings regarding ELF language usage, a list of research findings sorted by 'traditional' linguistic fields such as phonology, lexis, morphology and syntax, and pragmatics will be given. As it is not always possible to draw a clear line between different linguistic aspects of language in interaction, sometimes the categories overlap. Or rather, what is listed under one category could as well be listed under another category as it affects both. The use of certain forms such as *gambits* or *speech action augments,* e. g., will be listed under the heading of *pragmatics* rather than *lexicon* as they are categorised according to their interactional function. Other forms will be listed under the heading of their grammatical category. That is because some of the findings in the literature are sorted according to grammatical categories, whereas others are sorted according to functional or interactional aspects. It is a general problem of linguistics that categories are, in most cases, established according to structure rather than interactional function. But since this dissertation is not the place to solve this inherent problem of the field of study, I have decided to use classical grammatical categories first in order to make the overview more accessible.

'Linguistic systems' in the context of lingua franca interactions are primarily determined by the context of their language use. The linguistic repertoire of the speaker might not be as wide as that of so-called inner circle users who use the language for a wide range of purposes. Lingua franca speakers are likely to have a smaller range of linguistic expressions and to adapt to the context in which they find themselves. The data discussed in most publications so far is from university contexts. It is either elicited data, e. g. students fulfilling tasks given by researchers, but more often authentic data, e. g. students and university staff recorded during authentic activities such as seminars and lectures, presentations, international conferences etc. Another important source is social encounters, e. g. students or university staff recorded when socialising with each other (e.g. Meierkord 1996, Pölzl/Seidlhofer 2006) or interacting at conferences. Other data was recorded in business contexts (e.g. Firth 1990; 1996).

What all the empirical studies into the field of LFE have in common is that they take a 'look through the key hole' at communication in LFE. So each of them adds a piece to the jigsaw puzzle and helps us to hopefully one day see the overall picture of English when used as a lingua franca as well as to get a complete picture of the forms and possibilities of the English language.

The results of these studies will be listed here without differentiating them according to the context they stem from, but according to linguistic aspects. Furthermore, competence levels of speakers may vary a lot and are very seldom given in the publications of the research data. However, it is not only the level of competence of a speaker that is important for the different linguistic choices, but also different topics and, mostly, the communicative requirements. They, too, lead to different linguistic forms or communication strategies. To give just one example, topic changes were found, e. g. by Meierkord (1996), to be a communication strategy used to avoid misunderstandings in situations that are characterised mainly by consensus and social aspects. This strategy is not found in group work in university seminars (e.g. by Björkman 2010). In these rather high stakes settings, it is more likely for communicative problems to be overcome by strategies like explanations, paraphrasing, negotiation of meaning etc. Thus different studies come to different conclusions about lingua franca communication – sometimes despite using similar approaches – because the contexts and the participants' aims influence the form of discourse. And the linguistic and strategic choices speakers make can be more decisive than the fact that they are operating as users of a lingua franca. So the different interactions recorded for different research projects show some forms of LFE that are common to different settings. And they also show the use of forms that are unique to specific settings.

4.2 General findings

Since the 1990s, linguistics has become more and more interested in the phenomenon of LFE with different foci. For some time, the guiding research questions were whether or not ELF is a variety in its own right (e.g. Seidlhofer 2005) and whether a local variety that could be referred to as *Euro English* exists (e.g. Jenkins et al. 2001). The aim was to define a specific variety of English in its international use and to describe its features. Research projects like the VOICE project (Vienna Oxford International Corpus of English)[6] were started, and data was collected in contexts that were not dominated by so-called 'native speakers', but by those who use it as a means of communication in restricted and often specific purposes such as professional ones. These corpora enabled analyses of great masses of data of spoken language that were not gathered in the so-called *inner circle* (Kachru 1989; 1996).

As it turned out, no specific variety that could be called *Euro English* was found (Mollin 2005), although there are some specific terms used in the context of the European Union such as *Eurocrats* (Moriano 2006:233), and it is hard to define a separate variety that could be labelled LFE since its forms vary very much according to different contexts and speakers.

Another research focus of the past decades lay on deviations from standard forms (e.g. Björkman 2008; Breiteneder 2005; Mauranen 2003, Seidlhofer 2004, etc.), as well as on the question of whether misunderstandings or other communicative problems occur (e.g. Meierkord 1996; Mauranen 2006) and on how they are treated (e.g. Meeuwis 1994; Lesznyák 2002). These studies discuss forms that are different or used differently from their usage in so-called Standard English

6 https://www.univie.ac.at/voice/

or *inner circle varieties* (cf. Kachru 1985; 1989), e. g. the omission of the 3rd person singular –s (e.g. Ahvenainen 2005; Breiteneder 2005; Cogo/Dewey 2006), word formation (e.g. Björkman 2008; Hülmbauer 2007), redundant forms (Dewey 2007; Seidlhofer 2004) etc. Most of the studies, however, are descriptive and do not discuss communicative functions of these forms. When it comes to explaining these 'deviant' forms, they are often regarded as 'accidental' deviations rather than linguistic choices.

For a long time, linguists assumed that LFE, as it became known in the 1990s, was merely a form of learner language. So the focus of its research was mostly on mistakes speakers made. Or, to be more precise, on *errors*, i. e. deviations from standard forms that indicate either an overgeneralisation of a rule or an incomplete acquisition of the language (cf. Corder 1967).

In the 1990s, however, the focus changed and researchers like J. House, J. Jenkins, K. Knapp, C. Meierkord, B. Seidlhofer and many others tried to establish ELF or LFE as an independent and emancipated form of language use. They argued it ought no longer to be regarded as an incomplete, erroneous form of language use but as a successful – although not always unproblematic – means of communication.

Researchers started collecting data of lingua franca speakers and linguistically described its forms of usage. Seidlhofer started the VOICE corpus and Mauranen the ELFA (English as a lingua franca in Academic Settings) project[7] (cf. e. g. Mauranen 2006). At first, one of the aims was to describe language features that would allow researchers to identify and define a variety called *ELF*. For others, the focus was more on describing communicative strategies as well as aims that come into play (e.g. Knapp 2002). Forms varied so much that it was hard to identify a clear-cut variety that could be described and set apart from other varieties of English. So nowadays, the focus is on describing how the language works as a means of communication and how the language is adjusted, by its users, to communicative needs.

The greatest achievements of these researchers are the emancipation of the use of English in lingua franca contexts and the fact that they set it apart from language learning contexts. Of course, the two cannot always be separated completely. Speakers of a language were learners at some point and a lot of users will acquire new forms for the rest of their lives – be it in their first or any other language. But the difference lies in the focus – of the speakers as well as of the researchers (cf. chapter 3). And the new focus in research has been seeing speakers as mature, independent and to a great deal successful users of the language.

---

7 http://www.helsinki.fi/elfa

In general, it can be said that lingua franca communication is less oriented towards the so-called 'inner circle' norms than EFL communication. This shows in aspects such as the greater acceptability of non-standard forms in the fields of lexicon as well as morphology and syntax (see below, 4.5). Even more so, these different forms are accepted on the level of pragmatics, as the examples below show. That is because "[w]ithin ELF, intelligibility is of primary importance, rather than native-like accuracy" (Graddol 2006:87).

When it comes to the practical aspects of LFE, many speakers use versions of English that are simpler in structure than most inner circle communication. Speakers make less use of complex sentences and of verbal routines that are typical of inner-circle forms of English (Beerkens 2008). Besides, some researchers found a high tolerance of non-understanding, which was labelled differently. One of the first studies in the field was Firth's (1990; 1996) study of telephone business negotiations. In these negotiations, misunderstandings were not made explicit and the interaction was carried on without the problem being solved. Only when one of the interlocutors needed clarification, e.g. because they were supposed to answer a question, was the problem made explicit. This strategy was labelled 'let-it-pass' (Firth 1990) because comprehension problems were not solved when they occurred. Instead, hearers let the lack of understanding 'pass' if or as long as they did not appear crucial for the ongoing discourse.

Two further labels established by Firth (1996) were the '*make-it-normal*' principle or '*robustness of talk*'. According to the *make-it-normal* principle, participants act as if forms – sometimes not understood, sometimes marked – were 'normal'. So they do not see them in any way extraordinary or problematic in the context in which they occurred. Firth (1996) finds that lingua franca business communication is about achieving 'normality'. So deviancies, marked forms and problems of communication were not made explicit or commented on. Instead, according to Firth (1996), interlocutors strive for an unproblematic and smooth interaction. The so-called *robustness of talk* means that the focus is on intelligibility even if interpretation work is required on the side of the hearer. Both labels, '*let-it-pass*' and '*robustness of talk*', were used for similar findings about ELF interaction, e.g. by Ahvenainen 2005, Lesznyák 2004 or Mauranen 2006.

Although the majority of studies seems to indicate successful communication among users of LFE, House (1999; 2002) stresses a lack of orientation towards the interlocutor. In her studies (e.g. 1999, 2002), she shows that students in her (elicited) data do not really react to each other's contributions. Rather, speakers seem to engage in what seems to be monologues although they take turns as if communicating with one another.

One of the problems could be that there was no real aim for the participants in her study to be reached. Students had to complete no task other than producing talk for the purpose of the recording. However, her findings are alarming when reflected in the light of international educational programmes. If there is no coherence between different contributions, cooperation and communication, as required in many professional fields, are hardly possible. Higher education today is supposed to prepare students to work in international contexts, often in international teams, which, in all fields, means being able to communicate and cooperate.

Another aspect that seems to characterise lingua franca communication in a number of studies is co-operativeness. Interlocutors in lingua franca settings show a high willingness and readiness to help each other when linguistic problems occur. This is a feature of lingua franca discourse also found in House's (2002) study. Although participants did not take up the interlocutor's topic or stance in their contribution, they helped each other by co-constructing utterances or by scaffolding (House 2002). The finding echoes Meierkord's (1996) as well as Firth/Wagner's (1997) findings.

Knapp (2002) also found cooperative behaviour in small talk situations. However, he showed that speakers did behave uncooperatively in high stakes, competitive situations. Students at an international students' conference only helped one another as long as it did not bear any disadvantages for themselves. As soon as they were in situations where their contributions were graded, their linguistic behaviour became competitive. Knapp's study is one of the exceptions in the field, revealing uncooperative behaviour. Most studies on lingua franca discourse state cooperative behaviour as one of the main features of LFE discourse. However, speakers seem to change their linguistic behaviour towards the interlocutor depending on what is at stake for them, i. e. depending on their non-linguistic goals.

Another general finding regarding lingua franca interactions is the formation of so-called "novel signs replacing those that would conventionally be employed in standard L1-varieties of English" (Meierkord 2002:120). According to Meierkord's findings, e. g. laughter or pauses can be used to replace gambits which speakers lack, e. g. to introduce topic changes or to close a topic or a phase in the discourse (cf. Meierkord 2002). In general, "interactions between speakers of different individual Englishes – be they nativized or learner Englishes – are characterised by a number of processes of leveling and regularization at all linguistic levels" (Meierkord 2006:23). Accordingly, one of the most striking features of LFE usage certainly is the acceptance of non-standard forms. This is also an aspect that differentiates the use of ELF from language learning.

So-called 'deviations' from these standard forms have been studied on different levels. For reasons of limited space and time, I will list some examples starting with phonology and moving on to lexicon. Then I will list examples from grammatical categories such as morphology and syntax and finally turn to aspects of discourse (4.6).

4.3 Phonology

One of the first empirical studies on LFE was Jenkins (2000). Jenkins studied L2 speakers in interactions with a focus on what was important for intelligible pronunciation. She found that some deviations from native speaker realisations which are regarded as 'typically English' – and on whose teaching a lot of time is spent in EFL classrooms – are not relevant for communication. In international communication they can be, and ever so often are, replaced by other sounds. The sounds used as an alternative, however, need to differentiate the meaning of the word in question. Jenkins defined those pronunciation deviations that did not cause any comprehension problems as the *lingua franca core* (see Jenkins 2000; also Seidlhofer 2004:214 ff.). Consequently, deviation from native speaker norms on the level of phonology is acceptable and accepted in many contexts.

4.4 Lexicon

On the lexical level, non-standard forms of LFE seem to affect mainly nouns and verbs. Lingua franca users tend to employ more general rather than specific terms as well as "culturally largely neutral" ones (Meierkord 2005:101). The differences include applying a word that is related in meaning. However, it has a more general meaning rather than the specific one, e. g. *paper* for *sheet* (Hülmbauer 2007:16). This goes in line with Meierkord's (2005) finding that many users of LFE have a reduced lexicon. That would explain why they use terms that are similar in meaning to the standard form, but do not have the exact meaning.

Interlocutors are ready to help when lingua franca speakers lack a word or expression and negotiation of meaning is a common strategy in lingua franca discourse (cf. e. g. Cogo/Dewey 2006, Mauranen 2003; 2006, Meeuwis 1994, Pitzl 2005; for the exception see Knapp 2002, above). Sometimes negotiation of meaning leads to *coinages* (e.g. Hülmbauer 2007), i. e. speakers make use of other expressions that are given a new meaning or definition in lingua franca discourse. Speakers establish, at least for their temporary discourse situation, new terms that are not found in native speaker usage. *Testing time* for *probation period* (Ahvenainen 2005) is an example of a coinage that lingua franca speakers create for their specific language use. They also find new combinations of words to replace an expression, e.g. *far away uncle* for *great uncle* (Hülmbauer 2007:16) or *self exposition* for *Selbstdarstellung* (Cogo/Dewey 2006). They also use expressions from one of the L1 cultures involved and explain them to the partners in communication, e.g. *fleur bleu* or *kitschig* for *cheesy* (ibid.). This form of code switching can also be found for more pragmatic functions (see below) or when a specific cultural or national concept is being discussed (cf. Klimpfinger 2007). Users also create new forms, which tend to be accepted in the discourse, although sometimes they require negotiation of meaning or explanations.

A more specific form of language use is phrasal verbs and idioms. These are very much culture dependent and specific to groups of speakers who interact regularly. Meierkord (2005), e.g., finds few instances of the use of phrasal verbs and idioms. Lingua franca users seem to avoid expressions that are culturally determined as they may cause problems in communication across different languages and cultures.

In her 2006 study, Meierkord compares Englishes across the three circles using the wider definition of LFE. She found users oriented more towards L1 English varieties than towards nativised varieties, i.e. outer circle varieties, and use neutral or core lexical items (Meierkord 2006). Mollin (2005), who studied LFE in Europe, found a change of meaning of two words. *Possibility* was used in the sense of *opportunity* and *eventual* in the sense of *possible*. However, there is a semantic overlap, which indicates a shift of meaning or non-standard use of a word that carries the meaning, or part of the meaning, of the standard form. Another example is the expression *to stable*, used as a verb by students in Björkman's (2008) data. In other cases, speakers use morphemes to form verbs that native speakers would not use in the same form (see 4.5 below).

Speakers also seem to make flexible use of words that have a grammatical rather than lexical function: The relative pronouns *who* and *which* are used interchangeably, e.g. *things who* or *people which* (Seidlhofer 2004:38). Not surprisingly, language users seem to focus on meaning more than on form and do not differentiate between words whose distribution is defined grammatically rather than lexically. The same seems to apply to the pronoun *this*, which Seidlhofer found to be used with reference to plural nouns (cf. Seidlhofer 2004:38).

Another feature that affects lexical items is redundancy. Speakers in lingua franca situations are found to insert additional prepositions, e.g. *discuss about something, phone <u>to</u> someone* (Seidlhofer 2004), *my topic is <u>about</u>* (Dewey 2007) or nouns, e.g. *black <u>colour</u>, how long <u>time</u>* (Seidlhofer 2004) or even whole phrases: *I got two ideas <u>in my mind</u>* (Dewey 2007). Another form of redundancy in LFE is the addition of another noun with the same reference, e.g. *English this subject is in the national curriculum* (Dewey 2007; my emphases).

The focus of the above-mentioned studies is descriptive. However, there seems to be an underlying function to most of these 'additions' or redundant forms: They seem to be motivated by a pragmatic intention, i.e. to increase clarity. The added expression stresses or clarifies the meaning of the preceding noun or verb. And since in lingua franca situations understanding cannot be taken for granted, these words might be used to clarify the lexical meaning and avoid misunderstandings (cf. Seidlhofer 2004:38). So redundancy, although showing on the phrase level and referring to lexical aspects, could as well be listed under *Pragmatics* (see below).

Redundancy is also one of the features of ELF that Seidlhofer (2004:38) enumerates in her summary of features of ELF. She summarises features of ELF as follows:

- intensive use of semantically wide, general verbs such as *make, do, have, put, take*
- invariable forms for question tags such as *isn't it?* or *no?* instead of the forms of Standard English, e.g. *shouldn't we?* etc.
- enlarged redundancy (and thereby clarity) by inserting prepositions (*discuss about something, phone to somebody*) or nouns (*black colour* instead of *black* or *how long time* instead of *how long*).

The 'intensive use of semantically wide, general verbs' she mentions will be discussed under the heading *Verb frequency*; cf. chapter 8.2.2).

4.5 Morphology and syntax

On the level of morphology, speakers of LFE sometimes make use of forms that exist in the standard varieties, but apply them differently. For example, they may use a lexeme that fits the context. In order to also fit it in grammatically, they mark it as a noun or verb by adding a suffix. So they use suffixes that are available in the language but are not applied by (adult) L1 speakers. Examples of new nouns created through a non-standard combination of a standard lexeme plus suffix are *boringdom* or *discriminization* (Björkman 2008) or *dictature* for *dictatorship* (Hülmbauer 2007). Examples of word formations concerning verbs are e.g. *forsify, levelize* (Björkman 2008), which are not part of the standard lexicon of English. However, they are formed according to the rules of word formation.

Other non-standard forms are e.g. the analytic comparatives where standard varieties tend to use synthetic forms, e.g. *more easy.* Double comparatives like *more safer*, *more wider* are other examples of expressions in LFE that are different from inner circle uses. These forms are redundant yet – or rather therefore – easy to understand. Countability is also a semantic aspect that leads to non-standard forms, e.g. *how many hydrogen* (Björkman 2008). So is the non-marking of the plural on the noun, e.g. *all the detail* (Björkman 2008). Although not found in inner circle usage, none of these forms seems to cause communicative problems. They only affect the marking of grammatical categories of the word in question. Most of the phenomena described under headings like 'morphosyntactic features of ELF' (e.g. Seidlhofer 2002) do not affect communicative success negatively.

Björkman (2010) lists 12 different phenomena of non-standard language use of which only the non-standard question formulations caused any communicative problems. Questions like '*What other equation I would use?*' caused communicative problems because they were not interpreted as questions. Deviant forms of negation, like e.g. *It looks not good* or *This point is supposed to not move*, on the other hand, did not cause communicative problems. This might be because, although different to standards in form, they are semantically clear. So are other features, e.g. the use of articles, that affect different parts of speech.

4.5.1 Noun phrase

Some of the features of LFE use can be broken down into single features of parts of speech. And even though they affect e.g. the pragmatics of the language, they can be classified according to their grammatical function or the part of speech they affect. One feature is the non-standard use of articles (cf. Björkman 2008, Cogo/Dewey 2006, Meierkord 2006). Although it is not reported to cause any communicative problems, researchers found the phenomenon interesting enough to study it in detail. Interestingly, though, only Cogo/Dewey (2006) and Dewey (2007) explain the differences in article use to Standard English as a communicative strategy in ELF.

Cogo/Dewey (2006) interpret the omission of articles as an accommodation strategy. Some speakers seem to omit the article after the first speaker has done so. They do not explicitly discuss it as a marker of non-learning oriented discourse. However, the fact that speakers accommodate to the speaker with less proficiency could be an indicator of lingua franca discourse as opposed to learner discourse: Learners usually try to orient towards the more competent speaker. Lingua franca speakers, on the other hand, might accommodate to the less competent speaker.

Dewey (2007) offers an interesting explanation of non-standard article uses: According to his findings, the article in his data is used where it is not used in

Standard English, i.e. with abstract nouns like *abortion, euthanasia, nature* and *pollution*. He hypothesises that the article use increases the relative importance of the noun it precedes. According to his findings, speakers in lingua franca discourse make use of linguistic means in unconventional ways to stress the importance of parts of their speech and mark them for their hearers. So the function seems to be a pragmatic one.

Although not explicitly found in her interpretation, a similar explanation may hold for the examples of non-standard usage of the definite article given in Björkman (2010). Examples are *The Einstein* or *Pure hydrogen comes from the natural gas* and *So question. What is renewables? Anybody can define the renewability?* (Björkman 2010:232). They seem to indicate a similar function as Dewey (2007) assumes. The definite article seems to indicate enhanced importance of the noun it precedes. So Björkman's data could support Dewey's hypothesis that the definite article is used to emphasise a noun's relative importance in discourse. The examples of the zero article Björkman (2010) gives also seem to support this hypothesis: *Who has paid for the infrastructure? That's always ø interesting question* and *From those figures, you can have ø idea what reasonable speed [...]* (Björkman 2010:232).[8] Nouns like *infrastructure* and *figures* are marked with a determinator like *those* or the definite article and carry relative importance; *interesting question* and *idea*, on the other hand, seem to be less relevant and are thus not marked.

Dewey (2007:66) sees the use of articles as one aspect of language use that is different in LFE. He assumes that in ELF, the relative importance of a noun in discourse is the decisive criterium for the use of the article. He concludes:

> There are [...] some notable innovative patterns of usage emerging in much of the data, part of which involves a shift in the article system away from a distinction between specific and generic reference. A more significant factor determining whether the zero or definite article is the preferred option in ELF often involves the relative level of importance attached to a noun or noun phrase in a given stretch of discourse. If an item is deemed to be of particular importance it will often be preceded by the definite article, while if the item is relatively unimportant it will often more likely be used with the zero article. Therefore, a primary function of the definite article seems to be to provide additional emphasis to a noun and thus signify its increased importance relative to the discourse. This suggests quite strongly that in ELF, patterns in the article system are far more context dependent and meaning driven than they tend to be in ENL (Dewey 2010:66).

8 The third example in Björkman (2010:232), "L2 is ø liquid", cannot be interpreted without context since *liquid* could as well be an adjective.

So not all deviations from standard forms seem to be due to the user's mastery of the language. Sometimes, it seems, deviant forms fulfil a communicative purpose, usually a pragmatic one, e.g. stressing something. So in lingua franca (English), speakers guide the hearer's attention towards aspects the speaker considers important. This communicative function seems to be rated higher than grammatical correctness, i.e. inner circle standards.

Sometimes, however, deviations fulfil no communicative purpose but simply differ from standard language, e.g. due to inferences. An example is the use of prepositions. A street sign in Germany, which was up in the year 2009 in Düsseldorf, welcomed visitors to a trade fair. Although the preposition was not standard, the message on the sign was quite clear:

Street sign in Düsseldorf, Germany, (Kappeler Straße), October 2009 (personal source).

4.5.2 *Verb phrase*

When it comes to verbs in LFE, a frequently studied feature of morphology is the omission of the third person singular *-s*. It affects the morphology of the sentence predicate, but becomes relevant on sentence level because it affects the subject-verb-agreement. The use of the *-s* as the marker of the 3rd person singular of the present tense indicative active of the verb, or rather its omission, is observed and described in various papers, e.g. Ahvenainen 2005, Björkman 2008, Breiteneder 2005, Cogo/Dewey 2006, Dewey 2010, Seidlhofer 2004; 2005.

It is interesting how much this feature has been studied, even though it does not seem to have much influence on the communicative success of an utterance. Breiteneder (2005) as well as Cogo/Dewey (2006) discuss the feature in more detail. According to Cogo/Dewey (2006), the 'zero form', i.e. the omission of the

3rd person singular –s, and its use are two competing variants in LFE. According to their findings, its use is context-dependent. If a native speaker is present or the context is formal, speakers are more likely to use the 3rd person singular –s. Therefore, Cogo/Dewey (2006) conclude that "the 3rd person zero is emerging as the more characteristic, unmarked feature for present simple verb forms in ELF communication" (Cogo/Dewey 2006:80). One explanation might be that speakers monitor their language more consciously when a 'native speaker' is around. In lingua franca situations, speakers are more likely to see eye to eye, and their focus shifts to the content.

Breiteneder (2005) also focused on the 3rd pers. sing. –s. She found that 29 tokens in her data were marked out of 141 tokens that, according to Standard English grammar, required the marking of tense and number by the so-called '3rd person singular –s'. That makes 20.57%. The omission was independent of whether the sentence subjects were pronouns or singular nouns. She explains these findings by processes leading to "maximization of economy and simplicity as well as differentiation" (2005:13). So she holds linguistic and extra-linguistic principles as well as effects of language contact responsible for the omission of the third person singular marker. These principles are, e.g., the *principle of notion* and the *principle of proximity*. The first one explains that collective nouns are treated as plural, even though grammatically they are singular. And the *principle of proximity* explains that the verb is chosen in agreement with the preceding (plural) noun phrase which is closer to the verb than the actual (singular) subject.

Interestingly, however, she also found 15 instances of what she calls 'overgeneralisation', i.e. present tense verbs that are marked by an -s morpheme although they refer to a plural noun. This phenomenon was also described by Björkman (2010:232f.). Breiteneder (2005:21f.) tries to ascribe the occurring forms in her findings to phenomena like language contact, too. However, the linguistic principles and extra-linguistic circumstances she quotes fail to explain 6 out of 15 instances of the 'over-generalization', i.e. of the extended use of the 3rd person singular –s.

But the feature varies in the data, so an explanation should either encompass all the instances or explain the variety in use. And since no pragmatic reason could be found, a potential explanation might be that it is a feature of learner language. Although the representatives recorded for the study were proficient users of the English language, they might not have completed the acquisition of subject-verb agreement. Subject-verb agreement becomes automatised relatively late in the process of language acquisition (cf. Pienemann 1998). So the missing 'agreement' might have a psycholinguistic reason.

Besides, Breiteneder argues that dropping the 3rd person singular –*s* is a marker of "social identity and prestige" (2005:6). This goes in line with sociolinguistic processes that occur in English varieties. However, it does not hold for the given context. It may well be assumed that "representatives of the EU government and national agencies of higher education" (ibid.) carrying out official meetings will attempt to use a standard variety. In the given context, it is likely to be Standard British English. And that is characterised by marking of the 3rd person singular.

So the omission of the third person singular –*s* as a grammatical marker is a widely spread phenomenon; not only in lingua franca situations, but also in many varieties of English. Yet, it is not one that inhibits understanding. The question thus is why researchers spend so much effort on its research. As opposed to the tense and aspect of the verb, e. g., it does not carry a specific meaning and is a redundant grammatical form.

4.5.2.1 Tense and Aspect

The tense and especially the aspect of a verb carry a lot of information. The tense is relevant because it places the action at a certain point in time, i. e. in the past, present or future. Therefore, it is relevant for the hearer to place the action in the time continuum. The aspect, on the other hand, "marks the duration or type of temporal activity denoted to the verb" (Crystal 2003:36). It is not used in all languages – at least not in standard varieties, e. g. not in standard German (although in some dialects, cf. the *Rheinische Verlaufsform* (*Rhenish continuous form*)). Other languages, like Spanish or English however, use the aspect to provide further information concerning the duration of an action. It will be interesting to see in the long run, in how far speakers of LFE make use of the aspect since it is not marked in all (standard) languages. So the question is whether speakers regard it as relevant and under which circumstances.

Björkman (2010) discusses issues of the aspect, such as the use of the progressive instead of simple form for scientific or technical phenomena. The example *Do you understand how this is working not what it is but how it is working?* (2010:233) did not cause communicative problems. Ranta (2006) discusses the finding, too. She compares the use of progressive forms by native speakers and non-native speakers with the help of the Michigan Corpus of Academic Spoken English (MICASE). She found the same 'non-standard' use, i. e. the use of the progressive for static verbs and for verbs in statements of general validity, in the MICASE corpus. So native speakers of US American English used the progressive for these static verbs. However, they use it less frequently than lingua franca speakers. Lingua franca speakers also use the progressive for points in time in the past (Ranta 2006:109). Ranta assumes a pragmatic function as the reason for the attractiveness of the progressive. According to her interpretation, lingua franca speakers want to put emphasis on the verb and thus use the progressive. So the use of progressives, and thus of the aspect, represents, according to Ranta (2006:112), a communication strategy.

4.5.3 *Sentence structure*

Regarding the overall sentence structure, findings indicate that grammar in lingua franca communication is driven by simplification on the one hand and communicative aspects on the other hand. Meierkord (2004), for example, found a high conformity to the norms which characterise British or American English. But when marked forms occur, they can usually be ascribed to three different reasons: to interlanguage patterns, to transfer patterns or to communication strategies. Interlanguage patterns are forms that learners are reported to use in the process of learning. Transfer phenomena are forms caused by the influence of the mother tongue. Phenomena explained as communication strategies are, e.g. accommodation and simplification. Simplification is the structuring of talk into short utterances as opposed to long or complex sentences. This makes it easier for the hearer to process the given information. One example is *topicalisation*, i.e. the movement of focused information to the front of the utterance (cf. Meierkord 2004:125).

Topicalisation is also realised through *left dislocation*, also known as *fronting*. It is putting the element in question in the first position of the utterance regardless of its pre-determined position in the written (standard) sentence. Examples of fronting are *This rate you have it* or *This report we'll do it later* (Björkman 2008) and *Difficult culture, ours is* or *Three years you have to do* (Meierkord 2004:127). These so-called deviations are not learner errors, however. They are phenomena that occur in L1 communication as well (cf. Prince 1981 for a more detailed discussion). Fronting is used to put emphasis on the first part of the utterance as in *Macadamia nuts I yet have to buy* (Meierkord 2004:127) quoted in Meierkord/Dresemann (2009).

Although left dislocation is less frequent in English than in other languages, e.g. in Spanish, it is, according to Hidalgo (2002:1), a universal strategy with a topic marking function. And although it is a marked construction in English and restricted to oral language use (Hidalgo 2002:15), it is an interactional device that speakers, including native speakers, use to stress parts of a sentence. This way, they put it or keep it in the focus of a conversation. So they simplify focusing on relevant information for the hearer. Therefore, topicalisation is a communicative strategy.

Another tendency in LFE that, e.g. Hülmbauer (2007) describes is simplification through replacing question tags. Especially *isn't it?* is used regardless of the actual predicate of the sentence. The question tag as such is a communicative means to involve the hearer by inviting them to react to the utterance. In English, the question tag is supposed to morphologically agree with the predicate of the sentence. The question tag usually consists of a pronoun and a verb, often plus negation. This, however, requires a strategy that matches different parts of the sentence (cf. Pienemann 1998) and thus requires a lot of mental capacity. So replacing the matching question tag with a ready-made chunk is less psychologically demanding since it does not require agreement with the verb. So it serves the function of involving the hearer while at the same time sparing the speaker's mental resources.

Often, linguistic structures in LFE are described as grammatical, i.e. morphosyntactic, features only. Not always do researchers interpret them as communication strategies. However, it seems that many phenomena that are described only as structural features affect the discourse behaviour. So they might really be strategies used to minimise psycholinguistic effort for either the speaker or the hearer or both and at the same time ensure understanding.

4.6 Discourse

On the level of discourse, most lingua franca communication is said to be successful and cooperative (e.g. Meierkord 1993, Pitzl 2005, Mauranen 2006) and to run smoothly (Firth 1990). However, as research has shown, not all lingua franca communication that looks smooth on the surface is really successful: Meierkord (1996), for example, found that when mutual understanding turns problematic and communication becomes difficult, interlocutors change topics. House (2002a), similarly, shows that sometimes coherence exists only in the contributions of the same speaker. And Knapp (2002) found that the context, as well as the speaker's goals, determine whether or not competent speakers are ready to cooperate with others. Sometimes they use their competence to gain advantages over less competent speakers.

Most of the studies in the field were carried out in academic settings in the widest sense. Not all of these findings are applicable to all contexts of use of LFE, even though they give valuable insights into the structures applied by lingua franca speakers. In other professional contexts, however, communicative success ought to be determined by whether or not understanding is achieved. This could be measured by the non-linguistic consequences outside the communication. But if topics are changed or contributions left without reaction, communication may fail certain aims that lie outside purely social purposes. So the question is if communicative success can be measured by objective criteria. However, this is often not the focus of research.

When it comes to pragmatics, the focus of research is usually not on the non-linguistic goals, but on the achievement of effects on a local level. However, in the field of discourse, a lot of insights have been gained concerning aspects of pragmatics and communicative strategies. Some have used specific foci like accommodation, misunderstandings (and their avoidance) or intercultural aspects of lingua franca research.

Due to differences in context and data, findings in lingua franca research are sometimes contradictory. Meierkord (1998; 2002), for example, studied lingua franca speakers in social encounters. She found that topic changes were used as a communicative strategy when communication problems occurred. Firth (1990; 1996) on the other hand, as well as Björkman (2008), who studied business interactions and interactions in university courses respectively, found that participants did not change topics. Instead, they had to overcome communicative problems if they could no longer 'let it pass'.

These contradictory findings are due to the fact that high stakes encounters usually do not allow for topic avoidance or topic changes because institutional or professional objectives make it necessary for speakers to reach their objectives. Social encounters, on the other hand, are usually guided by the maxim of politeness (cf. chapter 9.6.1). This leads to the concentration of topics that are neither conflict-laden nor linguistically too demanding for one or the other participant. Thus comparisons across different forms of discourse in LFE are difficult to make. And many non-linguistic aspects influence linguistic as well as social behaviour.

However, it is interesting to see how users of English operate in the language and interact successfully in most cases despite their – sometimes reduced – language means. Research focused, among other aspects, on how they indicate meaning, especially illocution. Findings in the field of LFE come from different approaches, mainly from Conversation Analysis, but also from Discourse Analysis, Cross-cultural Pragmatics, and a few from Functional Pragmatics, etc. So terminology and research foci differ. However, in the following I have tried to organise findings from different studies according to different aspects of pragmatics. I adopted some of the well-known concepts and terms, mainly from Conversation Analysis, the approach used for the majority of research in the field, and ordered the findings according to these foci:

1) use of gambits
2) discourse strategies
3) misunderstandings/negotiation of meaning
4) interculturality
5) code switching

Again, categories may overlap and some findings may – like with the grammatical categories above – belong to more than one category or differ from the categories that were used in the primary study. However, these categories are only labels that help organise the findings in a way that I hope will make them more accessible.

4.6.1 Use of gambits

One of the first researchers concentrating on pragmatic aspects of LFE was House. Coming from a cross-cultural studies background, House, in some of her studies (e.g. 2002), compares the structure of lingua franca discourse and the use of gambits to that of native speakers of English. In other studies, House (2002a; 2003) concentrates on interactions between LFE speakers.

House found a lack of coherence between different interactants' contributions, e.g. questions were not answered. Subjects in House's study hardly used discourse markers or discourse particles with one exception, namely 'Represents' (i.e. the hearer repeats part of the utterance). She explains problems and discrepancies by the "Self-Centered Hypothesis". It accounts for subjects' lack of orientation towards the other, which leads to non-coherent talk (House 1999; cf. also House 2002a).

However, House found a high frequency of utterance-initial conjunctions like *but* or *and*, but not *I see, well, yes* etc., which would be used in inner circle discourse instead. Furthermore, subjects in her study used hardly any interpersonally active discourse strategies (i.e. moves supporting their main illocutionary intent) e.g. 'I'd like to ask a question'; 'I hate to contradict you but' (House 2002:254). And "violations of turn transition points and of relevance" (ibid.) marked their discourse. House also found abrupt topic changes in the conversations, but she also found what she calls a "marked demonstration of solidarity and consensus-orientation" (ibid.). Cooperation, scaffolding and the co-construction of utterances were common in her data. These findings are similar to what Wagner/Firth (1997) found in their study of LFE discourse. Cooperation was limited to the local level or problems of formulating single utterances. The overall discourse lacked coherence. And although participants were cooperative regarding these issues, the question is if they would have been able to achieve any non-linguistic goals, especially if it had been in high-stakes encounters. In high-stakes encounters, a lack of coherence is not acceptable and might threaten the non-linguistic objectives.

Using House's (1982) and Edmondson/House's (1981) theoretical background, Meierkord (1996) carried out one of the first empirical studies on ELF in authentic contexts. She recorded dinner table conversations in an international students' residence. So her data were authentic, informal conversations in LFE. In her analysis, she focussed on the organisation of talk and the use of gambits. Her findings include that speakers do not link opening and closing phases to the core of the conversation and change topics abruptly, and that speakers fail to use, e.g. extractors. Instead, speakers tend to use other indicators like long pauses or laughter to replace linguistic signs (cf. Meierkord 1996; 1998). However, she also finds a high degree of cooperation in utterance formulation and negotiation of meaning, which again equals cooperation on a local level.

4.6.2 Accommodation

Another discourse strategy that was found in LFE discourse – or sometimes applied to explain phenomena of lingua franca communication – is *accommodation*. Accommodation Theory interprets speech modifications as a means to identify with or distance oneself from the other speaker by using the same or distinct features of speech (cf. e.g. Giles/Coupland 1991).

Knapp (2002), for example, uses Accommodation Theory to explain differences in behaviour of the same speakers in different situations depending on what is at stake. He observed students at an international students conference. In general, they were cooperative as long as their linguistic behaviour in the respective situation was not assessed. Knapp differentiates between *native speakers (ns)*, *non-native speakers (nns)* and *quasi-native speakers (qns)*, i.e. speakers who were raised in inner circle countries or were attending school there. During the course of the simulations at the conference, the nns' contributions became fewer during negotiations and discussions. However, the most competent students showed cooperative behaviour in some instances, e.g. in negotiations of meaning. When their contributions to the conference were assessed, however, qns tried to make the partners in conversation appear less competent. They showed competitive behaviour in group discussions and negotiations because their contributions to the outcome of the simulation were graded. They made fun of nns' slips of the tongue or communicative deficiencies, ignored contributions if the meaning was not clear or rejected them. They even voiced aggressive criticism as in "Can't you say this in other words?" (Knapp 2002:232). They also limited the less competent partner's influence in the communicative process. They were cooperative as long as their own objectives were not affected, yet they showed uncooperative behaviour in high stakes situations, e. g. when being graded.

Knapp's study is one of the few observing uncooperative behaviour in LFE communication. Using Speech Accommodation Theory, he explains differences between uncooperative behaviour in students' interactions and business negotiations: In informal contexts, speech accommodation serves as an in-group marker. In the conflicting situations in Knapp's (2002) data, however, language differences were used as out-group markers and diverging goals lead to competition. In business negotiations, however, diverging goals are accepted and do not lead to uncooperative linguistic behaviour (cf. Knapp 2002:241).

Another form of accommodation is what Firth describes as 'make-it-normal' (Firth 1996). As explained earlier, subjects in his data, a set of business negotiations, pretend there is nothing extraordinary about the talk although the other's choice of words is marked. They accommodate by treating marked or unclear forms as if they were unmarked forms or as if they understood. They do so as long as the misunderstanding or non-understanding does not become obvious or hinders them from continuing the process (cf. above)

This strategy does not disturb the ongoing communication as long as both speaker and hearer know what the other means. It becomes problematic only when one of the interlocutors does not understand what is intended, yet avoids making the problem explicit. However, as long as no problems occur, participants in the business negotiations studied by Firth support each other linguistically by accepting odd linguistic forms. So Knapp's (2002) thesis that diverging goals are accepted in business contexts and do not lead to uncooperative linguistic behaviour goes in line with Firth's (1996) findings.

4.6.3 *Misunderstandings*

Misunderstandings do occur in lingua franca communication despite the fact that speakers go to a lot of effort to avoid them. The way speakers deal with them, however, seems to be very much dependent on the form of discourse.

Pitzl (2005) studied non-understandings and misunderstandings in business meetings and found that speakers try to prevent misunderstandings by self-initiated negotiation of meaning. According to her findings, speakers signal non-understanding directly if it is relevant, e.g. through requests like *Again?*, yet not through meta-discourse. This might be due to the fact that in business negotiations, time is a scarce resource. So elaboration of the problem is avoided and not regarded as a lack of politeness since it saves time. And since the communicative aim is quite clear and cooperative behaviour is given (cf. Knapp 2002, above), the short form of the request seems to be considered appropriate.

Mauranen (e.g. 2006) studied misunderstandings in academic exchanges. According to her findings, speakers actively try to ensure mutual understanding. They signal misunderstanding by using confirmation checks as well as interactive repair and self-repair. Academic discourse seems to show the highest level of cooperation between participants as well as linguistic awareness. Participants do not only avoid misunderstandings through their interactive behaviour, but also use interactional repair strategies if communication becomes troublesome. They also "maximize simplicity" (Mauranen 2006:123) in order to ensure understanding. They use simple structures that are easier to process for the hearer and make the communication process as efficient as possible. Furthermore, questions and backchannels like *hm* are used to signal possible sources of incorrect understanding or interpretation. Their use leads to clarification and explanation. Mauranen (2006) observes that "seemingly redundant signalling of comprehension also seemed to reflect a heightened awareness of a need for cooperation" (Mauranen 2006:135).

So speakers in professional contexts seem to be aware of communicative requirements and adapt their production to meet the hearer's needs. At the same time, they accept limited and shorter forms and hold efficiency over politeness. In purely social interactions, participants seem to avoid negotiation of meaning as it bears the risk of failure. Rather, they change topics and keep the interaction as simple as possible without the risk of communicative breakdown. Difficult or complex interactions might threaten the communicative and social situation and are therefore avoided. Participants in academic discourse or business negotiations, on the other hand, cannot avoid certain topics or change them if they become linguistically demanding. They have to pursue their professional and business aims and thus have to find ways to achieve understanding.

4.6.4 Negotiation of meaning

Negotiation of meaning is a very important discourse strategy in LFE discourse. That is because successful communication is not a given. And if communication is not successful from the beginning, negotiation of meaning is the key device to turn things around. It is possible, e.g. to repair the passage of discourse that went pear-shaped and to avoid misunderstandings through negotiation of meaning and clarification.

According to Clyne (1994:144f.), success in communication is based on the relation between "the speaker's communicative intention, the interlocutor's expectation of the message, and communicative effects of the message." So success in communication can only be reached if "the communicative effects match the intentions" (ibid.).

Clyne differs between five possible outcomes of a communicative act:

- Communication which is successful from the start
- Potentially unsuccessful communication, where a communication breakdown (including a pragmalinguistic failure in the sense of Thomas 1983) is averted through negotiation of meaning. Thus, communication is successful in the end
- Resolved unsuccessful communication. Due to the resolution of the communication breakdown is resolved. Thus, communication is successful in the end
- Unsuccessful communication which cannot be resolved
- Unsuccessful communication whose resolution has not been attempted.

In his view, communicative failure can be solved by negotiation of meaning if the interlocutors are aware of the problem and willing to solve it. So negotiation of meaning is a central procedure in communication, especially in communication that is not successful from the beginning; a situation that is not uncommon in lingua franca communication.

According to Varonis/Gass (1985), the communicative goal is decisive for the interpretation of an utterance, i.e. the hearer tries to interpret an utterance according to the context in which it was uttered or the context assumed by the hearer. Speakers and hearers have a "shared belief space" (Varonis/Gass 1985:336), a notion based on Marlos' (1981:554) definition of a belief space:

> [A] belief space 'contains both the set of propositions a participant believes to be true of the world, and any goals he holds that are directly relevant to or invoked by the speech event in question' (cited in Varonis/Gass 1985:366).

But if expectations differ and the hearer does not interpret the utterance according to the speaker's intentions, negotiation of meaning is necessary.

Negotiation of meaning seems to be a crucial feature of LFE, since 'meaning' is not necessarily a shared notion. Culturally determined interpretations of a word or expression are not always identical (as e.g. the concepts of 'breakfast' or 'tea' across cultures show). A further complication that comes in here is the fact that lingua franca communication is by definition intercultural. And so culturally determined meanings are deemed to becoming problematic, or they have to be negotiated.

4.6.5 *Interculturality*

The interpretation of complex expressions and sometimes also of single words is biased by cultural conventions that influence language use. The question regarding lingua franca discourse then is: To what extent do cultural notions influence communicative processes?

Although, theoretically, a strong cultural and L1 influence is assumed in lingua franca communication (cf. Meierkord 2002:110), this influence could not be confirmed in e.g. Meierkord's data (cf. Meierkord 2002). House (1999) even formulated the "Culture Irrelevance Hypothesis", which states that "[i]n ELF talk it is not interactants' affiliation with their native linguacultural norm and values that come to the fore, rather interactants act primarily as individuals and there is no strong attachment to their L1 groups" (House 1999:84).

Pölzl/Seidlhofer (2006) also concentrate on cultural influence and discuss the so-called *habitat factor*, i.e the influence of the culture that surrounds ELF discourses. It influences the use of language, especially discourse strategies. According to their findings, gambits and discourse strategies are transferred from a speaker's L1 to ELF if it seems appropriate. So they function as 'habitat markers'. The pre-condition is that the discourse in question takes place in the surroundings of some of the speakers. And that other speakers are familiar with the culture and the gambits/discourse markers and other forms of pragmatic behaviour. The *habitat factor* is meant to explain that the culture that surrounds the ELF discourses influences language use.

4.6.6 *Code switching*

Another discourse strategy found in LFE discourses is *code switching*. *Code switching* means that in an utterance – or sometimes a few utterances – a different language is used, usually the L1 of the speaker. Code switching can be the switching between different languages within an utterance or between utterances. Switching within an utterance and using different language for different parts of an utterance is sometimes also labelled *code mixing*. *Code mixing* implies that different languages are combined to create an utterance.

Usually, code switching is intended to achieve a communicative effect, either to establish a social identity (cf. Holmes/Stubbe 2004) or to be dramatic (Clyne 1997:309). Sometimes a phenomenon called *borrowing* is used. It means that a speaker 'borrows' a word or phrase from another language. Speakers usually 'borrow' because they lack a certain term or expression in the language of communication. So *borrowing* qualifies as a communicative strategy to enable understanding, whereas *code switching* and *code mixing* can enable communication, but usually serve a more rhetorical or psychological purpose.

In lingua franca contexts, speakers sometimes use borrowing by using a term from their first (or other) language and define it for their interlocutor. Also, speakers sometimes use the politeness formula from the hearer's L1 or from the surrounding or habitat in which they interact (cf. Pölzl/Seidlhofer 2006).

Code switching can also be used for strategic purposes, e.g. to exclude someone – sometimes even one of the hearers (or participants) – from part of the ongoing discourse. This happened in one of the recordings for this dissertation project. The incident was discussed in detail in Dresemann 2007.

In the following example, two speakers, the German distribution manager S1mGr and the Norwegian label manager S3mNr, discuss the option of using existing business connections with a distribution company to import goods to Germany. The idea came up earlier in the discourse. Since S3mNr did not favour the suggestion, they did not agree, but remained non-committal. At this point, the topic has come up again, and S4mGr, a co-worker of S1mGr's who joined them earlier, switches to German. He makes the suggestion of using the existing business connection. He speaks English to the two of them most of the time, but in se (847), he switches to German. He does so to open a side discourse with his co-worker and to exclude the Norwegian speaker (cf. Dresemann 2007). However, S3mNr manages to re-enter the conversation in se (863) in English after an unsuccessful attempt in se (852), in which he tried to interrupt the other speakers. (Original transcript; my translations):[9]

(842)	S4mGr	I will speak to Anthony tomorrow.
(843)	S4mGr	I'm not too sure if I can handle it at the moment.
(844)	S4mGr	But maybe there is a possiblility.
(845)	S1mGr	I think maybe there is a chance if, you know, I involve myself.
(846)	S1mGr	So we have to, we have to see how we can …
(847)	S4mGr	Kannst ja mit Righthand anfangen zu dealen. (*Why don't you start dealing with Righthand?)*
(848)	S1mGr	Nee, das ist … *(No, that is …)*
(849)	S4mGr	Das ist ja kein Problem. *(That's no problem.)*
(850)	S4mGr	Die haben ja alle ( ). *(They have all the ( ) anyway.)*
(851)	S4mGr	Ja, müssen wir mal gucken, wie wir das machen. *(We'll see how we're gonna do it.)*
(852)	S3mNr	It's up, it's up …
(853)	S1mGr	Es geht ja auch dann auch nur um die/um den Kontakt. *(It's only about the contact anyway.)*
(854)	S1mGr	Es ist ja das eine, die Warenbestellung. *(That's the one thing, the orders.)*
(855)	S1mGr	( )…
(856)	S1mGr	Ja, das ginge schon. *(Yeah, it would be possible.)*

9 The original transcript was published in Dresemann 2007:128 f.

(857)	S4mGr	Ja, du sagst uns, was bestellt werden muss. *(Yeah, you tell me what has to be ordered.)*
(858)	S4mGr	Ich mein, der Guido bestellt sowas fast immer bei Righthand. *(I mean, Guido almost always orders those things at Righthand.)*
(859)	S4mGr	Der bestellt dann auch meinen Kram mit, aber ich hab trotzdem sehr viel Kontakt direkt zu Y C K, weil Y C K mir dann auch die (die Labels)/die Infos rüberschickt. *(He also orders my stuff, but I still have a lot of direct contact to Y C K because Y C K then sends me the, (the labels)/ the information.)*
(860)	S4mGr	Weil anlegen und so tu ich alles selbst. *(Because the creating and so on I do myself.)*
(861)	S1mGr	Das würde ich dann halt auch machen. *(I would do that myself, too.)*
(862)	S3mNr	You are, you are not doing all the label, right?
(863)	S4mGr	No.
(864)	S3mNr	No, they have too many.

Example: Distribution deal (DIS)

In utterance se (847), S4mGr switches to German. Thereby, he opens a side-discourse with S1mGr and excludes the Norwegian speaker S3mNr because S3mNr does not share their common language. However, as I showed in Dresemann 2007, S3mNr applies professional knowledge and receptive multilingualism to first follow the discourse between the two and to stand his ground. And in utterance (842), he uses a productive strategy, in English, to become an 'active' participant, i. e. he speaks and thus takes the floor. The use of receptive multilingualism does require a lot of 'activity' even though it is a labelled a 'receptive' form of language use. S3mNr strategically applies a question to make the others turn back to English and to be part of the discourse again:

(862)	S3mNr	You are, you are not doing all the label, right?

At the beginning of his utterance (se (862)), S3mNr uses the personal pronoun *you* to directly address S1mGr and gain the attention of his hearer. The repetition of the first part indicates that his planning is still incomplete. However, he uses the opportunity of a falling intonation by S1mGr in se (861), which indicates a completed utterance. He starts his utterance to gain S1mGr's attention. And by asking a direct question, he makes both his hearers turn back to English. It makes the hearer not only code switch, but also adopt the topic S3mNr raises. Thus they create shared knowledge due to his initiative. And with the shared discourse knowledge and the re-established discourse language – LFE – the discourse can be continued between the original participants.

So code switching is used for two different reasons here: Firstly, for strategic reasons. It is used to create room for discourse that excludes one of the speakers. It enables those who share a language – in this case the two German label managers – to open a side discourse. This way, they (believe they can) discuss an aspect that is, to their interpretation, not meant for S3mNr to be part of. Secondly, code switching is used to gain influence and mark active participation. In se (862), switching back to English gives the speaker a chance to re-gain influence and demonstrate power by changing the topic. Thus in both cases code switching is used for strategic purposes.

Code switching was also found to specify meaning by administrative academic staff in a pan-European conference (Klimpfinger 2007). Code switching, which in Klimpfinger's interpretation covers code switching in the strict sense as well as code mixing and borrowing, was used when new keywords were introduced into the discussion that had a cultural or national notion. The new keywords were accompanied by explanations and translations to enable comprehension. So code switching served to transport a specific notion from the national language context to the lingua franca context. Contrary to House's (2002) assumption that LFE serves as a language of communication rather than as a language of identification, Klimpfinger (2007) found a different function. In her data, it served as a marker of identity. Similar functions were found on the lexical as well as the pragmatic level (Pölzl/Seidlhofer 2006). Meierkord (2005), on the other hand, found participants in lingua franca communication borrowing no lexical items from their L1s, even if their national languages were nativised varieties of English. Instead, they rather oriented towards inner circle varieties.

There may not be general agreement on whether or not LFE serves as a language of identification or not. However, it can be said that it first and foremost serves as a language of communication, especially in a professional context. In other, more social settings, it may also serve as a language of identification (*Identifikationssprache*) in the sense of Hüllen (1992).

All in all, language 'correctness' or inner circle standards can be said to be secondary in lingua franca communication. And speakers make use of unusual forms and communication strategies to enable the hearer to decode not only their message, but also their intention. Hearers, on the other hand, are very tolerant and for the most part cooperative in lingua franca communication. They focus on the speakers' intentions more than on form.

When it comes to ELF, it can be said that it

- takes on different functions and thus different forms depending on the discourse function as well as participants' language competence,
- takes on forms that may differ from inner circle language use,
- is mostly cooperative,
- is used for communicative rather than learning purposes,

- primarily serves as a language of communication, but sometimes also of identification,
- is a language whose actual forms depend on the speaker's and hearer's ability and on the context in which it is used.

5. Business negotiations

5.1 General definitions of *business negotiation*

Business negotiation is a type of discourse that is carried out not for the purpose of communication as such, but to fulfil a societal need. And the linguistic forms used in this specific form of discourse are evoked by the constellation. And although *business negotiation* is a very frequent term, its definition is not as clear-cut and obvious as one might expect at first sight.

If one enters the term *business negotiation* in a search engine like Google, they will receive literally millions of results in less than a minute (123,000,000 in 0.42 sec (accessed 25 July 2019)). Most of the entries contain keywords like 'successful negotiation', 'skills', 'tactics' etc.

One of the few definitions that do appear – albeit on a page about negotiation skills – defines *negotiation* as "a method by which people settle differences. It is a process by which compromise or agreement is reached while avoiding argument and dispute" (www.skillsyouneed.com/ips/negotiation.html). The 'differences' that make a negotiation necessary are mentioned, yet not defined. While the definition stays very much at a superficial level, it is explained that "individuals understandably aim to achieve the best possible outcome for their position (or perhaps an organisation they represent)". Thus, the function of negotiation is described as "the best possible outcome". So the focus is on the result rather than on the process. And although *negotiation* is defined as a 'method', this method is only broken down into stages. However, it is not defined or explained. So *business negotiation* is only seen as a means to get from an assumed 'problem' (diverging interests) to an ideal 'aim' (settle differences). However, no explanation of *method*, i. e. of procedures or actions that negotiators are to use, is given; neither is a way to measure its success.

The blog of the PON (Programme of Negotiation at Harvard Law School) starts with the heading *Business Negotiation*, but instead of a definition, the reader finds an entry explaining that "[e]ffective business negotiation is a core leadership and management skill" (www.pon.harvard.edu/category/daily/business-negotiations/; accessed 25/7/2019; original emphasis). So negotiation skills are defined as a "leadership and management skill". It is not explained how they can be noticed or which actions or abilities make this skill.

Most entries leave the definition aside and start by emphasising how important good negotiation skills or strategies are, like the website of Forbes Magazine.

It stresses: "Nearly every business deal requires a strategy for a successful *negotiation*"[10], leaving out the actual definition too. Instead, the entry jumps straight to the strategies that are assumed to be required.

One of the few exceptions is the government of Queensland, Australia, (one of the first three entries of the results). It defines negotiation, with reference to business, as "a process where two or more parties with different needs and goals discuss an issue to find a mutually acceptable solution"[11]. So it stresses the function of a negotiation: Finding a "mutually acceptable solution". This narrows down the successful outcome. More importantly, the process is defined through the use of the verb *discuss*. The most relevant part of the definition, however, is the fact that negotiation is defined as a "process of discussion". This definition makes the phenomenon of negotiation accessible from a linguistic point of view. According to it, the actions relevant for the process are verbal and observable (that is if one is allowed to observe and, ideally, record the negotiation).

The fact that *business negotiation* is defined on a government website shows how important business negotiations are, not just in the field of economy, but as a societal phenomenon. All in all, few definitions are given in the majority of entries. However, almost uncountable offers of suggestions and advice on negotiation are found. And even the English Wikipedia entry comes 13th place on the list, excluding ads and videos. This is an uncommon result and shows that the definition of negotiation is less frequently searched for than other pages, e.g. those offering advice.

The term is obviously so current – and thus important in our society – that its definition is not relevant for the majority of people. And although it is a frequently used term, its definition is not clear. And even among linguists, the definition lacks agreement. The following linguistic definitions from guide books and dictionaries will show that there is less agreement on the term than could be assumed (cf. 5.2 below).

5.2 Linguistic definitions of *business negotiation*

Researchers in the field of linguistics have defined *negotiation* in different ways. Wagner (1995) gives an overview of the different terms they have applied to the phenomenon, such as "language game" (Wittgenstein 1958), "activity type" (Levinson 1979), "frame" (Tannen 1979), "frames" and "scripts" (Goffman 1974; 1981),

10 www.forbes.com/sites/allbusiness/2016/09/16/15-tactics-for-successful-business-negotiations/#38ab55f22528 (25/7/2019)

11 www.business.qld.gov.au/running-business/marketing-sales/managing-relationships/negotiating (25/7/2019)

or “Handlungsmuster” (*pattern of action*) (Rehbein 1977, Ehlich/Rehbein 1972). He tries to overcome the problem that there is no generally accepted definition of *negotiation* and that most definitions refer to “a Western concept of negotiation” (Wagner 1995:11) (which has been a problem of many research areas for a long time). Wagner gives a definition that involves the negotiators’ awareness of the goals of the participants as the defining aspect of a negotiation. In his definition, he stresses that these goals are in one way or other controlled by the other party (Wagner 1995:11).

Rehbein (1995), who uses the framework of Functional Pragmatics to discuss the function of negotiation, defines *negotiation* as an *auxiliary device*. It is a means that speakers and hearers use within institutionalised patterns of action (*Handlungsmuster*) when a conflict of interest restrains them from resuming the pattern of action. According to Rehbein (1995), the *negotiation device* can occur at different points within different patterns of action if the speaker and hearer experience a discrepancy between their goals. This discrepancy needs to be overcome in order to move forward in the pattern of action. It is seen as a circular movement in which the hearer and the speaker take different ‘rounds’ trying to close the gap between their positions. Only when they have closed the gap between their positions can they resume the pattern of action. The ‘movements’ in the pattern lead them towards an exit point. At an exit point, an aim is reached, a decision can be made, and a future action is enabled (or required) that is supposed to fulfil a societal purpose.

Rehbein’s definition differs from Wagner’s in that Rehbein does not use ‘awareness’ and ‘control’ (cf. Wagner 1995:11) as determinators. Instead, he uses the linguistic and mental actions negotiators take to explain how agreements over details are reached. This is a necessary function to proceed towards the outcome of their discourse: a contract or the decision not to make a deal.

5.3 Definitions in guide books and dictionaries

Another area of publications on business negotiation is the field of guide books and dictionaries of business administration. Most of them also define *negotiation* as a process, and usually with a focus on the outcome or on strategic aspects, just like most entries of online sources of advice. The advice in most guide books aims at manipulating the other party and pursuing one’s own objectives.

Friedman (2007), for example, defines negotiation as the “process of bargaining that precedes an agreement. Successful negotiation generally results in a CONTRACT between the parties” (Friedman 2007:437; original emphasis).

In the same dictionary, under the entry *negotiable,* the following definitions are listed:

1. something that can be sold or transferred to another party in exchange for money or as settlement of an obligation
2. matter of mutual concern to one or more parties that involves conditions to be worked out to the satisfaction of the parties (Friedman 2007:436).

The second entry is one of the rare sources that stresses the process of jointly working out the conditions of something that will then be to the satisfaction of the parties involved. Thus it stresses a form of cooperation, at least as far as the process is concerned. Most other entries, definitions and advice alike, focus on the strategies leading towards a certain outcome. And the success of a negotiation is usually defined by the extent to which ONE party reaches its pre-set goal(s).

Most of the literature stresses different aspects negotiators are supposed to focus on, e.g. to have a 'battle plan' or 'floor plan', not to be provoked etc. (see e.g. Harvard Business Review on negotiation and conflict resolution 2000, Lewicki/Hiam 2006, Tracy 2013 etc.). These guide books do not analyse the process or give examples of actual encounters. And most guide books do not give a definition of *negotiation*. Rather, it seems that readers are supposed to draw on their own conception of *negotiation*. And negotiators are meant to focus on their own objectives as well as strategies rather than focussing on their interlocutor and the discourse that unfolds.

Two exceptions are Fisher/Ury 1981 as well as Ertel 2000. Fisher/Ury (1981) focus on the communicative processes and the importance of the decision-making process as well as the awareness of conflicting interests on the way to a common goal. And Ertel (2000) stresses that the aim of analysing and planning negotiations should be to make negotiators "feel comfortable walking away from a deal when it's not in the company's best interest" (Ertel 2000:102). This is exceptional because the focus is not on a specific outcome of a negotiation, i.e. a specific agreement that negotiators defined in advance based on their own interests and aims. And because it explicitly includes the possibility of *not* reaching an agreement.

However, Ertel (2000) does not discuss the behaviour or the specific language use that help to achieve the state in which negotiators feel comfortable walking away from a negotiation without having reached an agreement. Nor does he explain what speakers can do to create this state in which they "feel comfortable walking away from the deal" (Ertel 2000:102).

In order to make up their mind during the negotiation process, negotiators need a decision-making process. Grießhaber (2000) defines languages for specific purposes on the basis of the underlying (verbal and mental) actions that are taken in order to fulfil the purpose in question, i. e. carrying out business. And this decision making process is the underlying activity of the unfolding discourse (cf. e. g. Grießhaber 2000, Rehbein 1995). Therefore, it requires information about the other party and its objectives. It takes place not only in the negotiators' minds, but involves a communicative part in order to gain information on which negotiators can base their decision. Hence, it requires a phase in which negotiators are able to explore different options.

More general definitions of the term *negotiation* in language dictionaries, for example, also combine critical aspects, such as the ones described by Rehbein (1995) as well as Wagner (1995), e. g. the element of *agreement* as the goal. It is, according to Rehbein, the precondition to be able to continue within the pattern of action. The important element, from a linguistic point of view, however, is exploring these options through a verbal process, i. e. through *discussion.*

The *Oxford Dictionary of British and World English* as well as the *Oxford Dictionary of US English,* for example, define *negotiation* as a "discussion aimed at reaching an agreement"[12]. Although these dictionaries do not restrict the meaning to business contexts, the problem that underlies most definitions is the focus here: Two or more parties share an interest, i. e. they want to achieve a common goal – hence the agreement. At the same time, there may be a conflict due to different interests regarding aspects of that goal or their own input – hence a *discussion.* So what characterises and defines any negotiation is a common goal yet conflicting interests that require a *discussion.*

A *discussion* can be regarded as a verbal conflict. Etymologically, the term stems, according to the Oxford English Living Dictionary[13], "[f]rom Middle French *discuter* (French *discuter*) to examine the case for and against (something), to contest, dispute from classical Latin *discutere* to dash to pieces, to shake violently" (Oxford English Living Dictionary; my emphasis). So a discussion can be seen as a way of examining the option of achieving a common goal or a subgoal. That is, not only to overcome a conflict of interests on a lower level, but also to examine something by taking it apart (i.e. by examining the different aspects of an often complex deal) and focussing on single aspects one at a time (e.g. the different conditions, different versions of a product, different amounts or simply the price (a part of the negotiation which is called *bargaining*)).[14]

---

12 http://www.oxforddictionaries.com/us/definition/american_english/negotiation?q=negotiation (accessed 18/2/2014)

13 https://en.oxforddictionaries.com/definition/discute (accessed 31/5/2019)

14 *Bargaining* is not considered here because it is a simpler process that usually focuses on one aspect, e. g. the price, and is defined as trying "to make someone agree to

In this sense, a negotiation does not necessarily have to lead to a business agreement or contract. It can be a means of finding out whether or not an agreement is preferable for the parties involved. And the parties, i.e. the negotiators, need to consider not only their overall goals, but also their sub-goals; e.g. what they are or are not willing to offer as their part of the agreement.

This view opens options for focussing on the decision-making processes, which are carried out verbally as well as within the negotiators' minds, rather than focussing on the outcome of the discussion. It is thus a definition based on a decision-making process and goes in line with Grießhaber's (2000) definition. It focuses on an examination of linguistic means that participants use to carry out the discussion. Speakers need to build common ground with their hearers by creating discourse knowledge. They build discourse knowledge by learning what each one is ready to offer. This is also the main difference between *bargaining* and negotiating. Speakers need to take the hearer along to the different stages of the process so that they are 'on the same page'. This way, single aspects of a potential agreement can be examined and – if necessary – changed so that the parties involved can adjust their offers to the requirements of the other party and vice versa.

Rehbein (1995) calls this phase of the discourse 'negotiation device'. And Wagner (1995) defines it as a strategic interaction in which the parties involved modify their goals and exchange relations (Wagner 1995:11). In this thesis, I will refer to it as the *core negotiation*. It is the critical phase within a form of discourse that, in Wagner's (1995) definition, is a *business negotiation* as a whole and, according to Rehbein (1995:70 ff.), the pattern of *buying/selling*. It is the phase where different objectives are at the centre of the discussion and participants exchange information and evaluate different options. The aim is to investigate different options for cooperation. The evaluation process can be a mental one and is often not verbalised. Neither is the decision that negotiators may take during the actual negotiation or later in a different surrounding, e.g. back at the office.

The overall discourse, however, will be labelled *negotiation*. It involves not only the phases of strategic interactions, or the *core negotiation*, but also other phases such as homeleic discourse and phases of other patterns of action. The core negotiation is the actual phase in which different forms of cooperation are discussed. In it, ideas, comments, questions about different options are exchanged, and different options are evaluated. Sometimes decisions are verbalised during this phase.

---

give you something that is better for you" (Cambridge Dictionary online (http://www.dictionary.cambridge.org; accessed 01/08/2020)

5.4 Contract

If an agreement is reached in business negotiations, it is usually called a *contract*. In a business negotiation, the aim is to find out or establish the conditions for a contract – or sometimes it is just to find out whether the establishment of a contract is preferable at all.

A contract is "in the simplest definition, a promise enforceable by law" (Encyclopaedia Britannica)[15]. According to the Encyclopaedia Britannica, "[t]he making of a contract requires the mutual assent of two or more persons, one of them ordinarily making an offer and another accepting. If one of the parties fails to keep the promise, the other is entitled to legal recourse."[16] Thus in Great Britain, as in other European countries, a contract does not come about in explicit, i. e. written form. Rather, it can be established through mutual assent. This is also the way it is defined in the German Civil Code (Bürgerliches Gesetzbuch (BGB), cf. BGB § 433 ff.).

And according to Article 11 of the United Nations Convention on Contracts for the International Sale of Goods, "[a] contract of sale need not be concluded in or evidenced by writing and is not subject to any other requirement as to form"[17]. If both enterprises are based in countries that signed the UN convention, the UN regulations for contracts apply.[18] Thus negotiators operating in international markets that signed the Convention are not required to establish contracts in any specific form. According to the UN convention, contracts are – legally speaking – not established in writing. Any agreement – written or oral – can be regarded as a contract.

This is the case for all the home countries of the companies who were involved in the data for this dissertation. The companies were from Germany, Norway and France. So for none of them, a written agreement is required to establish a contract. When it comes to making clear what is going on in a negotiation, it is essential for all speakers to avoid any misunderstandings as to whether they are discussing an option or making or accepting an offer because accepting an offer would, by definition, constitute a contract and therefore oblige both parties to further actions (delivery, payment, etc.). So they need linguistic forms that ensure their hearer interprets the intention.

15 http://www.britannica.com/EBchecked/topic/135270/contract (accessed 18/9/2013)

16 http://www.britannica.com/EBchecked/topic/135270/contract (accessed 18/9/2013)

17 https://www.uncitral.org/pdf/english/texts/sales/cisg/V1056997-CISG-e-book.pdf

18 IHK Rhein-Neckar: Vertragsbestimmungen im Export (https://www.rhein-neckar.ihk24.de/international/export-import/ausfuhr-eu/vertragsbestimmungen-export/AnwendRecht/950856; accessed 22/3/2016).

5.5 Commissives and negotiations

Since no specific form is required to establish a contract, an oral agreement is sufficient to come under a legal obligation. Therefore, the forms of language used in negotiations are decisive. Speakers have to indicate to the hearer whether they are forming a contract or are merely discussing options. And as pointed out above, negotiators are not always in the interaction to reach an agreement at all costs. They often want to evaluate different options, i. e. to discuss different forms of cooperation. Negotiators thus need to open space for these discussions. They need to linguistically create 'room' to examine and discuss different options. And the actual decision about the establishment of business cooperation or a contract is not necessarily taken during the actual encounter. Often, they are taken back at the company, depending on the organisational and hierarchical structures of the business unit in question. Also, the decision rights of the representatives may vary so that they are not necessarily in a position to decide about potential deals.[19]

So negotiators, as representatives of businesses, must create 'room' to discuss different options. They need 'room' in which offers and suggestions are not legally binding and where suggestions, discussions, evaluation and also rejections can happen without consequences. And this room needs to be opened through linguistic means.

And since their linguistic behaviour also determines, to a large extent, how the hearer sees them as a person, negotiators need to consider the impression they make on the hearer. It is therefore important that speakers appear reliable and approachable as individuals and as the 'other party' in a potential contract. Especially in business encounters like trade fairs, business representatives need to consider the impression they make as a person. They might want to establish business relationships in the future even if no business cooperation or contract is established at this point. And since in a lot of markets the number of businesses and thus potential business partners is limited, they need to make a good impression in order to keep the options of future cooperations open. So, on a social level, they need to connect to the hearer and appear likeable and reliable.

At the same time, they might negotiate with different businesses at the same time. They need to check out different options. They might engage in different negotiations before deciding which offer to accept. In this sense, a trade fair resembles the original 'marketplace', where vendors (sellers) and customers (buy-

19 The German label manager used this fact strategically by claiming at one point that he needed to consult his boss about a decision when he actually was authorised to decide.

ers) meet. It is the location where customers, in this case businesses, 'go shopping' for potential business partners. Thus, they need to find linguistic forms that show they are trustworthy and reliable as a person and potential business partner. At the same time, on a business level, they want to investigate what the potential partners are willing to bring 'to the table'. So they need to mark their contributions in the negotiation as suggestions rather than offers as long as they are negotiating. And they want to discuss the terms of a potential business agreement. However, they do not want to legally commit to the aspect in question yet. Linguistically speaking, they will avoid *commissives* in order not to come under any legal obligation.

Even if there might not be legal consequences, negotiators may find it crucial to avoid misunderstandings as to what they are ready to commit to, i.e. to promise. So they need to communicate these different messages. Speakers therefore need to find linguistic forms that indicate whether or not they commit to something or are 'only' discussing it as an option.

So sometimes contradictory messages have to be transmitted linguistically: Speakers want to appear reliable as a person, i.e. on a social level. At the same time, they do not want to commit to a specific suggestion in the sense that it is not legally binding. And they have to transmit all these different linguistic aspects at the same time. So messages are manifold because speakers pursue different aims on different levels. Table 1 below indicates the different intentions speakers, i.e. negotiators, might pursue on different levels at the same time.

Tab. 1: Speakers' intentions in business negotiations

Level	Aim
social	presenting oneself as a reliable person and business partner
propositional	possibilities of cooperation are presented, discussed, evaluated, criticised, modified, withdrawn
illocutionary	+/-commissives: certain illocutionary acts are avoided
legal	+/- contract: a legal obligation might be formed or not (yet)

+/- indicate the decision of the speaker whether or not the aspect in question is intended.

As indicated in Table 1, the different aspects or 'messages' affect the different levels of communication: Speakers might present themselves as reliable and trustworthy on a social level, while on a propositional level, they need to present, discuss and evaluate, or maybe criticise, reject, modify or withdraw suggestions. Juristically, they need to do this without coming under any legal obligation. They do not want to form a contract as long as they are not ready to accept an offer and to commit to the economic and legal consequences. On an illocutionary level, they have to be linguistically clear about the degree of commitment to the proposition of the utterance. So they have to indicate how far they are or are not ready to make a promise or accept a suggestion. They thus need to indicate whether or not they are using *commissives*.

Their linguistic work and their responsibility thus lie in making it clear whether they *promise* a certain future action or *suggest* or *evaluate* it etc. So they want to avoid misunderstandings concerning their commitment to the function of an utterance[20]. Speakers therefore have to transmit these different messages at the same time. Especially in lingua franca situations, they might need to do some extra work in order to ensure understanding, not only on the propositional level, but also on the illocutionary level. This might be the critical issue that sets business negotiations apart from many other types of discourse. As long as speakers do not want to form a contract, they have to avoid speech acts that bring them under any obligation, such as commissives. And in order to avoid any misunderstanding, they have to make sure their utterances are not *interpreted* as commissives. Speakers therefore need means to guide the hearer's perception accordingly.

There is a certain tension if not contradiction between the different aims. Linguistically speaking, speakers in negotiations will need to separate the proposition from certain illocutionary acts. They thus need to express the right 'quality' of the verb and need to separate the proposition of their utterance from the current situation, i.e. from the actual discourse or speaking situation.

20 Unless, of course, someone uses or creates misunderstandings on purpose, thus using linguistic or communicative ambiguity strategically, something which did not appear in my data and which would need to be discussed further on a different data base.

6. Research aims and data

6.1 Aim of this dissertation

The aim of this dissertation is to add to the description of LFE from an applied linguistics point of view. Its guiding question is if there are forms of language that are used in business negotiations that fulfil communicative functions that were not found in other contexts such as separating the illocution from the proposition of an utterance.

Therefore, the first question is if the forms of LFE described so far show in the data for this dissertation, the BusinessELF corpus (chapter 7.2). Once it has been established that the forms of usage are the same as in other LFE discourses, the question is in how far the data differs from other usages of LFE. The data in the BusinessELF corpus shows a high amount of conditional sentences. 64 out of 3,784 utterances are complete conditional sentences. Therefore, the focus of the main part of the dissertation will be on the forms and functions of the different conditional sentences and potential reasons for their usage (chapters 9 and 10).

Business negotiations are high stakes encounters that are defined by non-linguistic goals, i. e. goals that lie outside the discourse. So are the consequences of business negotiations and the obligations that may arise from the discourse situation. Sometimes further actions are required, or legal obligations are established (see chapter 5.4). And since these obligations can be severe, negotiators need to decide well if and when to agree to certain suggestions in negotiations. Therefore, forms of language are required that set the pure discussion of aspects, i. e. the negotiation process *per se* (cf. definitions in chapter 5.3) apart from the actual establishment of a contract. And since these are both linguistic processes, forms of language are required that make the different aspects distinguishable for the hearer. So negotiators need to avoid misunderstandings concerning their communicative intentions: agreement to certain suggestions or offers needs to differ from suggestions, questions or discussion (cf. Table 1).

And in lingua franca situations, speakers might not only encounter difficulties on the production level. Speakers also need to consider the receptive part of communication. Sometimes, what they might be able to express may not be interpretable to the hearer or not interpreted in the intended way. So speakers need to ensure, through their linguistic choices, that the hearer understands their message accordingly. In business negotiations, the hearer needs to know if the speaker sets suggestions, questions, inquiries etc. apart from promises or acceptances of suggestions. This might require extra linguistic work. So speakers, in order to avoid legal obligations, e.g. contracts, need to be linguistically very clear about their communicative intentions. And as long as they are still negotiating, they need to avoid misunderstandings concerning legal obligations. And it is the aim of this dissertation to show how this is marked linguistically.

6.2 Hypotheses

I base my hypotheses for the dissertation project on the definition of a *contract* as a legally binding yet not necessarily written promise to complete a future action and on the definition of *negotiation* as a form of discourse by which negotiators establish whether or on which conditions they are willing to form a contract (cf. chapter 5.4).

My first hypothesis therefore is that speakers in business negotiations will avoid formulations that may be regarded as commissives, i.e. speech acts that oblige them to further actions (Austin 1962) in order not to come under any legal obligation. They will do so if or as long as they are not ready to form an agreement, i.e. a contract, and commit to a certain action that would follow it.

My second hypothesis is that, as long as they find themselves short of reaching their goal in the negotiation, they will indicate to the hearer that their utterances are contributions to a discussion and not to an agreement. They will thus use linguistic forms that mark an utterance as a proposal, question, summary or contribution to a discussion etc. rather than a promise.

My third hypothesis is that the linguistic forms in the corpus like marked forms of conditionals, as well as matrix-constructions, inversions etc., are used to indicate to the hearer the degree to which the speaker does or does not commit to the proposition of the utterance.

7. Method

7.1 Data collection and function

In his study of simulations of job interviews in preparation classes, Grießhaber (1987) showed that language use differs between simulations and authentic language use. Grießhaber compared simulations to authentic job interviews and showed a fundamental difference: that the underlying decision-making processes were decisive for the language use. Since the necessity for actual decisions was absent in the simulations, the language use of the participants was different to the authentic situations. As these findings show, it was important to use authentic data for this dissertation project. The aim was to gain insights into the language forms that are actually used in business negotiations. And while mere simulations would have provided more data and appeared statistically more reliable, the language forms are likely to have differed. And in order to be able to describe the actual language use in business negotiations, it was paramount to find participants in this dissertation project who needed to pursue non-linguistic goals and who provided authentic language data.

That is why the data base is a – although small – corpus of authentic business meetings. They were recorded at an international music trade fair. The corpus consists of three audio-recorded negotiation encounters, taken out of eight that were originally recorded. Unfortunately, the other recordings could not be used for acoustic reasons.

Authentic data of business encounters is hard to come by (cf. Ehlich/Wagner 1995:2). It proved difficult to find participants who were willing and, more difficult yet, allowed by their employers to be recorded for research purposes. I am therefore extremely grateful to the participants in this study for allowing me to do the recordings, especially to the German label manager. He not only allowed me to accompany him to the trade fair (twice!), but he also introduced me to the other participants (before the recordings, although it as a very short encounter due to their busy schedules) and patiently answered all my questions.

Since I promised to keep all data anonymous, I will not use his or the other participants' real names. Neither will I use the real names of the companies, artists or labels involved. Instead, I chose pseudonyms for labels and artists and acronyms for the speakers involved.

I was present at the trade fair, yet not during the meetings. Participant observation was not an option since it might have changed the language behaviour and thus the outcome of the project. I did not want participants to feel observed, mainly because I did not want them to monitor their language any more than they do in these encounters anyway. Furthermore, it would have required further permissions if I had been present in person.

The recording was carried out with a portable mini-disc recorder (the Sony Mini Disc recorder) and a clip-on microphone that was placed on the table (or in one case on a bench) between the participants. Originally, the project was planned to consist of 10 recordings including short interviews with the participants about their position and function in the company, first and other languages, training in their second language(s) and experience on the job. These were supposed to be transcribed for the project too. However, it turned out that some of the meetings I had planned to record could not be recorded because participants did not feel happy about the idea; others could not be transcribed because either the background noises were too loud (since it was a music trade fair, music was playing all the time and sometimes at a very high volume), sometimes the number of speakers was high (up to 8 in one meeting), voices overlapped, and long passages of the discourse were incomprehensible or speakers could not be identified.

For organisational and time reasons, it was not possible to interview the other participants or to elicit further data about them, as I had planned when designing the dissertation project. Most of the participants in the study were on a very tight schedule and had back to back meetings during the trade fair. They were asked on site if they allowed the recordings. Fortunately, most people were so kind as to agree to be recorded.

Being able to record them was an opportunity that enabled this project and helped me gain an insight into the authentic language use of professional people who use English successfully in their daily work even though they were not explicitly trained for it. This is true for the German label manager who was in all the recordings. And since most people in this line of business do not have official training for their job, but come from different backgrounds, this source is especially valuable. I am very grateful for their support, open-mindedness and readiness to help.

7.2 The BusinessELF corpus

The corpus on which this project is based consists of the recordings of 3 encounters. All were carried by the above-mentioned label manager of a German record company (called *Lingua* in the data) and different representatives of his potential and actual business partners from other countries.

I identified all speakers with the help of acronyms. The acronym starts with an 'S' for speaker and an individual number for their identification. Then follows their gender (m or f for *male* or *female*). Then two letters for their first language, i. e. the language that they use primarily as the language of communication in their country. It was also their language of socialisation in all cases. So the German label manager is identified as S1mGr; *S1* standing for 'Speaker 1', *m* for his gender, male, and *Gr* for German, his first language.

One meeting was with the Head of Distribution of a French record company, whose first language is French. She is identified as S2fFr, short for "Speaker No. 2 (S2), female (f), French (Fr)". The two other recordings were with the same representative of a Norwegian record company whose L1 is Norwegian, identified in the transcripts and examples with the abbreviation "S3mNr" for "Speaker 3, male, Norwegian".

At one point, a work colleague of the German label manager, who is also German, joined the meeting with the Norwegian distribution manager (see example 'receptive multilingualism' under 'code switching'; 4.6.6 above). He left again after approximately two minutes. Since he is another male speaker, his identification number is 4, his acronym is S4mGr. Table 2 below lists the speakers in the different recordings.

Tab. 2: Speakers' acronyms, functions and L1s

Speaker	Gender	Language of origin	Function	Recording
S1mGr	male	German	Label manager	Marketingcooperation Distribution Backcatalogue
S2fFr	female	French	Head of Distribution	Marketingcooperation
S3mNr	male	Norwegian	Distribution manager	Distribution Backcatalogue
S4mGr	male	German	Label manager	Distribution

Table 2 indicates the gender of each speaker in the corpus, their language of origin, their respective professional function or title as well as the recording or recordings in which they appear.

Unfortunately, it was not possible to assess the participants' language mastery, e. g. by measuring it with the help of an objective, and preferably standardised, assessment tool such as the C-Test, for example.[21] An objective assessment

21 The C-Test is a test format developed by Klein-Brailey and Raatz (1984) that is based on the cloze test format. For its advantages and a detailed discussion of its application, see e. g. Baumeister et al. 2005, Traxel/Dresemann 2010.

would have made the results of the study more comparable to other research work. A test anchored in the Common European Framework of Reference for Languages (CEFR)[22], would have been even better because it would have enabled a precise determination of each participant's language level. However, it was not possible to gain test results or a self-assessment of any of the speakers. Although an objective measuring was not possible, the fact that each of the participants carries out business and business negotiations with negotiators from other international businesses on a regular basis and holds responsibility for their own area of business indicates a very advanced mastery of the language.

The three different meetings were named after their main topic. The first was about possible cooperation in the marketing and distribution of products, mainly CDs, but also vinyls, of the French record company and the German company represented by S1mGr, Lingua. The negotiation was labelled *Marketingcooperation* (short: MARK). The topics were the different forms of a distribution and marketing deal and the type and range of products S1mGr's company might be interested in distributing in Germany. S1mGr's main aim was to find out which forms of cooperation would have been possible and what the French company was offering as its part of the deal in addition to the product as such. He wanted to know, e.g. if they were willing to provide a marketing budget and support his company in the marketing of the products. These were, as he explained before the meeting, the decisive criteria for the potential business cooperation.

The second recording was labelled Distribution (short: DIS). It was a meeting of the German label manager with the Norwegian representative (S3mNr), whose company had already closed a deal with Lingua. The deal obliged Lingua to distribute publications by the Norwegian record company in Germany. The contract was established by other departments of the companies beforehand. And S1mGr and S3mNr, who were in charge of the realisation of the deal, had never met before. And although the legal deal had already been closed, many of the aspects that are usually discussed and negotiated beforehand were still open. So the two met in order to work out the details of the cooperation. This recording is also a negotiation because details of how to put the legal agreement into practice, such as a budget for certain operations, the logistics etc. still needed to be settled. And although the overall aim – a business deal – had already been closed, many decisions were still to be made and therefore negotiated.

Both S1mGr and S3mNr had very tight schedules on the trade fair. However, both enjoyed discussing their own tastes in music and other related topics.

---

22 Council of Europe 2001: Common European Framework of References: Learning, teaching, assessment. Strasbourg: Council of Europe; https://rm.coe.int/1680459f97 (accessed 2/12/19)

So they decided to meet again the following day to discuss further aspects, like the distribution of past publications. 'Past publications' is a technical term from the musical industry and refers to a catalogue of earlier publications that are still available yet not advertised, the so-called 'back catalogue'. Therefore, the last recording, in which S1mGr and S3mNr continued the negotiations and also their – partly private – conversation of the day before, was labelled Backcatalogue (short: BACK).

All in all, the corpus consists of approximately 3 hours of recordings, all involving S1mGr. The recordings were transcribed in a relation of approximately 1:20 with the programmes SyncWriter® as well as NisusWriter® for the utterance list using the conventions of HIAT 2 (*Halbinterpretative Arbeitstranskription* (Ehlich/Rehbein 1976). The utterance list was then converted into an MSWord® file. Search for forms, words and expressions was carried out with the help of the programme BBEdit®.

The transcripts add up to 3,784 utterances, made of 37,915 words, including augments like *uh, uhm* and *hm*. These augments are relevant in communication because they fulfil communicative functions, e.g. indicating doubt, agreement, misunderstandings etc. However, the utterances, as well as the number of words, were distributed unevenly over the three recordings. Table 3 shows the number of words, utterances and the time as well as the speakers involved in each recording:

Tab. 3: The BusinessELF corpus

Recording	**# words**	**# utterances**	**time (h:min)**	**speakers**
Marketing cooperation	7,696	821	0:43	S1mGr, S2fFr
Backcatalogue	19,235	1,734	1:49	S1mGr, S3mNr
Distribution	10,984	1,229	0:30	S1mGr, S3mNr, S4mGr
total	37,915	3,784	3:02	

As Table 3 indicates, Backcatalogue (BACK) was the longest recording with a duration of 1 hour and 49 minutes and 1,734 utterances. Distribution (DIS), the first meeting of the two participants, was only 30 minutes long and consists of 1,229 utterances. Marketingcooperation (MARK) is 43 minutes long and is made of 821 utterances.

The duration of each recording is not proportional to the number of utterances or words. Yet it does indicate that utterances in all the recordings were, on average, rather long, with an average number of 8 to 11 words. Even though this does not directly indicate the quality of a discourse, it does go to show a rather complex context. Long utterances usually indicate that the exchange is content-based and complex as opposed to e.g. learner discourse which its typically short utterances.

All names, titles and place names have been changed for reasons of anonymity. As agreed with the participants beforehand, the audio files will not be published or made accessible.

7.3 Quantitative analysis

In order to first define what has to be considered as LFE features in my data, I will compare the features of LFE described by other scholars (chapter 4) to the language forms in my corpus. I will use the same categories of description as used in the literature overview. I will show that the majority of forms discussed in the literature on LFE also can be found in my data. The comparison will prove that the data can be regarded as 'typical' of LFE. It sets the prerequisite for going into detail about the communicative function of features that are not found in all forms of lingua franca discourse, i.e. the use of conditional sentences (cf. chapter 9).

I will discuss some of the findings from other studies in more detail, e.g. the "intensive use of semantically wide, general verbs such as make, do, have, put, take" (Seidlhofer 2004:38) by questioning this thesis. I will calculate the likelihood of the appearance in my corpus against the appearance of the same verbs in the British National Corpus (BNC). The aim is to see if the quantitative use qualifies as 'intensive' (Seidlhofer 2004). 'Intensive' use implies an over-average use of these tokens in LFE usage. I will show with the help of the *loglikelihood* that for most verbs, the claimed 'intensive' use does not hold true on a mathematical basis (cf. *Verb frequency*, 8.2.2.).

Therefore, the appearance of certain verbs in my corpus was electronically counted with the help of the programme BBedit, then the grammatical function was determined (e.g. to exclude the use of *do* as an auxiliary), and the adjusted number of overall appearances was compared to the appearance in the BNC with the help of loglikelihood calculator (LL Wizard) provided by the University of Lancaster. I thus determined whether or not in my corpus these verbs were used 'intensively' or not.

I used a structural approach to describing the grammatical forms of the conditionals first. I ordered the conditionals in my corpus by the tense of the predicate of the protasis first and then of the apodosis, as is done in classic grammatical description. Then I grouped the conditionals based on the order of the verb tenses and modal verbs. I will analyse the use of these conditionals for different purposes first on a descriptive level before analysing their communicative function using the qualitative-interpretative approach of Functional Pragmatics (Ehlich/Rehbein 1972); see 7.4 below.

7.4 Qualitative analysis: Functional Pragmatics

After using a quantitative approach to describing their appearance and function, I will, in chapter 9, analyse the use of conditionals with reference to time, place, politeness as well as speakers' stance. However, these analyses focus on the use of conditionals from the point of view of the speaker. They focus on the grammatical form without explaining the mental processes such as the decisions that negotiators take during the process.

I will analyse the communicative functions of different forms of conditionals in different phases of discourse using the qualitative-interpretative approach of Functional Pragmatics (Ehlich/Rehbein 1972; Grießhaber 2001; Rehbein/Fienemann 2004). It is an approach that is based on speech act theory and allows for the analysis of underlying mental processes. It orders linguistic processes in patterns of actions. It allows to explain the effects and thereby communicative functions of utterances by taking the hearer into consideration. Rehbein (1995) defines Functional Pragmatics as follows:

> Functional Pragmatics is based on speech act theory (linguistic pragmatics) and takes on a functional view of communication. Compared to Conversational Analysis, it takes not only interactions, but also mental and perceptible actions into consideration. Compared to Discourse Analysis, it operates on a higher level of schemata ("patterns"), which are analysed as non-linear structures, i. e. as potentials of actions and interactions, represented in diagrammatic form. [...] Functional Pragmatics draws conclusions about underlying mental decisions from perceptible (inter)actions. [...] It must be stressed that the pattern structure has its own typical features, but each individual sales talk can be analysed against the background of this basic structure (Rehbein 1995:70 f.).

Those mental actions, especially decisions that interactants take, are decisive for the process of negotiation. Although this dissertation does not contribute to the discussion of patterns of action (*Handlungsmuster*), the basic concepts of Functional Pragmatics, such as the goal orientation (purposes), apply.

A pattern of action is a way of acting through speaking. It is determined by forms of interaction (linguistic and otherwise) that occur on a regular basis (cf. Ehlich/Rehbein 1972). These patterns determine certain alternatives, e. g. in the linguistic expressions that are considered adequate. So verbal and non-verbal actions trigger certain responses. These responses can be realised by a certain number of culturally determined linguistic forms. Within each pattern, speakers can choose between different forms of expression. Within the pattern, speakers and hearers move towards certain decision points and – ideally – towards a shared aim.

Functional Pragmatics focuses not only on the actual interactions, i. e. observable utterances, but takes mental operations like decision making processes and speakers' intentions into consideration. On the basis of these processes, Grießhaber (2000) defines the language of business as a language for specific purposes. It is based on the non-linguistic goals that users need to fulfil. It is characterised by interactive as well as decision-making processes. The main function of any language of specific purposes is to enable actants to fulfil purposes with the help of language and linguistic actions. In order to fulfil them, speakers and hearers need to go through different phases such as the estimation of the situation, motivation, planning, determining the aims, etc. And while most aspects of doing business can be analysed in stages of the overall process (cf. Rehbein 1977), the discourse of business negotiation is not subject to these different stages since it is, by definition, a cooperative pattern of action.

Grießhaber (2000) criticises that former approaches to defining the language of business focused primarily on the lexicon. In his view, the language of business negotiation is mainly determined by the purposes that actants need to fulfil and by the interactive, i. e. linguistic, decision-making processes. He states that the language of negotiation is a specific kind of discourse within the different types of discourses that are required in business (Grießhaber 2000:409). Furthermore, business negotiations are determined by external factors like the resources that are available. Another aspect that needs to be considered when analysing the language of business negotiation is the aspect of legal consequences of possible certain formulations (Grießhaber 2000:410). And although Grießhaber does not want to include the aspect in a basic determination of the analytical concept (Grießhaber 2000:410), it is an important factor for language use within the type of discourse (cf. chapter 9, 10). It therefore needs to be considered when analysing functions of language, especially so if it concerns a language that is not the speaker's 'strongest suit', as is the case for many lingua franca speakers.

I will explain the forms of conditionals before the background of business negotiations as a high-stakes discourse. It is a high stakes discourse because it bears the risk of potential legal consequences, e. g. by obligations that result from an agreement, aka a contract. Business negotiations are, according to Grießhaber (2000), a domain that defines a language for specific purposes. And the legal consequences are, in the end, what decides about the participants' actions and utterances in a business negotiation. Since an agreement, e. g. a contract, obliges negotiators to future actions, they need to decide what to agree to. And they need to avoid misunderstandings concerning their agreement to certain suggestions or offers. I will define these legal and linguistic aspects as the determining factors for the use of linguistic forms such as the conditionals in the negotiation in chapter 10.

Speech act theory

Some of the conditionals in my data are 'unconventional' in that they use grammatical forms in a different function to inner circle usage. Some are 'ungrammatical', i. e. the combination of tenses is not what inner circle speakers use. Other conditionals are in line with what is defined as the rules for conditionals in standard English. I will offer an analysis of their different communicative functions and how it is reflected in the grammatical form. By matching them first with the discourse phases and then analysing the effect on the hearer, I will show that these forms are not accidental. I will draw on speech act theory (Austin 1962, Searle 1969) to explain their function by distinguishing between illocutionary acts and the propositional acts of an utterance.

Proposition is a term in semantics that goes back to Searle (1969). Searle used it in the discussion of different speech acts and their illocutionary force. It describes a level of 'non-linguistic' content of an utterance or 'force' which comes with the utterance (e.g. Green 2007). Utterances consist of an illocutionary and a propositional part. The propositional content of an utterance is the 'non-linguistic' content that remains the same even if the illocutionary content (e.g. promise, prediction etc.) of an utterance changes. In the interpretative analysis of my data, I will use the term 'proposition' to refer to the non-linguistic content without the illocutionary force of the utterance, and 'illocution' for the 'force' that may or may not be carried by an utterance and that may change and that determines the effects of an utterance.

According to speech act theory (Austin 1962; Searle 1969), commissives are speech acts by which the speaker is committed to a future act through promising or offering. And through the illocutionary force of the speech act, the speaker is (under certain circumstances (cf. Austin 1965:14 ff.)) obliged to a certain act, determined by the proposition of the utterance. A commissive contains an illocutionary act whose performance produces an obligation for the hearer. And in business negotiations, these speech acts need to be avoided as long as speakers are not willing to commit themselves to a future act, i. e. to agree to a suggestion and thus, by definition, form a contract (see chapter 5.4).

With the help of Functional Pragmatics and Speech Act Theory, on which it is based, I will explain how conditionals are used – in conventional and unconventional forms – to use or 'suspend' the illocutionary force of an utterance. I will explain how language forms are used to reinforce a specific illocutionary aspect and how some of the forms are used to make the interpretation of an utterance easier for the hearer and thereby avoid misunderstandings.

8. Lingua franca features in the BusinessELF corpus

The data collected for this dissertation project is LFE in the conservative sense (cf. chapter 3). All the speakers are users who were not raised in the language and use it for restricted purposes. For them, it is a language that enables communication and allows them to fulfil a societal goal, in this case, carrying out business. In the following, I will describe the features of language found in the BusinessELF corpus using the same categories as in the overview of the literature (chapter 4).

8.1 Phonology

Speakers in the BusinessELF corpus are from three different linguistic backgrounds (cf. Table 2): Two speakers, S1mGr and S4mGr, speak German as their L1; one speaker, i. e. S2fFr, speaks French as her L1; and speaker S3mNr speaks Norwegian as his L1. All of them live and work in the country where their L1 is the national language and use it in their everyday life, inside and outside their profession. These speakers use English in professional contexts on a regular basis, which is a common situation in the European Union. So they are all expanding circle speakers and LFE speakers by definition.

All speakers have a so-called 'accent'. An accent is defined as the "cumulative auditory effect of those features of pronunciation which identify where a person is from" (Crystal 1980:3). However, their pronunciation does not cause communicative problems. The linguistic background of all speakers can easily be identified, in the case of S2fFr through the quality of her vowels; in the cases of the other three speakers mainly through the quality of their consonants. The German speakers in the study in particular tend to use devoiced consonants at the end of the word, pronouncing *hard* as [ha:t] for example.[23]

Furthermore, SmGr1 has what is commonly referred to as a 'German accent', which is notable in his rather monotonous sentence patterns and pitch as well as in the clear pronunciation of most of his words, i. e. he does not contract syllables or shorten words as most inner circle speakers do. However, based on the lack of repair work and the rather fluent conversation, it can be concluded that his interlocutors do not find it difficult to understand him.

All speakers in the data have a clear pronunciation, and their respective vowel quality does not cause problems, probably because Englishes, in general, vary

23 Due to his accent, S1mGr also drops the *r* after the vowels *a* and *o*.

with regard to the pronunciation of vowels. Communication in the corpus works smoothly, and there are very few comprehension checks.

8.2 Lexicon

8.2.1 Flexible terminology

Although speakers in the study are all very competent speakers and use English for professional purposes, most of them have not reached complete mastery of the language. On the lexical level, this shows in the occasional lack of a specific word or phrase.

When realising a lexical gap, speakers can use different strategies to prevent communicative problems. They can and do use strategies like *negotiation of meaning, coinages* or *borrowing* when they realise a lexical gap. In the corpus, they use *coinages*, i. e. of expressions that are used differently to inner circle conventions (cf. e. g. Ahvenainen 2005). However, it is something that happens rarely. In the two examples below, two different speakers, S1mGr and S3mNr, apply an item – a phrasal verb in one case and a noun in the other – that would not be used in the same way in inner circle Englishes. In the two cases when it is used in the BusinessELF corpus, it is a successful strategy and understanding is achieved. (A third example is a little more problematic and is therefore discussed under the heading of *communication strategies* below.)

In the first example, S3mNr explains why he has only brought a limited number of 'samples', i. e. CDs, referred to as 'records', to the trade fair. He uses the phrasal word 'pick up' in the meaning of 'to choose':

(172)	S3mNr	And I/so I picked up three records for him.
(173)	S1mGr	Right.

Example: picked up (BACK)

The combination 'pick up' usually has a different meaning in inner circle contexts. However, the form – which would be *pick* or *pick out* in inner circle varieties – does not cause any problems. So the use is not commented on or referred to, and the discourse continues without hesitation or questions. If the hearer realised the form as non-standard or in any way unexpected, he does not let it show and interprets the meaning as intended.

In the second example, S1mGr uses a lexical deviation. He uses the noun *support*, which is an anglicism used in German as *opening act* for musical concerts. However, both speakers seem to know what he is referring to when he explains that one of the bands he represents played as an opening act for a band, Jam Jumpers, his hearer represents:

(328)	S1mGr	This band, New Yorkers, they played in Bruegge as the support for Jam Jumpers.
(329)	S3mNr	Yeah´·
(330)	S3mNr	They did?
(331)	S1mGr	Yeah, they did.
(332)	S3mNr	Okay.

Example: Played as the support; BACK

In the excerpt, S1mGr explains to S3mNr the coincidence that their two bands played in the same concert, despite S1mGr and S3mNr never having met before. S1mGr seems to be surprised at remembering the event. He uses the noun *support* in the phrase *they played as the support* (se (328)). He actually means that the band *New Yorkers* were the *supporting act* or *opening act* for the other band, Jam Jumpers. However, S3mNr interprets the utterance accordingly. So the discourse is continued without any signs of mis- or non-understanding, and the coinage, even though not consciously used, is a successful way of enabling understanding.

Although S3mNr reacts with two questions – a *Yeah* with a rising intonation and the more explicit *They did?* – neither of the questions are asked for clarification. They are not communicative strategies to clarify any comprehension problems, but rather requests of confirmation. This request, however, is an expression of S3mNr's surprise at the proposition of S1mGr's utterance. It expresses not linguistic difficulty, but his involvement in the construction of shared knowledge. And S3mNr infers the intended meaning on the basis of his professional and world knowledge. Thus the expression in question, *support*, although not used in the same way in inner circle varieties of English, does not cause any comprehension problems.

The examples demonstrate that in the corpus of this dissertation project, there are instances where speakers use forms that can be regarded as 'typical lingua franca' forms, e. g. forms of *coinage*. However, quantitatively speaking, most of the applied forms in the discourse do not differ from inner circle Englishes.

8.2.2 Verb frequency

Seildhofer (2004:38) finds an "intensive use of semantically wide, general verbs such as *make, do, have, put, take*". It seems logical at first sight that speakers from the expanding circle, whose exposure to the language has been limited, would use what she refers to as "semantically wide" verbs. These are likely to be focussed on in instruction or found in the language sources such as the media rather than specific lexical items.

However, Seidlhofer does not define what qualifies as an "intensive" use. The question thus arises how 'intensive' the use of these verbs is or could be expected in the context in question. In order to see how 'intensive' the use of these verbs is in the BusinessELF corpus, i. e. how many times these verbs are used in relation to other corpora, I will compare the use of verbs in two corpora. In order to see whether they are used with a higher rate or *likelihood* in BusinessELF than in a representative corpus of inner circle English, I have compared the likelihood logarithms (*log likelihood*; *LL* in short) of certain verbs in the BusinessELF corpus and the British National Corpus (BNC).

In order to do so, I used the *log likelihood* calculator provided by the University of Lancaster (http://ucrel.lancs.ac.uk/llwizard.html; accessed 13/04/2014) and calculated the use of the verbs in question. Then I compared their frequency in the BusinessELF corpus to the use of the same words in the spoken part of the British National Corpus (BNC) (http://www.natcorp.ox.ac.uk/; accessed 13/04/2014).

Likelihood determines "[t]he probability of a set of observations given the value of some parameter or set of parameters" (Everitt/Skrondal 1998:222). The LL calculates the frequency distribution of a specific item, in this case a verb, and shows, with the help of a statistic calculation, whether or not the item is 'overrepresented' or 'underrepresented'. If it is overrepresented, its frequency, i. e. its occurrence in the corpus, is higher than its frequency in the corpus used as a reference. If it is underrepresented, its frequency is lower. The likelihood is calculated by constructing a contingency table like the example in Table 4 below:

Tab. 4: Verb frequency

	Corpus 1	**Corpus 2**	**Total**
Frequency of word	a	b	a+b
Frequency of other words	c-a	d-b	c+d-a-b
Total	c	d	c+d

Verb frequency (http://ucrel.lancs.ac.uk/llwizard.html; 13/04/2014)

Table 4 shows how the likelihood is established. In the first step, the frequency in absolute numbers is established. Value *c* corresponds to the number of words in corpus one, and *d* corresponds to the number of words in corpus two (*N* values). Values *a* and *b* are called the observed values (*O*). The aim is to calculate the expected values (*E*). Using the calculator provided by the University of Lancaster, the expected value is calculated by the calculator with the help of the following formula:

$$E_i = \frac{N_i \sum_i O_i}{\sum_i N_i}$$

Formula 1:
Expected value[24]

The LL is then calculated with the following formula:

$$-2\ln \lambda = 2\sum_i O_i \ln\left(\frac{O_i}{E_i}\right)$$

Formula 2:
Calculating G2 as follows:
G2 = 2*((a*ln (a/E1)) + (b*ln (b/E2)))[25]

One needs to compare the occurrence of the item(s) in question to a second corpus. As the second corpus I chose the spoken part of the BNC because it is a purely spoken corpus. The BNC is one of the largest and best-described corpora of inner circle English available to date. It is supposed to give a reliable and statistically relevant example of oral language use in the inner circle. In order to see whether subjects in my corpus 'overused' semantically wide verbs, i. e. whether they used them more often than inner circle speakers, I first selected all forms of each of the verbs Seidlhofer (2004) lists: *make, do, have, put, take*. After the first search, I eliminated the auxiliary use of *do* and *have*.

I decided to add the verb *work* to the list because it is also 'semantically wide', yet less so than *have* and *do*. And it is more relevant in the context. Speakers used it in its traditional meaning like in the example below, in which it is used to express that it is their job or profession:

(59) S1mGr And most of them are really experienced and pretty much dedicated to, to music and, and to the labels they work for.

Example: Dedicated (BACK)

They also use it as a transitive verb, indicating a process, as the following sentence shows:

(510) S1mGr I think • it makes sense to, to work (it) like that rather than, say, • • paying kind of a flat fee or something.

Example: Work it (BACK)

24 cf.http://ucrel.lancs.ac.uk/llwizard.html (accessed 13/04/2014)

25 cf. http://ucrel.lancs.ac.uk/llwizard.html (accessed 13/04/2014)

In BusinessELF, which consists of 37.915 words, *work* is used 77 times. It is thus used more frequently, in absolute numbers, than *put* (19 occurrences), *make* (45 occurrences) and *take* (47 occurrences). The only verbs used more frequently were *do*, which was used 274 times as a full verb (as opposed to 209 occurrences where it served as an auxiliary) and *have*, which was used 312 times as a full verb.

The adjusted value of absolute occurrences of a verb was calculated, i. e. the absolute times it was used as a full verb, in different forms and tenses. The number of occurrences of the forms *did* or *had* and of the past participle were added before the overall occurrence was calculated against the same forms of the verbs used in the spoken part of the BNC.

Table 5 below shows the results in absolute numbers, the percentages with which each verb was used and the LL compared to the corpus of reference, the spoken part of the BNC, here called BNC for short:

Tab. 5: Verb frequency and log likelihood (LL)

Verb	#BusinessELF	# BNC	%1	%2		LL
make	45	1902	0.12	0.02	+	88.47
do	274	13017	0.72	0.13	+	486.20
have	312	12373	0.82	0.12	+	646.52
put	19	1828	0.05	0.02	+	14.10
take	47	1793	0.12	0.02	+	100.90
work	77	931	0.20	0.01	+	322.14

KEY to table 5: #BUSELF is the observed frequency in the BusinessELF corpus, #BNC is the observed frequency in the spoken part of the BNC, %1 and %2 show the relative frequencies in the corpora, + indicates overuse in BusinessELF relative to the BNC spoken corpus, - indicates underuse in BusinessELF relative to the BNC spoken corpus, LL is the log-likelihood

The BusinessELF corpus with its 37,915 words is relatively small. So the statistical relevance of these data can be questioned on the grounds of the size of the BusinessELF corpus. However, the calculation of the LL can serve as an indicator of the overuse of certain verbs. For a statistically relevant statement, however, a more representative corpus would be required.

The calculation of the LL of these verbs shows that in the BusinessELF corpus the 'semantically wide verbs' in the sense of Seidlhofer (2004) were all 'overused' relative to the spoken part of the BNC corpus. That indicates that they might in general be used more intensively in lingua franca settings than in spoken British English. This is true especially for the verbs *do, have* and *work*.

Their 'overuse' in particular can be explained with the help of the topics discussed. In all three discourses studied, participants meet for the first and second time and do so to discuss potential business cooperations. They ask each other various questions about products, procedures and the organisation of the company the other one works for. So it does not surprise that in the corpus at hand, the most frequently used verbs are the ones used to talk about procedures and products distributed by the companies in question. So the use of these verbs appears to be influenced by the context in which they occur. It is very likely that the context is more decisive here than the fact that the verbs are used in a lingua franca situation. So in order to really see if the 'semantically wide verbs' are over-represented in lingua franca contexts, one would need a broader database. And the corpus to which to compare the data would have to be more specific regarding the context. It would have to be data from spoken discourse in a professional setting, preferably from business negotiations. However, such as specific corpus was not available at the time of the analysis.

Another verb that was used very frequently in the corpus – and, as the numbers suggest – probably overused in comparison to the BNC was the verb *distribute*. Again, this is a verb that is used frequently due to the very topic of the encounters recorded for the corpus. Its total frequency is 17 in the BusinessELF corpus. It was not listed in the BNC, however. Its percentage is 0.04, its LL 189.68. So its likelihood of usage is higher than that of *take*, *make* and *put*. *Distribute*, however, is not a 'semantically wide, general verb' (Seidlhofer 2004:38), like the other verbs studied for the question. On the contrary, it is a specific verb used in English for specific purposes. On many occasions, speakers, especially the male speakers, replace it with *make available*. *Make available* is a rather colloquial term that might again be used in order to appear more 'laid back' or 'cool'. The aim of speakers to appear 'cool' was stressed by one of the speakers. He considers it an issue in the specific context of the music fair. Still, the frequency of *distribute* is higher than that of many 'general' verbs.

Again, the question arises if the frequency of certain verbs is really a typical feature of LFE use or of the context in which a conversation is recorded, or both. Or whether there might be other explanations. In the data at hand, it seems to be the case that both hold true: Certain semantically wide verbs such as *make*, *do*, *have*, *put*, and *take* are used very frequently and 'overused' in relation to the BNC. They might be a feature of LFE. On the other hand, certain specific verbs such as *work* and *distribute*, which are not 'semantically wide, general verbs' (Seidlhofer 2004:38), are also overused in relation to the BNC. This could be caused by the context. The question thus is if the BNC contains enough data from comparable contexts such as business to represent specific data. Then again, it is not a specific corpus. Maybe specific lexical items speakers use in the context are indeed overused, e. g. due to a lack of alternatives and a reduced lexicon on the side of the speakers. This is a question, however, that requires a much larger database and a separate study.

8.3 Register

Regarding their language register, the speakers' linguistic choices vary widely. However, all speakers make use of a wide variety of colloquial as well as formal expressions and of very general as well as specific forms. None of the speakers in the corpus stands out due to an extraordinarily high number or remarkable form of linguistic choices.

Speakers apply specific terms like *distribute* and *release* (see 8.2 above). *Release* is used frequently as a noun and as a verb and is a specific term of their profession. On the other hand, they alter it with the less formal expression *make available*, a rather unmarked and unspecific term with a less restricted, yet comparable semantic meaning. *Make available* is used 13 times in the corpus, just like *distribute*, whereas *release*, the most specific of the three terms, is used 31 times in the whole corpus. The informal language choices also show in comments like the following:

(149) S2fFr So I actually just grabbed • a couple of things …

Example: Grabbed (MARK)

The verb *grab* here is chosen to support the rather careless and hasty way in which the action (choosing products to bring as samples to the trade fair) was carried out. The utterance serves as an apology for not bringing the specific samples S2fFr wanted to present to her hearer, S1mGr. The rather casual choice underlines the supposedly laid back attitude that all negotiators in the data tried to transmit to their hearers.

Another example of marked language choices is the use of adjectives like *cool* and *weird*, which again shows a tendency to use an informal register. S1mGr commented on this observation: He tries to use informal language frequently, just like all other speakers in the corpus.

Their overall range of linguistic choices indicates a large linguistic repertoire of the speakers. And the use of different registers within the same discourse seems to be specific to this special constellation: competent lingua franca speakers with a vast knowledge of specific vocabulary in a business context that requires its participants to be 'cool' and 'hip'. Being 'cool' seems to be equalled in the context with being informal. This also shows their ability to consciously choose a specific register in order to achieve a certain effect; an ability of highly competent language users.

So regarding their lexicon and language awareness, speakers in the BusinessELF corpus are highly competent and flexible in their language use. Still, occasional lexical gaps and grammatical choices show, but they are rare. And if they occur, speakers handle them cooperatively, another typical feature of lingua franca communication in most contexts. At no point did the communication fail or become troublesome due to lexical gaps.

8.4 Grammar

When it comes to 'grammar', lingua franca speakers use some linguistic forms that are unlikely to be found in inner circle varieties. In the following I will look at some aspects of grammar, first on the level of the noun phrase, later at the level on the verb phrase. Although communication problems were rare in the corpus, they did appear occasionally (see 8.4.2 below). Regarding the overall appearance, however, they were very rare. Yet, some of the features considered typical of lingua franca communication were found in my corpus as well. Regarding one specific aspect of grammar, the use of conditional sentences, chapters 9 and 10 will list and discuss this rather outstanding form and its use in the corpus.

8.4.1 Noun phrase

Two features that – apart from lexical gaps that were discussed above – affect the noun phrase are the use of articles and the plural forms.

One feature described for lingua franca communication is the use of definite articles where the so-called *zero article* is used in inner circle varieties, i. e. where the noun is used without the definite article as a determiner. In inner circle varieties, this constitutes a difference in meaning. In lingua franca communication, the use differs. However, it does not seem to hinder communication. Dewey (2007) noticed a communicative function behind this feature, i. e. increasing the relative importance of the following noun.

In my data, however, there was only one example of an article use that might be due to increased importance of the noun. And it is the indefinite article rather than the definite article which is used instead of a zero article:

(99) S2fFr Because uh, because I think there is a potential for some (synchronisation) as well.

Example: A potential (MARK)

It might be the case here that S2fFr tries to stress the advantages of one of her products, putting emphasis on it with the help of an (in this case indefinite) article, yet the communicative relevance seems to be little. All in all, the use of articles in the BusinessELF corpus is almost always the same as in inner circle varieties.

Linguistic forms that differ from standardised Englishes are quite rare in the noun phrases of the data in general. At one instance, however, there is a form of a determiner that is not typical. S2fFr uses the plural form of the number word *thousands*:

(254)	S2fFr	And each time it's about twenty-five thousands, you know, copies • of each.

Example: Thousands (MARK)

Although the plural form of the number *thousand* exists in English, it is not normally used in front of a noun and after another number. In S2fFr's L1, French, the plural form *milliers* exists, which would be used like the English *thousands of*, yet not with a concrete number. In the example, however, S2fFr mixes two forms: the equivalent of the English *thousands of*, which uses *thousand* as a noun and puts it into the plural, and a concrete number, *twenty-five*. In this case, though, one would use the non-declined number. However, this might be an indicator of planning processes. In speech production, speakers often change the structures halfway through a sentence or are distracted by other thoughts. Sometimes this leads to constructions that they would not use in written English or planned speech.

All in all, linguistic forms on the level of the noun phrase that could be regarded as typical LFE forms are very rare in the corpus. With the exception of some of the flexible uses of the lexicon, as described above, more noteworthy forms as well as more communicative effort were found regarding verbs.

8.4.2 Verb phrase

Researchers studying LFE have studied forms of verbs with a focus on form and deviations from inner circle uses. Functional problems, on the other hand, are seldom, if ever, discussed. Yet sometimes so-called 'deviations' are forms that are also found in inner circle varieties. Linguistic forms that look like inner circle forms, on the other hand, might cause misunderstandings that go unnoticed. This will be shown in section 8.5.1 below. In the following, I will first discuss some formal aspects of deviations regarding the verb phrase before coming to communicative problems caused by the form of the verb.

3rd person singular –s

One of the features of LFE that was often observed and described is the missing third person singular -*s* in the present tense, also referred to as *zero–s* or *–s omission* (cf. e.g. Ahvenainen 2005, Seidlhofer 2004, Björkman 2008, Breiteneder 2005). Cogo/Dewey, who also studied the phenomenon, state that "the 3rd person zero is emerging as the more characteristic, unmarked feature for present simple verb forms in ELF communication" (Cogo/Dewey 2006:80).

Although it is often discussed as a typical feature, speakers in the BusinessELF corpus do not omit it. Rather, they use it very regularly. Only one utterance could be found where the speaker did not use the -*s*, but it might be inaudible because the whole utterance was spoken fast, and there was background noise.

So, all four speakers can be said to be rather advanced speakers of English as they have automatised the use of the 3rd person singular -*s*, a grammatical form that is automatised only at a quite advanced state of language acquisition (cf. Pienemann 1998). It is interesting, however, that their English is in line with inner circle standards as far as the use of the –*s* in the present tense is concerned.

8.4.3 *Adjective instead of adverb*

One feature that can be noticed in the data is the use of adjectives instead of adverbs. The example below shows a typical sentence in which an adjective is used where – according to 'rules' of Standard English – and adverb would have to be used. It is, however, a form that would probably go unnoticed in many contexts, even in inner circle constellations:

(1312) S3mNr ((1s)) Yeah, it's kind of/described the music quite good.

Example: Described good (BACK)

The usage of adjectives instead of adverbs is quite common in American English, especially in oral language use. Thus it would not be adequate to call it a typical feature of LFE, but perhaps rather of oral English usage. Or, as Liberman (2007) points out: "The adverb is an endangered species in Modern English". The speakers in the BusinessELF corpus, at least when it comes to the use of adjectives and adverbs, do not seem to differ much from inner circle speakers.

8.4.4 *Prepositions*

Another feature of English usage in the corpus is the omission or replacement of prepositions. Whereas in the example above (se (172); see *Lexicon*), where the speaker used *picked up* instead of *picked* or *picked out*, in the example below the speaker omits the preposition.

(102) S2fFr And he (hasn't listened) the C D, I just gave him yesterday, but he was interested, I mean just, you know, from what I could, I could say.

Example: Listen the CD (MARK)

Although the speaker did not use the preposition *to*, which usually follows the verb *listen*, the omission did not cause any problem. It is redundant anyway – or an idiomatic preposition, i. e. "[it] has an idiomatic relation to the verb and is otherwise meaningless" (Levelt 1989:195) because *listen* does not have various meanings, as many other verbs do.[26]

8.5 Discourse

8.5.1 Covered misunderstandings

Most forms of lingua franca communication are successful, and in general few misunderstandings occur (e.g. Meierkord 1996). And despite some non-standard forms, communication usually seems to run smoothly. It is also the case in the BusinessELF corpus. However, one example causes communicative problems. Although the utterance in question (se (150)) looks correct on the lexical and grammatical level, it does not express what the speaker intended. And it causes a communicative problem. However, the problem only becomes detectable further down in the discourse after the speaker has realised that he was not interpreted as intended. What looks unproblematic on the local level turns out to be a misunderstanding: The question in se (150) and the following answer, se (152), which is further explained in se (154), (158) and (159) in the following excerpt, look unproblematic as they occur. Compared with the second excerpt (see excerpt *Are you actually promoting* (MARK); next page) a misunderstanding becomes obvious:

26 In the second part, the speaker leaves out the pronoun that would be used to refer back to the object in question, i. e. the aforementioned CD. However, this seems to be due to planning processes. In the first 'sentences', i. e. at the beginning of the utterance her focus is on the 'not listening'-fact; in the second part she realises the possible reason for this. Had not the intonation fallen and a very short break appeared between 'CD' and 'I', the construction would have been transcribed as a complex sentence with a relative clause. However, her intonation changes, and she seems to shift her focus to the temporal aspect in the second part of her utterance, here transcribed as a new sentence.

(150)	S1mGr	But, but how is it going in, in, in France?
(151)	S1mGr	And …
(152)	S2fFr	Ah ((1s)) it's/uh well as far as promotion, I mean, we get amazing reviews, you know, in all those very/uhm ((2s)) uh, uh you know, I know those magazines such as uh/I don't know if you know the ( )?
(153)	S1mGr	Hm`.
(154)	S2fFr	It's like uh the magazine.
(155)	S1mGr	Okay.
(156)	S2fFr	You know, for all the people who are like, you know, kind of into the Pop/Pop and new tendencies and, and also those magazines like Dove or G'do which are more oriented electronic music.
(157)	S1mGr	Right.
(158)	S2fFr	So national publication.
(159)	S2fFr	A big, a big amount of uh readers.

Example: How is it going (MARK)

Utterance (150) looks grammatically correct and appropriate in the situation. It is a question and as such requires a direct answer from S2fFr. S2fFr directly reacts to it and explains the situation in France: Her company is getting good reviews of the artists she is offering S1mGr for distribution. He gives polite backchannels using augments like *hm* (with a falling intonation) and *Okay,* indicating attention. He listens to her explanations concerning the relevance of the media that cover the concerts and publications by the artists in question (se (156)).

The exchange goes on in a similar manner without any topic changes or questions and looks smooth and trouble-free until, more than 10 utterances later, in se (168), S1mGr interrupts S2fFr. He thereby stops her from giving further information about the press reviews. It becomes clear here that the press reviews, or the artistic success of S2fFr's company which they stand for, were not what he was looking for. So he initiates a topic change in se (168). With a new question, he refers directly to the procedures at her company and inquires about their activities and the organisation of her company. This time, he reformulates it, first into a question about the type of company (or an interrupted verbal construction that was going to use another progressive tense), then reformulating it into an active structure inquiring about the actual function of her company:

(167)	S2fFr	All the press reviews we get now …
(168)	S1mGr	Is this your/is your company also/uh are, are you actually promoting ((1s)) uhm the, the, the stuff you release or …?

Example: Are you actually promoting (MARK)

Despite some planning issues, indicated through the two changes in structure, the hesitations and the pause between *promoting* and the repetition of *the*, he reformulates the question into *Are you actually promoting the stuff that you release?*

It becomes clear that the intended meaning was not 'how things are going' but rather 'how things work'. He wants to know how the French company is organised and what exactly their mode of operation is.

So the present continuous tense was interpreted as a request for information about the situation of S2fFr's company. His real intention, however, was to request information about their *modus operandi*. The misunderstanding was triggered by the aspect of the verb. English is a language that expresses *aspect*, "the way the grammar marks the duration or type of temporal activity denoted by the verb" (Crystal 1980:36). In the English verb phrase, it is realised by the use of *progressive* vs. '*non-progressive*' or *simple* tenses.

S1mGr triggered the misunderstanding through the use of the progressive form, making his hearer interpret the question as referring to a temporal state. S2fFr interprets the question as referring to the situation at the time being and explains the reviews and feedback to the products on offer.

S1mGr used a form of the present tense that is marked in English and thus triggered this interpretation while he really wanted more general information. Instead of reformulating his question, however, he breaks the more general proposition down into smaller, more specific elements. He asks about the organisation of the company. This shows later in the data. In se (182), he makes a clarification request. He summarises the information he inferred from different utterances after the question above. He announces the intention of clarification in utterance (182), in which he opens a form of meta-discourse expressing the function of the following question and sums up his discourse knowledge in se (183) before specifying his request for information in se (184):

(182)	S1mGr	So just, just for my under/for my better understanding.
(183)	S1mGr	So, Black and White is a distribution company.
(184)	S1mGr	Do you have in-house labels as well or just distribute stuff?

Example: Do you have in-house labels (MARK)

He makes his hearer aware that he sees a necessity to clarify certain aspects in order to create discourse knowledge: knowledge, or common ground, that the speaker and hearer have achieved through their joined linguistic efforts. It enables them to interpret following utterances by comparing their interpretation to the knowledge that has been exchanged and established throughout the discourse. This form of summarising information for a clarification check is part of patterns of action like negotiations in order for negotiators to compare their discourse knowledge (cf. e.g. Rehbein 1995).

S1mGr starts this part of the discourse by explaining the purpose of his utterance: "So just for my better understanding". He states that he needs further information to help him understand how the company operates. In utterance (182), he announces the function of the following passage of discourse (*For my better understanding*), while in se (183) he summarises his knowledge of S2fFr's company.

Even in linguistic interactions between speakers from the same linguistic background, some patterns of action, e.g. *buying and selling*, have pattern positions where speakers sum up their discourse knowledge (cf. position 40/buying-selling, e.g. Rehbein 1995:81) to double-check their understanding with the hearer. Summaries in negotiations are usually indirect requests to the hearers to 'double-check' their understanding of the discourse's outcome by comparing it to the speaker's. It is the hearer's opportunity to confirm what has been discussed or agreed so far or to correct whatever aspect of the discourse they find critical. And since in lingua franca communication language barriers a higher, speakers might feel the need to be 'extra sure' about comparing their understanding. So it is likely that they are more explicit especially when it comes to the illocution of utterances.

In the example above, S1mGr double-checks his understanding of the situation against S2fFr's. In se (184), he asks a direct question, requesting specific information about the company structure. He breaks this down into single aspects and thereby builds discourse knowledge together with S2fFr. Having done so, they can continue their negotiation based on the knowledge they share. This way, he repairs the misunderstanding he caused earlier and establishes a new, shared basis for their further discourse.

The example shows that, although his grammatical choice was not 'deviant' or 'incorrect' on the surface level, it did not fulfil the intended purpose and caused a misunderstanding. The situation thus required further communicative effort, i.e. repair work, to achieve understanding and fulfil the speaker's needs. If the stakes are high, speakers need to make sure their needs for information, clarification and understanding are fulfilled. So they may go to some extra effort to achieve understanding. The principle of 'let-it-pass' (Firth 1996) did not apply in this situation because S1mGr required the information to base his decision on whether or not to accept S2fFr's offer on it.

8.5.2 Discourse strategies

Regarding the study of the discourse of lingua franca communication, the focus in research has mainly been on cooperation. 'Politeness'-strategies and cooperative behaviour were two elements that were stressed in the literature. Basically, transitions between different phases were found to be handled rather abruptly (cf. e.g. Meierkord 1998), and the lack of 'gambits', which would make their talk appear more coherent and 'smooth', was pointed out critically, e.g. Lesznyák 2002.

In the BusinessELF corpus, however, phases of so-called *small talk*' or *homileic discourse* (Ehlich 2007), i.e. the phases of discourse for social purposes, are rather short. This can be explained by the time limits. Participants had different meetings scheduled for the day and were under pressure to cover the topics they needed to discuss in order to fulfil their business aims. However, they still took some time to meet and get to know their potential business partners. So they used homileic discourse to learn more about the other person. Interestingly, though, these phases were at the end of the meeting. Short phases of polite exchange about matters at hand like where to sit, asking for permission to smoke and offering cigarettes were at the beginning of the encounter. There were also some comments about the surroundings or the trade fair. Otherwise, the more homeleic phases of discourse can be found after the core business had been discussed. Topics like holiday plans or different parties that were scheduled for the evening were discussed in the homeleic discourse at the end of the meeting.

Transitions of the phases, like found in other studies, are rather abrupt in my data as well. But phases of silence, as found e.g. by Meierkord (1998), were rather short. One of the few occasions is the example below. S2fFr asks for permission to smoke. The pause of 2 seconds before the start of the 'core' topic – which is introduced quite directly – is, however, due to her lighting a cigarette:

(67)	S2fFr	Is that okay?
(68)	S1mGr	Yeah, sure.
(69)	S1mGr	I don't mind at all.
(70)	S2fFr	Thanks.
(71)	S2fFr	[((2s)) Uhm so tell me what about ((1s)) uhm ((2s)) Double Moon. *[lights cigarette*
(72)	S2fFr	So you said – that's the label – y, you like it, I mean that's/you, you were interested.

Example: Double Moon (MARK)

After offering S1mGr a cigarette, which he rejects, S2fFr asks for his permission to smoke in his presence. Having received his permission and thanked him for it, S2fFr lights a cigarette for herself. This causes the 2-second-break between her utterances. She then raises the decisive topic of their meeting: whether or not S1mGr is interested in distributing a label she has offered him, i.e. his company, for distribution in Germany. She enters into the pattern of buying and selling very directly and without any introduction. Thus she directly starts the negotiation, which is the aim of the meeting. So in this incident, speakers in the

BusinessELF corpus show the same abrupt linguistic behaviour that Meierkord (1998) described.

The break in her utterance (71) is caused by planning processes and seems to be prolonged by her lighting a cigarette and what sounds, in the recording, like her putting away things in her handbag. However, her start of the core negotiation is rather sudden. She directly asks a question and puts her hearer, S1mGr, into the position of having to answer the question. In doing so, he has to take a stance and express his position regarding their potential cooperation. This behaviour does not cause and hesitation or irritation on his side, though. He seems to have expected the direct start of the negotiation and was prepared to directly answer her question.

Although communication in the BusinessELF corpus can be said to run smoothly most of the time, there are occasional communicative problems. These are solved in a cooperative manner. The cooperative behaviour is a feature of lingua franca communication that was stressed by most researchers (cf. chapter 4), with the exception of Knapp (2002), which is one of the few who stresses that participants' behaviour was rather un-cooperative in high stake situations.

In the BusinessELF corpus, speakers are, of course, focused on their business goals. But they also need to be aware of the image they create of themselves as a person and potential business partner. In Marketingcooperation, the conditions for a potential cooperation are negotiated, yet no agreement is reached. However, speakers remain friendly and cooperative all the time and stress their willingness to meet again in order to discuss other business opportunities in the future.

In very few instances, one of the speakers has trouble producing an utterance. If this occurs, as in the example below, speakers need support, e.g. due to a lexical gap. But meaning is negotiated and interlocutors help each other. Thus, on the linguistic level, they co-construct utterances as well as meaning. On the personal level, they remain cooperative and ready to help at all times. And even if on the content level, they do not reach an agreement, their behaviour remains polite and cooperative, as can be seen in the example below. S2fFr has trouble producing an utterance (171), and S1mGr offers a term (*freelance people*; (se (172)). Although she does not use the term he offers, they manage to find a different solution together to construct the utterance:

(168)	S1mGr	Is this your/is your company also/uh are, are you actually promoting ((1s)) uhm the, the, the stuff you release or …?
(169)	S2fFr	Yeah.
(170)	S2fFr	Yeah.
(171)	S2fFr	When, when we don't hit/uh in house we hired uhm, uhm independence …
(172)	S1mGr	Freelance people.

(173)	S2fFr	Yeah.
(174)	S2fFr	Independent [uhm, uhm, uhm]…
(175)	S1mGr	I see.
(176)	S2fFr	How do we say?
(177)	S2fFr	*((laughs))*
(178)	S1mGr	Eh independent companies.
(179)	S2fFr	Yeah, yeah.
(180)	S2fFr	So, and eh so it was two girls who worked on the ((1s)) on Merchand D R.

Example: Independent companies (MARK)

In the extract, S1mGr asks for information about the organisation and approach of the company by posing a clarification question concerning the form of business. He starts out with a nominal construction. Then he changes the construction to a less formal one using the active verb *promote.* However, he uses it in a progressive form: *Is this your/is your company also/uh are, are you actually promoting ((1s)) uhm the, the, the stuff you release or …?* (se (168)). S2fFr understands the illocution: a request for information. She confirms that her company does promotion and starts with an explanation, which she cannot complete, though, because she lacks a specific term: *When, when we don't hit/uh in house we hired [uhm, uhm] independence …* (se (171)). She expresses the concept she has in mind: hiring people who work independently.

S1mGr understands what she is trying to express. He suggests the term *freelance people* (se (172)), his informal version of the technical term *freelancers.* He does not use the standard term here either, but he makes use of the lexical item *freelance.* S2fFr however does not take up the term. She repeats the word *Independent* (se (174)), an adjective that expresses the concept which determines the word she is looking for. She is obviously seeking an adequate noun to follow it, and she holds on to the concept as well as the expression. S1mGr understands what she means and confirms so by his utterance *I see* in (se (175)). S2fFr, however, does not let go yet. She explicitly asks for help with her question *How do we say?* (se (176)). Her laughter at this point is used to ease tension. She seems to be under pressure to come up with a comprehensible answer, although S1mGr has already received the information he was looking for.

S1mGr is linguistically flexible and ready to help, as can be seen in the following answer. After a short hesitation, in which he seems to look for an alternative term that might be easier for her, he fills the gap and offers her *independent companies* (se (178)). The phrase is not entirely correct in this context, yet obviously easier to process for S2fFr because it takes up her construction of the adjective *independent.* She combines it with a noun (i.e. *companies*; (se (179)). It is easier for her to process because it uses the same semantic concept she started out with.

She acknowledges his contribution in se (178) with two *Yeahs* in se (179), but does not repeat the term. However, she confirms their shared construction of knowledge – "some independent agent carried out the job". She goes on to explain, with the help of an example, that in the case of a successfully released album by the artist Merchant DR, her company hired two freelancers to help take care of the marketing. She labels them "two girls" (se (180)). Since, according to her explanation, two individuals were hired, the term *independent companies* is not the exact term here. However, it is the term S2fFr can easily use as it is compatible with the concept she activated and the term she was looking for. It is the one she agreed on with her hearer. So he helped her close the vocabulary gap and the two negotiated the term and co-constructed the utterance successfully.

S1mGr's own formulations are usually standard or even technical expressions, but, as explained above, he often seems to be trying to appear less formal. He uses expressions like *freelance people* and tries to be more colloquial in his linguistic choices by avoiding the specific term. He does so throughout all conversations recorded for this study, as explained above. However, what makes this exchange so valuable for research in LFE is that:

- both speakers share professional knowledge,
- do not share the linguistic knowledge to express this knowledge,
- negotiate a specific linguistic form to express this professional concept,
- are successful communicators because they apply their lexical knowledge flexibly.

So their general attitude is more decisive than their actual knowledge of the language – which is, however, true for most lingua franca speakers. But it is their shared professional knowledge that makes this exchange successful and a valuable example of professional lingua franca discourse.

And, as Knapp (2002) observed, contrary goals are accepted in business negotiations and do not jeopardise friendly and cooperative behaviour. Furthermore, speakers in the corpus are rather polite. Their communication runs smoothly and with very few misunderstandings or interruptions. If misunderstandings occur, they are solved and not 'let pass'. Topic changes or omissions, as were found to be used in more socially oriented lingua franca encounters (cf. e. g. Meierkord 1998), did not occur in the corpus. They are, of course, barely an option in business negotiations, but were also not necessary: Speakers were competent enough to cover all topics that were required. And if an incident occurred in which one of the speakers lacked an expression, the other speakers were competent enough to solve communicative problems if they were indicated.

All in all, speakers in the BusinessELF corpus use the same forms of English on the surface level; they use the same strategies as other lingua franca speakers. Most of their discourse is thus typical lingua franca discourse. However, all these forms occur in all parts of the discourse.

As the comparison of my data with the research literature has shown, almost all the features defined by other researchers as LFE features can be found in my corpus too, such as the use of more general terms, especially verbs, instead of those based on more specific lexemes, the use of non-standard prepositions, or the use of continuous forms instead of simple tenses etc. Compared to the data on lingua franca forms that is available, however, speakers in the BusinessELF corpus seem to be more competent than many other speakers. This shows in their grammatical forms as well as in their flexibility when faced with communicative problems such as lexical gaps.

All in all, speakers in the BusinessELF corpus can be said to be 'typical' and successful lingua franca speakers in that they

- are very cooperative in their linguistic behaviour,
- are flexible regarding the use of lexical items,
- use some general terms, especially verbs like *make, take, put, do* and *work,* more frequently than inner circle speakers.

9. Types of conditionals in the BusinessELF corpus

Though this be madness,
yet there is method in't.
(Shakespeare: Hamlet, Act 2, Scene 2)

Despite the high language competence of the speakers in the BusinessELF corpus, there are some constructions, namely different forms of conditional sentences, that stand out. Out of the 64 complete conditional sentences in the BusinessELF corpus, only a minority has what can be regarded as a 'standard' form (see details below). The majority of conditionals has a combination of tenses that is not common in (written or standard) English, namely the present tense in the protasis and *would* + infinitive in the apodosis.

In English, however, the forms of conditionals are not as straightforward as in many other languages. In the verb tense of the predicate in English, for example, different functions overlap, like the marking of time and probability. In this chapter, I will first define conditionals in English and discuss their functions in standard language. Then I will list different forms of conditionals found in the BusinessELF corpus and discuss their function. I will do a quantitative analysis to show a regularity in the use of different forms of conditionals (cf. chapter 9.4, 9.5). Then I will discuss the communicative effects with the help of a qualitative-interpretative analysis (Chapter 10).

9.1 Conditionals and grammar

All languages have means to separate reality and ideas. In many Indo-European languages, the *conditional* as well as the *subjunctive* are forms that operate on the edge between language as a representation of the world, i.e of 'reality', and language as an expression of ideas, i. e. of 'hypotheticality'. By 'hypotheticality' I will refer to different degrees of likelihood of an action or state expressed in the form of the predicate of a clause or a conditional sentence as a whole.

Forms and functions of conditionals have interested philosophers, psychologists and linguists for a long time. And a lot of work on conditionals has been done, either in formal semantics or in the field of psychology, focussing on the estimation of probabilities and applying conditional reasoning to different mental models. For more information on conditionals from these viewpoints, readers are referred to the vast literature in the field. Oaksford/Chater (2010), for example, offer an overview of developments in the fields of the history of the psychology of conditional reasoning and the history of conditional logic and its formal semantics (Oaksford/Chater 2010:3). For a discussion of the function of modality and conditionals from a semantical point of view, see e. g. Kratzer 2012; from an analytical philosophical point of view, see e. g. Jackson 1998.

Works in the field of formal semantics consider formal and logical aspects and the *truth value* of conditionals. However, they do not consider the *context*. And since the context is decisive for the choice of linguistic forms in authentic contexts (cf. Grießhaber 1987), these works will not be discussed in this dissertation.

While many linguists agree that conditionals are expressions of some kind of 'hypotheticality', i. e. probability or marking of not being real, few go into detail when it comes to explaining how this 'hyptheticality' comes about. Neither do they explain how it influences the perception of the sentence or utterance. When it comes to 'rules' of usage, most grammars give categories and a set of rules for the forms and functions of conditionals. However, in reality, ever so often different forms are acceptable and used, especially in oral language, even if they are not forms that are used in formal or written contexts, i. e. so-called 'standard forms'. And an increased awareness of these variations becomes visible in the content of grammar books.

One example is Swan's (1995) *Practical English Usage*, a reference book teachers and students of English have been using for generations. In the second edition of Practical English Usage, he gives a very detailed description of the various uses of *if* as well as of forms of the conditional. He gives a list of exceptions for most 'types' of conditionals. In the fourth, fully revised, edition (Swan 2016), however, he explicitly states:

> The "rules" given [...] are intended to be useful for learners. They describe what happens most of the time, and are generally valid for formal speech and writing. However, usage is far from fixed, and educated speakers and writers quite often mix structures (Swan 2016:237).

So when it comes to forms of conditionals and to grammar in general, a paradigm shift can be seen: From a set of rules and a prescriptive function to a more liberated view and a descriptive view of language. This has been the case ever since linguists started focussing on the oral use of language, and since technical developments allowed linguists to record, transcribe and analyse oral data. And more social and psychological awareness in society in general increased the acceptance of varieties, and speakers' needs are put over form. Furthermore, forms and linguistic needs change over time. In the following, I will explain some developments in English and other European languages concerning conditional(s) and explain how conditionals are described in grammars – in learner as well as teacher's grammars and linguistically oriented grammars like Biber et al. (1999).

9.2 Subjunctive vs. conditional

All languages have means to express hypothetical statements, yet do so differently. And what is more, the systems and ways of expression change over time, as can currently be seen in Spanish, for example. Spanish is one of the languages that have a synthetic verbal system for the subjunctive and the conditional. And although de Bruyne (1993), for example, classifies the *conditional* as a tense rather than a mood of the verb (cf. de Bruyne 1993:417f., also Pons 2010:6/73). The conditional is used to express possibility, assumption etc. The *subjunctive*, on the other hand, is considered a mood used to express attitudes such as wishes and possibilities (de Bruyne 1993:427).

The use of the conditional (*condicional*) and subjunctive (*subjuntivo*), however, mix in modern Spanish. Though theoretically equivalent (de Bruyne 1993:418), they are used differently with some verbs. For verbs like *querer*, the use of the past subjunctive (*imperfecto de subjuntivo* = (*yo*) *quisiera* (*I would like*)) instead of the conditional (*condicional*) *querría* is considered polite. With most verbs, however, the use of the conditional is considered rather archaic, and the form of the subjunctive is used instead, e.g. with verbs like *diría* (*I would say*) or *trabajarías* (*you would work*).

In German, a similar development has taken place, and the conditional (*Konditional)* is replaced by the analytical form of *würde* + infinitive or, for some verbs, the Konjunktiv II (*subjunctive of the past*) (cf. Bußmann 1990:407).

In English, this development has gone even further. The use of the subjunctive is widely reduced and is mostly replaced by conditional constructions. Its use and semantic function is not often discussed in detail in grammar books. Alexander (1998:239), for example, observes that "[t]he subjunctive (rare in English) refers to what could or should happen in hypothetical situations". Crystal (2003:442) defines the subjunctive as a "term used in the grammatical classification of sentence types, usually seen in contrast to indicative, imperative, etc., moods". He uses the terms *subjunctive* and *conditional* interchangeably when explaining that the term *subjunctive* is used to refer to

> verb forms or sentence/clause types used in the expression of many kinds of subordinate clause, for a range of attitudes including tentativeness, vagueness, uncertainty (Crystal 2003:442).

In his definition, he states that forms that "come nearest to the subjunctive occur in hypothetical constructions of the type *If she were going*" (Crystal 2003:442), which he contrasts with *If she was going* (ibid.). Furthermore, the subjunctive is used for fixed expressions like *So be it!* (Crystal 2003:442), after expressions, i. e. mainly verbs, like *demand, insist* etc.

Svartvik/Leech (2002) refer to these verb forms as the *productive subjunctive*, which is used after "governing expressions that express will (or volition)" (Svartvik/Leech 2002:395). They see it in contrast to formulaic expressions like *Come what may* (ibid.). They also observe elsewhere that the use of the subjunctive is more common in American English than in British English (Svartvik/Leech 2002:29).

The fact that the moods in English are not clearly distinguished can also be seen in different definitions: Cowan (2008), for example, explains that "extraposition with *important* requires the bare infinitive, often called the *subjunctive* form (e.g. *It is important that he complete the entire course*)" (Cowan 2008:492). Biber et al. (1999), on the other hand, explain that the use of the subjunctive in fixed expressions like *damn you* "have the appearance of imperatives, but are clearly not" (1999:1102). They argue that the example would contain *yourself* instead of *you* if it were an imperative (ibid.).

To complicate matters further, the term *conditional* not only refers to grammatical forms of verbs, but usually refers to a clause (or sentence) type (Crystal 2003:442). It is defined, from a structural point of view, as "a conditional clause, i. e. one beginning with *if*" (Hornby 1995:239), or, from a semantic point of view, as "clauses whose semantic role is the expression of hypotheses or conditions" (Crystal 2003:94). Or, in yet more detail, conditionals are defined by Alexander (1998) as "clauses [that] are not about events that have occurred, but about events that can or might occur or might have occurred" (Alexander 1998:273). So the term as such has different meanings: verb forms or a type of sentence.

Although definitions as well as terminology vary, what all linguists agree on is that conditional sentences either involve a reference to a condition, i. e. a situation or an event that does not occur in its own right or without some other event, action or situation related to, and the verb forms can be used to express the speaker's attitude.

In the following, the term *conditional* will be used with reference to a sentence structure that mostly consist of two parts, the *protasis* and the *apodosis*. The *protasis* is a subordinate clause that begins with a conjunction (mostly *if*) or has an inverted order of predicate and subject. It states the condition on which the proposition expressed in the main clause, the *apodosis*, is based. The order of the two sentence parts may vary. And in conversation, the two clauses may be separated. Furthermore, sometimes only one part of the sentence, i. e. one clause (protasis or apodosis), is expressed.[27]

In line with classical grammar, however, I will cite conditionals in the order *protasis – apodosis* when referring to their grammatical form, i. e. to the verb tenses (cf. Table 6). I will use their actual order in the recordings, i. e. here: the transcripts, when discussing their communicative function. In order to explain communicative functions that are context-dependent, I will use excerpts from the discourse in which they occurred.

9.3 Categorisation of conditionals in standard English

Most classifications divide English conditionals into three categories, often naming them *type I, II and III*, (e.g. Alexander 1988). They group them according to the probability of the condition described in the protasis and the tenses that are used. In "the most common type" (Cowan 2008:449) of a conditional, the present tense (in the protasis) is used to mark a realistic condition, which is usually followed by the result in the *will*-future as in the example below (Cowan 2008:449):[28]

If John leaves now, he will arrive at the airport in time to make his flight.

While most grammars further define two more separate categories, the *hypothetical* and the *unreal* conditional, Cowan (2008) only defines two main categories: *Real conditionals*, i. e. "conditionals in which the condition, and hence the result, can be fulfilled" (Cowan 2008:450) and *unreal conditionals*, i. e. "conditionals in which the proposition in the *if* clause is an imagined condition and the proposition in the result clause [or *apodosis*, B. D.] is its imagined outcome" (Cowan 2008:454). All conditionals, real and unreal, can express present, past and future.

Eastwood defines two basic types of conditions, *open* and *unreal*. He then describes 4 types of conditionals: *Type 0* with the verb pattern "(if)…+present …+present", *Type 1* conditionals with "if …+present ….+*will*", T*ype 2* conditionals with "if ….+past …+*would*". He explains that the 'type 2' conditional "expresses an unreal condition." (Eastwood 1994:336). However, he also states

27 In the data at hand, only one example was found that contained only one part of a conditional sentence.

28 In grammars, the order of the clauses given is usually subclause (or *protasis*) first, followed by the main clause (or *apodosis*). However, according to Biber et al. "[c]onditional clauses in conversation have no strong preference for either position. In the written registers, there is a slight preference for initial position." (1999:833). So the order of protasis and apodosis may vary and does so throughout the corpus.

that "[w]e can use a Type 2 pattern as the past of a Type 1" (Eastwood 1994:337). So the problem with verb tenses in conditionals is twofold: On the one hand, they can refer to the degree of likelihood or to the time (past, present, future) in which the situation or action occurs or occurred. Furthermore, different tenses can be mixed (Cowan 2008). Thus, English is not quite clear when it comes to differentiating between the degree of likelihood (sometimes referred to as 'subtypes', e.g. Cowan 2008:450). That makes the "boundaries between [them] blurry" (ibid). And "in certain cases, context may determine whether a sentence belongs to one or another category" (ibid.).

However, so-called 'type 1' or realistic conditionals seem to be the most productive type of conditionals. Different grammars list different tense combinations for it (e.g. Alexander 1988), as well as different sub-categories (Cowan 2008, Eastwood 1994). Some add explanations about different meanings, e.g. of the modals used in this conditional (e.g. Cowan 2008:453). So the 'category' of a conditional seems to be only a scheme of tenses to which there is a number of exceptions, even in inner circle usage.

In Cowan's scheme, *unreal conditionals* are further divided into *hypothetical conditionals* and *counterfactual conditionals* (Cowan 2008:454). Other grammars usually classify as a *type II conditional* a hypothetical conditional that refers to an unlikely or impossible condition. Or they define it as a means to "talk about imaginary situations in the *if*-clause and speculate about their imaginary consequences in the main clause" (Alexander 1988:277) in the present or past tense. A *type III conditional* is usually defined as one that uses a past perfect tense in the protasis and is classified as 'counterfactual' or 'unreal' or used when speakers "assume something purely imaginary" (Alexander 1988:280). It refers to a condition and its consequences that occurred in the past and can therefore no longer be changed. According to Cowan (2008) and most other definitions – regardless of whether they consider a hypothetical conditional a sub-category of unreal conditionals or a category in its own right –, hypothetical conditionals about the future usually have a verb in the simple past tense. However, it can also take other forms. It can, e.g. "be accompanied, [sic] by a modal like *should*, or consist of *happened*, *managed*, or *were* and a following infinitive" (Cowan 2008:455).

Counterfactual conditionals deal with events in the past that did not obtain (Cowan 2008:456). They contain a verb in the past perfect tense in the *if*-clause (or *protasis*) and *would* (or *could* or *might* + *have* + past participle) in the result clause (*apodosis*). They can also talk about the present, in which case the verb in the result clause (*apodosis*) is or may contain *would* or *could* plus other forms, e.g. infinitives, as in the sentence below:

> If the French *had won* the battle of Quebec, we *would* probably *be speaking* French today instead of English. (Cowan 2008:456; original emphasis)

The sentence speculates about a different outcome of a situation in the past and its hypothetical consequences in the present. It therefore combines the past perfect in the protasis with *would* and a marked present tense form in the apodosis. So the relation of tense, time and probability in English is more complex than is indicated by the three (or two) categories most grammars use. And some verb tenses can be used to mark both: different forms of the conditional and different references to time. And marking the modality through the tense of the verb can be more ambiguous than the dichotomy put forward by most grammars. A sentence like the following, for example, with the simple past in the protasis and *would* plus infinitive in the apodosis, can refer to an unrealistic conditional in the present or express a *habitual* conditional, i.e. a conditional expressing a recurring situation in the past (cf. Cowan 2008:450):

> *If he had business in Boston, he would stay at the Ambassador.*

So in English, the mood of the verb is not always clear from the form of the verb alone. And when it comes to conditionals, more categories are needed than 'realistic' vs. 'unrealistic'.

All in all, the simple scheme of three different types of conditionals with a set of tenses – simple present plus *will*-future or simple present tense for realistic conditions, simple past and *would* + infinitive for hypothetical conditions and past perfect tense + *would* + *have* + past participle for unreal conditions – is not sufficient. And although it is taught in schools and used in students' grammars (see e.g. Murphy 1985), it is only a basic scheme. In reality, different forms and tenses can be found in conditional clauses. As Alexander (1988:274) puts it: "Sense and context permitting, any tense sequence is possible".

Declerck/Reed (2001) offer a corpus-based analysis of conditionals from a semantic point of view. They criticise that earlier work on conditionals mainly recognised categories such as 'factual' or 'closed' (to refer to conditions that are treated as fulfilled), but do not recognise both. To solve the problem, they base their model on the speaker's (assumed) treatment of the condition, i.e. whether or not the speaker knows or assumes a condition to be fulfilled or presumes that the condition will or will not be fulfilled in the future.

Declerck/Reed (2001) suggest a model that does not only consider the location in time and the possibility, but uses various subcategories such as *closed*, *open*, *tentative* and *counterfactual* referring to the attitude the speaker expresses (or does not express) towards the likelihood of the condition to become real. They differentiate, e.g. between *Factual-P conditionals* as conditionals whose

P-clause (protasis, B. D.) refers to a situation that forms part of the actual world, and *Theoretical-P conditionals,* conditionals whose P-clauses refer to a theoretical (=counterfactual) world (Declerck/Reed 2001:62).

They take this differentiation further by subdividing theoretical P-conditionals into *neutral theoretical-P conditionals* and *nonneutral theoretical P-conditionals. Neutral theoretical-P conditionals* are also known as *nonfactual-P conditionals.* They are conditionals with a P-clause that expresses a supposition "without presupposing anything about the relation of compatibility between the supposed world and the actual world" (Declerck/Reed 2001:62). *Nonneutral theoretical P*-conditionals, on the other hand, are conditionals "with a theoretical *P*-clause which expresses a supposition accompanied by an assumption (presupposition) about the relation of compatibility between the supposed world and the actual world" (ibid.). So, according to Declerck/Reed 2001, the speaker expresses a *stance* towards the proposition of the conditional.

Declerck/Reed match different categories with the same form. It does not become clear in their explanations, however, *how* the speaker's presupposition (or stance) is linguistically transmitted. Neither do they explain how the hearer is enabled to decode such a presupposition. Sometimes the 'counterfactual' aspect is expressed through the tense, but the hearer has to know whether or not the expressed condition is counterfactual or not in order to interpret the implied supposition (cf. Declerck/Reed 2001:52).

Basically, Declerck/Reed (2001) make assumptions about the speaker's attitude towards the proposition expressed in the conditional clause. However, semantics does not consider the hearers and explain their perception. Working in the field of semantics, Declerck/Reed (2001) do not give examples of the communicative effect of clauses in oral conversation. Therefore, one is not able to see how the interpretation of the forms in question is supposed to work. Declerck/Reed (2001), however, sometimes give examples of the hearer as the addressee of the *if*-clause, but do not analyse the effect the utterance has on the hearer's perception or the unfolding discourse.

In the present dissertation, however, I intend to discuss the effects of conditionals on the discourse, i. e. on the hearer's perception of what is communicated. Thus Declerck/Reeds' (2001) categories cannot be used to analyse the effect on the hearer. The advantages of Declerck/Reeds' (2001) categorisation for the current discussion, however, lie in the fact that they consider the speaker's *attitude* towards the proposition. So they do not just look at the relationship between the actual world and what is expressed in the conditional sentence. Instead, they focus on the speaker's *assumption* about the factuality or potential of the proposition to be fulfilled. And although they do not use the speaker's commitment to the proposition as an explicit category, they do consider conditional sentences as a linguistic expression of attitude rather than grammatical categories that depend on the dichotomy of *real* vs. *unreal*. Instead, conditionals are – amongst other things – expressions of the speaker's attitude towards the content, i. e. proposition of an utterance. Reservations or disagreement, for example are, according to Declerck/Reed (2001:344), two aspects that can be transmitted through the use of conditionals. So Declerck/Reed go beyond the dichotomy of 'real' and 'unreal' or 'open' and 'unrealistic'. They consider, in their classification, the fact that the speakers' attitudes, like reservation, disagreement etc., influences their grammatical choices.

In the following, I will discuss some forms of the conditionals with a focus on pragmatic functions. I will take a similar starting point as Declerck/Reed (2001), assuming that the speaker's intention lies beyond the pure categorisation of the content of the conditional clauses. I will show instead that there is more to conditional constructions than a separation of *counter-factuality* and *factuality* (or realistic vs unrealistic). I will rather assume that they express a view of the consequences and therefore the degree of commitment to the proposition (cf. chapter 10.2).

The German subjunctive (*Konjunktiv II*) is a mood that is primarily used in conditionals in German. As Redder (1992) explains, its function is to separate knowledge from reality. So it ascribes a purely mental quality to what is being said. I will assume a similar function for conditionals in English. I will therefore hypothesis that the function of certain conditionals, which replace the subjunctive in English, is twofold: On the one hand, they enable the speaker to differentiate different levels of reality vs. hypotheticality. On the other hand, they express the speaker's attitude towards the proposition of the conditional.

Taking both Declerck/Reed's (2001) as well as Redder's (1992) arguments as a basis, I will argue that the communicative function of the conditionals lies in separating reality, i. e. the speaking situation, from discourse knowledge, i. e. the shared knowledge speakers and hearers develop during discourse (cf. Rehbein 1995). So the speakers are able to express, with the help of the subjunctive and the conditional sentences, in how far they regard the proposition as 'realistic' or 'preferable' and in how far they are ready to commit to it.

At the same time, the hearer is enabled, through the form of the conditional sentence, to decode the underlying attitude of the speaker. So hearers understand the degree to which the speaker regards the proposition of the conditional as 'binding' and is ready to commit to it. This way, the illocutionary force can be differentiated and a *promise*, for example, can be told apart from a *suggestion* or *inquiry*.

9.4 Quantitative use of conditionals in BusinessELF

In the overall corpus of 3,784 utterances, 64 are conditional sentences. Not only does the quantity of conditional sentences seem high, but many of the forms also differ from the 'common' forms described above. However, none of these forms causes any communicative problems such as misunderstandings.

It is not easy to define how often conditional sentences can be expected to appear in a discourse at all. Using the log likelihood (LL), for example, one would need to define the type of corpus first – or just decide to use a mixed corpus. A mixed corpus, however, might not help to explain the occurrence of specific linguistic forms since it is the context that evokes their use. Furthermore, researchers do not agree on a definition of a discourse type that classifies as a 'negotiation' (cf. Chapter 5). Thus it would be hard to define which data to include or exclude and which corpus to consider representative of the purpose.

And even if one relied on the definition by the participants, one would not be allowed enough recordings – and the publication of the data for reasons of confidentiality – to create a statistically relevant corpus. Therefore, it is not possible in the scope of this dissertation to mathematically define, find or create a data base which provides enough statistically relevant data to determine how often conditionals can be expected to be used in a negotiation. Therefore, it is impossible to say whether or not certain conditionals are overused or underused in the corpus.

Secondly, identifying conditionals would pose a problem because of lexical and syntactic variation. The 'standard' form of a conditional combines a grammatically complete protasis (usually containing the subordinating conjunction *if* (cf. Hornby 1995:239)) with a complete apodosis. Sometimes conditionals are 'covert', i.e. the appearing sentence may only be the apodosis, but the protasis is hidden, e.g. because it was not uttered or because one protasis refers to two different apodoses. And these might appear in different utterances. Furthermore, some conditionals are expressed through inversions, e.g. *Had he not been there, I do not know what would have happened.* They would need to be annotated or would otherwise not be identified as conditionals.

Other conditionals are only implied as in *With luck, we'll be there by tomorrow* (Alexander 1988:282). In this sentence, an elliptical form is used instead of the full conditional *If we are lucky*. These forms are also hard to identify as conditionals in a corpus search unless they are identified and annotated in advance. Annotated corpora of spoken discourse with enough data from professional contexts, however, are still rare and usually not available for public use.

Usually, the internet is a good and easy source of data and information. In order to come by more data, a search engine like Google (google.com; a search engine owned by Google Ireland Ltd.; Reg. No. 368047) or any other search engine can be used to give a fast overview of the use of the linguistic form in question. Regarding the word *if*, for example, Google finds 9,740,000,000 entries within 41 sec (16/7/2016). The results, however, reach from definitions of *if*, such as a *Wikipedia* entry, to musical titles and utterances containing *if*. So a general search was not helpful to identify types of conditionals, let alone specify their function.

A more accessible means are concordancers, i. e. computer programmes that automatically search concordances. Some concordancers help find specific combinations like *'if*would'*, e. g. *Webcorp.org*[29]. A case insensitive search by *Webcorp live* generated 102 concordances from 80 websites in which *if* was the conjunction of the protasis of a conditional sentence. Yet they do not differentiate between *if* as a conjunction introducing a conditional subordinate clause and *if* as the conjunction introducing a different subordinate clause, e. g. in the meaning of *whether*. And not enough context was given to identify the different functions and meanings of the sentences in question. These circumstances make the search for specific forms difficult and the results hardly usable for this dissertation project. But since a lot of work is being done these days in the field of computational linguistics and in gathering authentic data, things might change in the future. Chances are high that in the near future, users will be able to use a reliable, perhaps annotated corpus. And users might be able to compare the quantitative occurrence of conditionals in business negotiations with their occurrence in other types of discourse.

For now, the more practical way would be to look for the subordinating conjunctions. Conditional sentences are connected with only a number of subordinating conjunctions. The most common one is *if*. *Provided, given that, unless, as long as* and *in case* can also mark the condition. This type of search would, however, still exclude covert conditionals and inverted conditionals. Thus the online searches for the quantitative uses or the expected quantitative use – represented, e. g. by the log likelihood – did not provide reliable statistical data. That is why I could not compare the actual use of conditionals in my corpus to the use in other corpora. So I could not reliably determine whether or not conditionals are used more or less in the BusinessELF corpus than in other, comparable, ones.

Data regarding the quantitative appearance of conditionals in discourse in general was not easy to find. The only hint at the overall occurrence of *if* I found was in Biber et al. (1999), in a discussion of subordinators (Biber et al. 1999:841). Biber et al. state that "[o]nly 15 subordinators occur at least 200 times per million words". This equals 0.02% for all subordinating conjunctions. In the BusinessELF corpus, which consists of 3,784 utterances, 64 utterances form a complete conditional, i. e. one consisting of a protasis and an apodosis. Not all are complete

29 http://www.webcorp.org.uk

utterances, but they contain a predicate. One uses *provided* instead of *if* and one *as long as*. In all other conditionals, the condition is marked by *if*. That equals 1.691% of all utterances. 1.691% is a high share. So, quantitatively speaking, based on the finding of Biber et al. (1999), the number of conditionals in the BusinessELF corpus is high.

9.5 Forms of conditionals in BusinessELF

Conditionals in the BusinessELF corpus have so-called 'standard' forms, i.e. forms that are in line with conventional grammars as well as non-standard forms. When combinations of tenses differ from standard use or the use of conditionals in a specific sociolect or dialect, linguists often regard them as *mistakes* or *errors*.

According to Corder (1967), who analysed errors as indicators of the language acquisition process, a *mistake* is "a deviation in learner language that occurs when learners fail to perform their competence" (Ellis 1994:714). An 'error', on the other hand, is a deviant form that "results from lack of knowledge of the correct rule" (Ellis 1994:700). However, in the BusinessELF corpus, the majority of the different combinations of tenses appear more than once. And in most cases, the combination of tenses is used by different speakers. So it is unlikely that these forms are 'mistakes' or slips of the tongue. Some might regard them as 'errors', i.e. forms that speakers use because, according to Corder (1967), they did not acquire the standard form. However, their regularity as well as their communicative function (cf. chapter 10) indicate that these forms are language choices.

Table 6 (below) shows all complete conditionals in the corpus. In line with standard grammars, they are organised according to the combination of tenses. Notwithstanding the original order of the clauses in the utterance, the protasis is given first to make the table more accessible and indicate the different categories. In the table, conditionals are sorted first by the tense of the predicate in the protasis. It indicates, theoretically, the probability of the event or situation and classifies the category (C1–C5) conditional sentence. Within these categories (C1–C5), if different forms were found, e.g. in C4, they form sub-categories organised by verb forms or tenses.

The first column lists the number by which the conditional sentences will be identified and quoted and the category (C1–C5). The second column indicates the tense used the protasis with a sub-group for modals. The third column lists the tense of the apodosis sorted further according to whether a modal plus infinitive is used or by the tense of the full verb. The last column indicates the discourse from which the example is taken (BACK, MARK, DIS (cf. Table 3)), the speaker and the number of the utterance (se) in the transcript.

Although *could* and *would* are modals, their use differs from that of other modals: They refer to hypothetical situations rather than expressing more semantic aspects such as moral, attitude or capabilities. So in the following (the text as well as Table 6), when using the term *modal,* I will refer to the modals *can, have to* and *should* unless otherwise indicated. I will mention *could* and *would* explicitly since they have a marked function and are used in hypothetical conditionals or to stress a hypothetical meaning. Examples from the core negotiation are printed bold.

Tab. 6: Combination of tenses in conditionals

Example	protasis	apodosis	source
C1	**present tense**	**present tense**	
1	if you want to	So you're free to take them	DIS S3mNr 57
2	if they want	everybody in my office is taking records from my office	DIS S3mNr 1009
3	If I don't have any	it's another thing	DIS S3mNr 1013
4	**If you, • if you uh give the whole label to Vital, because uhm • • they're not that good at sending out • • promos and stuff.**	**I don't know how it's • uh for your (work)´**	**DIS S3mNr 219/220**
5	if I have a cigarette?	Do you mind	MARK S2fFr 47
6	if I • take these two?	Do you mind	MARK S1mGr 371
7	**if we decide only to make • like ten percent of your catalogue available**	**then there are still ninety percent which, you know, which are not available in Germany**	**MARK S1mGr 527**
8	**if you only work with us**	**then we only make • • a few titles available**	**MARK S1mGr 565**
9	**if you make an offer**	**we give you exclusivity (for this).**	**MARK S2fFr 519**
10	if we stay there for two weeks	then I'm wasting • (work)	BACK S3mNr 459
11	If we/uh ((1s)) if I ask for promos and if we get promos	we get like four or five or something	BACK S3mNr 1017

Example	protasis	apodosis	source
12	**if Portugal releases it three months after us**	**that's fine with me**	**BACK S1mGr 1084**
13	if it's a cool t-shirt, the/ with good quality and nice colours	people (are) very happy about that	BACK S3mNr 1359
14	If I have a meeting at two	I don't th_•_ink so	BACK S3mNr 1692
15	if you say uh after two, between two and, • two and five,	then it's fine	BACK S1mGr 1700
16	if I'm coming	I'm coming quite late, I think.	BACK S3mNr 1769
17	if, you know, I involve myself	I think maybe there is a chance	DIS S1mGr 845
	GOING to-future		
18	if you are going to, to work this label and you, you believe in the potential	then • do it!	BACK S1mGr 880
	present tense	**modal verb**	
19	if you like	I can give you uhm the contact to my colleagues in, in Belgium	MARK S1mGr 490
20	**If you deal with like three companies and everybody says: Well, I would like the Precious Sousa**	**and then you have to, you know**	**MARK S1mGr 538**
21	**if we are not able to give/ you know to be flexible**	**I think we can easily die**	**MARK S2fFr 643**
22	if all of a sudden the whole Reaggae thing goes down and you are very specialized in that field	you have to uh make sure that you still, you know, have income	MARK S2fFr 656
23	if you are in charge of the label	then it can be done	BACK S3mNr 82
24	If they show a football match on TV, for example if there is one Norwegian player on the, on the field	they can, they can show a, uhm ((2s)) uh a match from uh the second eh division in, in England	BACK S3mNr 706
25	**And if it says „out now"**	**it should really be out now**	**BACK S3mNr 1099**
26	if I just work Big Time	it shouldn't be a problem	BACK S1mGr 1160

Example	protasis	apodosis	source
27	if you want to´	And the ones that uh you can do	BACK S3mNr 1494
28	if you don't,	we can, we can catch up to-morrow	BACK S3mNr 1620
29	If I, If I say: I need • twen-ty-five promos, in one week	I have them in my office	BACK S3mNR 995
30	if they are available	you can meet them	DIS S3mNr 119
31	if you want to	you can talk to them af-terwards	DIS S3mNr 160
C2	**present tense**	**will/won't**	
32	If I drop an email to • • Adrian	I will get them	DIS S4mGr 226
33	if you go out buy (news) of Madonna	you will get it for • thirteen Euros.	DIS S4mGr 639
34	**if you tell me: Uh okay, I am only interested in re-leasing Precious Sousa**	**it will be a problem for me to give you this exclusivity on our whole catalogue.**	**MARK S2fFr 548**
35	**if you ask me to give you the exclusivity on the whole catalogue and you don't do anything with (Déja-vu) because I will lose a lot of money.**	**Uhm it will be a problem for me**	**Mark S2fFr 594**
36	if I quit the company	they will uhm have a hard time	BACK S3mNr 700
37	And if you have to chase them now	that will be in two years time, you know.	BACK S3mNr 940
38	So if he • likes the music and wants to do that	think I will go with them	BACK S3mNr 1109
39	if they wanna do it	we won't do it	BACK S3mNr1241
40	even if they want	We won't do (Snap)	BACK S3mNr 1244
41	if I'm/I get it out and/if we get it out, which I think we will	And I will probably	BACK S3mNr 636
C3	**present tense**	***would/could***	
42	if they are at the Norwe-gian stand	I wouldn't mind to • yeah just introduce myself	DIS S1mGr 82
43	if one day (they) go to Vital	I guess it would be • • easy for you to do it	DIS S3mNr 79

Example	protasis	apodosis	source
44	if it's only the uh commercial aspect which uh decides about taking a certain label on or not	(it) would be very boring	DIS S1mGr 1053
45	**provided the label uhm, you know, does proper promotion** **if there's like a marketing budget**	**This could be, could be a good thing for us**	**MARK S1mGr 81**
46	**Even if we have let's say a distribution agreement**	**I think the/for me the best way first uh • would, would be uhm to let you decide if you want to release it or not.**	**MARK S2fFr 281/279**
47	**if we uh make, make certain titles available**	**I think that, that could be a way**	**MARK S1mGr 336**
48	**if you decide to release an album/I mean to distribute an album**	**would you ask also for the European territories?**	**MARK S2fFr 470**
49	**if we only take certain titles**	**then it probably would make sense for you to deal with other territories**	**MARK S1mGr 522**
50	**if I say: Well, Déja-vu is a great label, we would like to • • make the whole catalogue available**	**We could do a label deal**	**MARK S1mGr 632**
51	**if we are talking about • say twenty-five titles • uhm or fifteen priority titles and then ten or fifteen ehm • • titles**	**then we/I really would focus on the fifteen first and then • try to make the whole catalogue available**	**BACK S1mGr 1497**
52	If you have one.	I would prefer large actually.	BACK S1mGr 1634/35
53	**as long as no other company decides to • uh ((1s)) take on a certain • label • • exclusively**	**Okay, (1.5s) through, through the whole catalogue I would/• • or from the whole catalogue I would, would pick like ((1s)) ten, twenty titles, whatever, and make them available.**	**MARK S1mGr 634**

Example	protasis	apodosis	source
C4	**past tense**	**past tense**	
54	if I went with Viral	I had to • quit with eh Fame and, and, and eh Pineapple.	BACK S3mNr 1150
	past tense	***would***	
55	if I had money and a really big (electric) label	I would sign her quite • • fast	DIS S3mNr 192
	would	***would***	
56	If the faith would be a little bit stronger	everything would be cool	DIS S4mGr 544
57	**If, if I would say: Well I would like to make certain titles available in Germany**	**would that • then be an exclusive ((1s)) deal?**	**MARK S1mGr 517**
58	**((1s)) provided, you know, we would do like a distribution agreement**	**So you could give, give those titles to us and we would …**	**MARK S1mGr 275**
C5	***VOLITIONAL WOULD***		
59	if you could • keep me updated on things.	I really would appreciate it	MARK S1mGr 670
60	if we would have one European • release date	I really would appreciate	BACK S1mGr 1081
61	if we could wait till I'm back in the office	I really would appreciate	BACK S1mGr 1257
62	if you could send me hum a discography of the label	So it w, would really ((clears throat)) great	BACK S1mGr 1328
63	if you could send me • • twenty or twenty-five of the ehm label samplers´	What I really would appreciate is	BACK S1mGr 1334
64	if you could send it as a Jpeg sample	I would appreciate	BACK S1mGr 1427

Combination of tenses in conditionals (examples from the core negotiation are printed bold)

Regarding the tenses of the predicate in the protasis, there are basically five types of conditionals in the BusinessELF corpus: Conditionals with a present tense in the protasis combined with the present tense in the apodosis (C1), conditionals with the present tense in the protasis and the *will*-future in the apodosis ("type 1 conditionals" in standard grammar; C2 in Table 6), conditionals with the present tense in the protasis and *would* or *could* in the apodosis (C3), conditionals with the past tense in the protasis and different tenses and moods in the apodosis (C4), and conditionals that use *would* in both the protasis and the apodosis and are used for politeness purposes (C5).

As Table 6 indicates, the vast majority, that is 53 out of the 64 conditionals used in the corpus, uses a present tense form of the verb in the protasis (cf. sentences 1–53, C1–C3); one however uses a *going to*-future (example 18; explanation see below). The remaining 11 sentences all use a form of the past tense or *would* (or *could*) in the protasis, yet they form two different categories: Examples 54 to 58 form a category of hypothetical conditionals ('type 2' in traditional categorisations, C4 in the table), while examples 59 to 64 form a separate category, i. e. C5. Conditionals in C5 are what Cowan labels '*speech act conditionals*' (Cowan 2008:458 f.). They are requests using *would* in both the protasis and the apodosis. This form is pragmatically driven and a means of politeness (see definition below).

Sentences 54 to 58 form a category, C4, since they all make use of the past tense in the protasis or *would* plus infinitive in the protasis. These conditionals are considered *hypothetical conditionals* (or 'type 2') in traditional grammatical categories. However, there are 3 different types of conditionals within C4: Conditionals that combine a form of the indicative of the past in the protasis with a modal in the past tense (example 54) or conditionals that use a verb in the indicative of the past tense combined with *would* + infinitive in the apodosis, i. e. the 'standard' form of hypothetical conditionals. Other conditionals in the category use *would* or *could* in both the protasis and the apodosis (examples 56 to 58). Despite this form, these conditional sentences are not speech act conditionals. They are used to indicate the speaker's attitude towards the utterance, as I will explain below (cf. chapter 9.5.4).

9.5.1 *C1 conditionals:* present tense + present tense

The use of the present tense both in the protasis and the apodosis is the most common form of the conditional in the BusinessELF corpus. In inner circle Englishes, conditional sentences with a full verb or modal in the present tense in both parts of the sentence are usually used as so-called *generic conditionals* (Cowan 2008:450). They usually express "a fact that appears to be a scientific truth" (Cowan 2008:450) and thus are a marked form. In the BusinessELF corpus, however, most examples using the present tense in both parts of the sentence are unmarked. They refer to conditions in the present or future that are likely to be fulfilled or are fulfilled on a regular basis, as in example 13 below:

13	if it's a cool t-shirt, the/ with good quality and nice colours	people (are) very happy about that	BACK S3mNr 1359

In example 13, the speaker uses a present tense in both the protasis and the apodosis referring to a situation that happens on a regular basis. The topic is 't-shirts as a give-away', a means of promotion. He asserts that if the quality of the t-shirt is good, the recipients are happy; an observation of a situation that is common in his professional life. So the content of the utterance is not extraordinary in the context. Neither is there a pragmatic function in the sentence. Since there is no further pragmatic function than the observation, for the speaker, it is an unmarked combination of tenses.

This can also be seen in the quantity of this construction: 31 out of 64 conditionals in the corpus belong in this category. Three different speakers, i. e. S1mGr, S2fFr and S3mNr, use this form of the conditional, as the examples 1–29 (except 18; see below) show. So it is not a specific construction of one speaker that could be ascribed to incomplete learning or another person-centred explanation. Furthermore, none of the sentences seems to mark a specific regularity or 'scientific truth' (Cowan 2008:450), as would be expected in inner circle usage. Rather, speakers in the BusinessELF corpus use this form of a conditional for their own means and without regard of inner circle 'rules'.

Regarding form, examples 2, 10 and 16 stand out because they use a *present continuous tense*, also referred to as *progressive*, in the apodosis. This is an expression of aspect and is a marked form by definition: "A progressive form does not simply show the time of an event. It also shows how the speaker sees the event – generally as ongoing and temporary, rather than completed or permanent" (Swan 1995:450). However, the three sentences, all uttered by S3mNr, do not deal with ongoing events. Example 2 refers to a regular occurrence, while examples 10 and 16 refer to single future events. S3mNr is the only speaker who uses the present continuous in conditional sentences.

The majority of his present tense conditional sentences is in the simple present tense. There is no pragmatic function detectible that would explain the use of the continuous tense in the three examples. One possible explanation for the form could be an orientation towards American English, which has a stronger preference for the present continuous than, e. g. British English. The variety in the forms S3mNr uses, however, might indicate that he either has not acquired the difference between the forms or, more likely, that he is a competent speaker who varies forms. (S1mGr uses a continuous form, too, when he asks S2fFr a question and causes a misunderstanding (cf. chapter 8.5.1 above).) Two speakers in the corpus, S1mGr and S3mNr, use the continuous form instead of the simple forms in some utterances. And it is the only feature in the corpus that actually causes a misunderstanding. In the conditionals, however, its use is not problematic and does not cause communicative problems.

Regarding the use of modals, there are 12 conditionals within the first group, C1, that are formed with the modals *can* and *have to*; two have the modal *should* in the apodosis. *Should* can replace *would* in some sentences when its function is to "describe the consequences of an imagined event" (Hornby 1995:1091). However, that is not the case here. In example 25 (see below), *should* expresses that the following action would be appreciated (cf. Hornby 1995:1091). In this case, it refers to *being out,* i. e. being available for purchase, by the time to which the announcement *out now* refers:

25	And if it says „out now"	it should really be out now.	BACK S3mNr 1099

Even though in example 25, the speaker uses the deictic form *now* in the apodosis, he is referring to the release date in question. The deictic form indicates that he mentally puts himself in the time of the release. So for him, the difference between the time of speaking and the time of reference is 'void'. It shows a strong identification with the proposition of the utterance.

In the apodosis, the speaker uses *should* plus the adverb *really*, which reinforces the obligation indicated by the modal. In his opinion, it is important that if their companies announce that an album is 'out now', the album ought to be available for purchase. Here, he uses *should* as a modal expressing that the action in question is "appropriate" (Hornby 1995:1091) or the "right thing to do" (Hornby 1995:1092) rather than referring to "a possible event or situation" (ibid.). He stresses the obligation that comes with the announcement referred to in the apodosis of the sentence. So it is a semantic choice and not a grammatical one. It does not express probability here and thus does not replace *would*. Therefore, it does not belong in C2, but rather in C1.

In example 26, *should* has a different meaning. It expresses the speaker's, i. e. S1mGr's, certainty about the proposition and his commitment to it:

26	if I just work Big Time	it shouldn't be a problem	BACK S1mGr 1160

In the example, he uses the conditional with *should* in the apodosis. He reinsures his hearer that the procedure discussed in the passage of discourse before will work out. This will happen on the basis that he only use one distribution company, Big Time, to carry out deliveries to S1mGr's company in Germany. Both negotiators agreed on using Big Time for carrying out the deliveries between

Norway and Germany. The idea is that they coordinate release dates and organise the distribution of Norwegian products in Germany. S1mGr stresses the importance of a reliable delivery. He puts the proposition of the protasis in the present tense and thereby indicates his commitment to it. He reinforces that by the conditional and the use of the modal *should*, which can also be "used to say that [… something] is true or will happen" (Hornby 2015:1436).

The two conditionals, even though they use *should* in the apodosis, are listed as present conditionals, i. e. C1 conditionals, because example 26 expresses certainty, while the other, example 25, expresses a moral obligation which is based on a likely condition expressed in the protasis.

One sentence in this category (example 18) stands out because it combines a *going to*-future with an imperative. Strictly speaking, this conditional does not belong in a present tense category. However, since it refers to a realistic condition in the future, its meaning and function belong in C1.

18	if you are going to, to work this label and you, you believe in the potential	then • do it!	BACK S1mGr 880

Example 18 is an indirect quotation of SmGr1's boss. It differs from the other examples in that it makes use of the *going-to* future, an unusual tense for an *if*-clause, as well as the imperative in the apodosis.

For the expression of realistic conditionals, most grammars call for the use of the *will*-future in the apodosis (or, in the categorisation of Alexander 1988, other future tenses such as the *future perfect* (273 ff.)). According to Swan (1995), however, different tenses can be used. Yet, as he points out, usually the *will*-future is used. He observes that "the same tenses can be used after *if* as other conjunctions" (245) and explains: "When we do not want to suggest that a situation is unreal or imaginary, we use ordinary tenses with *if* – the same tenses as with other conjunctions". Even though the *going to*-future is not usually used after conjunctions, it is used to express plans. In example 18, S1mGr refers to a conversation he had with his boss. So the *going to*-future may have been used to express the decision taken by S1mGr, and he is indirectly quoting his boss.[30]

Declerck/Reed (2001), who use authentic data taken from different corpora, quote examples of the use of *going to* in the protasis, such as: "If you *are going to work* in another EC country for a UK employer for more than 12 months or to work for a foreign employer, form E 111 is not appropriate" (Declerck/Reed 2001:143; example from Cobuild Corpus of English (UK, written)). They explain

30 As no hesitation or change in tone or pitch could be heard in the recording, no quotation marks were inserted in the transcript.

that future markers like *going to* can be used in *neutral theoretical-P conditionals* [conditionals that express no supposition about the relation between the supposed world and the actual world, B. D.] because it "implies that the speaker takes it for granted that there are at least some people for whom the future P-situation will actualize" (Declerck/Reed 2001:142). "[T]he condition represented by the P-clause [the protasis, B. D.] is not an open one: the condition is represented, not as possible, but as one which the speaker assumes to be fulfilled in the future" (Declerck/Reed 2001:150). Applied to the example above, the tense could indicate that S1mGr's boss found it likely that he would "*work this label*," i. e. decide to distribute it. So the form is grammatical, even though it is not a typical example of a conditional clause.

All conditionals in C1, even though they do not use the 'standard combination' of tenses, express realistic conditions and their likely or factual consequences. They are not standard forms, but linguistic choices of competent (L2) speakers.

9.5.2 C2 conditionals: present tense + will*-future*

The standard form of realistic conditionals with reference to the future or present, also known as 'type 1' conditional, consists of the combination of present tense in the protasis and a form of the *will*-future in the apodosis. It is labelled C2 in Table 6. It is used less frequently than the present tense/present tense combination (C1); only 10 out of the 64 conditionals have this combination of tenses. All refer to realistic conditions and their likely consequences or to consequences that the speaker knows will come true because it has happened before, like in examples 32 and 33:

32	If I drop an email to • • Adrian	I will get them	DIS S4mGr 226
33	if you go out buy (news) of Madonna	you will get it for • thirteen Euros.	DIS S4mGr 639

In example 32, the speaker talks about Adrian, an employee at a record company who sends him sample CDs whenever required. He works with Adrian on a regular basis. Here, he uses the realistic conditional to stress Adrian's reliability: Adrian sends him the sample CDs without delay or problems. So the conditional is a means of stressing that the cooperation works well, and an email is all it takes for the desired result to come about (receiving the required samples). This is a regular and certain situation and outcome, and he expresses it with a 'regular', i. e. standard, form of a conditional.

Example 33 (above) is a statement about the price-drop in musical media, an issue that was discussed frequently at the trade fair and that concerned the speakers a lot. In the discourse passage, the speakers discuss the situation, and S4mGr gives an example of how low the prices for their goods are. To illustrate this, he uses the example of a then new publication by Madonna. She serves as an example of a well-known and established artist. He uses the example and a realistic conditional to back up and strengthen his argument that prices will drop.

Standard realistic conditionals of this category are used by speakers S2fFr (examples 34, 35), S3mNr (examples 36 to 41), and S4mGr (examples 32 and 33), but not by S1mGr. All speakers still seem to prefer present tense/present tense construction (with or without the modal) instead of the standard construction: 31 conditional construction belong in C1, while only 9 belong in C2, i.e. only 9 are formed according to standard grammar. However, conditionals in C1 do not have a specific, i.e. marked communicative function. So speakers in the BusinessELF corpus seem to show a preference for the form of C1 conditionals and use them as the unmarked form of realistic conditionals.

9.5.3 *C3 conditionals: present tense +* would

What catches the eye is that out of the 64 conditional sentences, 12 combine the present tense in the protasis with a form of *would* or *could*. This is rather extraordinary since *would* and *could* are the two most common verbs in the hypothetical conditional sentence. However, they are usually used in combination with a past tense in the protasis in English. The modals *could* and *would* are the typical, i.e. standard, markers of the hypothetical or *type 2* conditional. Unless the combination is used as a means of politeness (Alexander 1988:275).

In the BusinessELF corpus, however, the combination of present tense in the protasis with *would* + infinitive in the apodosis (C3) is the second largest category after C1. In the BusinessELF corpus, it is used more frequently than the combination with the past tense, i.e. the 'standard' form. Category C3 combines two aspects: A condition that the speaker regards as realistic or as part of their experience in the protasis, and an outcome that the speakers consider as either unlikely or that they dis-prefer in the apodosis. This can be seen in example 44:

44	if it's only the uh commercial aspect which uh decides about taking a certain label on or not	(it) would be very boring	DIS S1mGr 1053

In example 44, the speaker, S1mGr, uses a present tense in combination with *would*. However, it is not a form of politeness. Instead, *would* is used here to indicate his critical attitude towards the proposition of the apodosis. So there is difference between the two parts of the sentence: The protasis is in the present tense, so the proposition of the protasis is likely, i. e. something that may happen or happens. The attitude expressed in the apodosis is different. He differentiates between what is likely (the protasis) and his attitude towards it (the proposition of the protasis does not apply to him; hence the *would*).

So the intended message might be twofold: Sometimes it is the case that these aspects are decisive. But if it were the only reason for doing things, he would not appreciate the situation. He expresses this part with the help of the subjunctive in order to lift the proposition to a different, more hypothetical, level and away from the speaking situation and the situation in the protasis.

In example 43, the same combination of tenses is used, but for a different reason. Here, the speaker wants to be indirect. So the function is indeed close to a politeness form. S3mNr talks about a band that want to be distributed by S1mGr, but are still under contract with a label he does not distribute. S3mNr is talking about the plan of the musicians in question to go to a different label (Vital). He states it would be easy for S1mGr to sell their records once they changed the contract and signed a contract with the new label. He uses a present tense for the condition and thus expresses a high likelihood. He thereby implies that it is the band's plan.

43	if one day (they) go to Vital	I guess it would be • • easy for you to do it	DIS S3mNr 79

The use of the present tense in example 43 instead of a past tense indicates that the speaker does not see a 'distance' or difference between the speaking situation and the expressed proposition. The proposition of the protasis, however, is expressed with the help of *would* and the infinitive (*would be easy*). The matrix construction with *I guess*, the indirect formulation with the neutral pronoun *it* and the hesitation before *easy* as well as the relatively open and vague verb *do* all make the formulation indirect and rather vague. The speaker does not want to put pressure on the hearer (S1mGr). Although he suggests that S1mGr take care of the band after a change of labels, he does not directly ask him to. Instead, he uses different indirect forms. This makes the suggestion less pressing on S1mGr. On the one hand, he expresses an option in the future, on the other hand, he uses an indirect request. Through the construction, he makes it look like he is 'transmitting' the request on behalf of the band, and his indirectness can be considered polite.

Although the combination of present tense and *would* + infinitive is a grammatical one, it is not a standard form in inner circle usage. Quantitatively speaking, however, it can be considered a 'common' form in the BusinessELF. Speakers use this construction in 12 out of 64 conditionals. It is therefore an unmarked form. Speakers in the corpus use it not only as a politeness strategies (see below) like native or inner circle speakers do. They also use it to indicate to the hearer in how far they identify with the proposition of the apodosis. This way they use the form of the subjunctive to distance themselves from the content of the apodosis although they regard the condition as likely.

9.5.4 *C4 conditionals: past tense*

Another standard form of conditionals is the combination of a past tense verb in the protasis and a form of *would* + infinitive in the apodosis. It is the so-called 'hypothetical' or 'type 2'-conditional. In the BusinessELF corpus, only one out of the 64 conditional sentences actually has this form. It only appears in example 55 (see below), in which S3mNr talks about an up and coming female musician:

55	if I had money and a really big (electric) label	I would sign her quite • • fast	DIS S3mNr 192

The speaker uses the 'standard' combination of tenses for hypothetical conditionals: simple past in the protasis, *would* + infinitive in the apodosis. Since the proposition of the utterance is purely hypothetical, he marks this with the verb forms: The past tense is used to mark that the situation is not real; and the subjunctive (*would sign*) is also used to stress that the proposition is hypothetical.

The example shows that the speaker is aware of the standard conditional form that expresses hypothetical contents. The conditional is, however, the only example in C4 – the most varied category – of the 'standard' form of the hypothetical conditional. Out of the 5 conditionals in this category, only examples 54 and 55 make use of a past tense verb in the protasis; yet example 54 uses the past tense in the apodosis too. The apodosis was actually in first position in the utterance:

54	if I went with Vital	I had to • quit with uh Fame and, and, and uh Pineapple.	BACK S3mNr 1150

Since the apodosis in example 54 was uttered before the protasis, it is likely that the speaker had another consequence on his mind. Both parts of the utterance seem to express a condition. This might have been triggered by the reverse order of the sub-clause and the main clause. The protasis, again, has various indicators of planning processes such as the hesitation before *quit*, the repetition of *and* as well as the two *uhs*. So it is likely the speaker processed both parts of the utterance as the protasis; one because it preceded the other and the other because it is the logical protasis.

All other conditional sentences in C4 use *would* in both parts of the sentence. However, they are not speech act conditionals.

9.5.5 *C4 conditionals with* would *in the protasis*

The construction of conditionals with *would* in the protasis as well as in the apodosis is the most productive subcategory of C4. Even though different modals can be used in the protasis, the use of *would* after *if* is usually marked and motivated by a pragmatic function, i. e. politeness, in inner circle English. It is also the motivation for the conditionals in C5 (cf. 9.6 below). However, the form is not used to express politeness in this subcategory, but to express the speaker's attitude.

Examples 56, 57, and 58 are all formed with the modal *would* in the protasis. Example 56 expresses a wish by the speaker, whereas examples 57 and 58 are part of the core negotiation. They have a communicative function: they suspend the illocution and will be discussed in the following chapter (cf. 10.2). Example 56 is not a request, but an expression of a wish:

56	If the faith would be a little bit stronger	everything would be cool	DIS S4mGr 544

The protasis, *If the faith would be …*, is formed with the modal *would*. It expresses the speaker's realisation that the proposition (faith being strong) is not the case. However, the speaker would enjoy his job more if people believed more in their projects. So the second part, the apodosis, is formed with the modal *would* as well. It is the 'standard' form in the apodosis of hypothetical conditional sentences. The double use of *would* thus has two functions: In the apodosis in standard forms, it marks the consequence of hypothetical conditions. In the protasis, however, it expresses the speaker's wish for something he realises as not existing. Here, the original function of the subjunctive comes in: expressing a wish.

The formulation might be considered an 'error' and could be explained as an interference of S4mGr's mother tongue, German. German uses syntactic constructions with *würde* + the infinitive to replace the subjunctive (cf. above; Bußmann 1990:407). However, Kellerman (1989) found speakers whose mother tongues use analytical forms to express probability with the help of syntactic forms. So these grammatical forms are likely to be a communicative means rather than an error.

Kellerman (1989) explains that Dutch advanced learners of English formed sentences like *If I would be able to live all over again, I would be a gardener* although Dutch uses the past tense (preterit) as one option for marking hypotheticality. Kellerman does not explain the use of *would* in both protasis and apodosis as a potential L1 interference, as e.g. Swan/Smith (2001) do. He explains it as the learners' way of explicitly marking hypotheticality. According to Kellerman, not only Dutch learners of English use *would/would* constructions for the protasis and the apodosis although their L1 allows for other markings. French learners do the same, although French is one of the languages that mark probability by the preterit.

Trévise (1979; quoted in Kellerman 1989:103) found that French learners of English (1st and 2nd year university students) not only marked probability "wrongly" by *would* in the protasis as well as the apodosis, but in some cases even altered the correct form, i.e. marking with the preterit, into incorrect *would/would* in a subsequent editing phase.

Since French, like English, does not mark probability morphologically, but through the use of a past tense, both Kellerman's and Tévise's findings show that the use of the non-standard forms cannot be explained as interferences with the learners' respective L1s per se. Kellerman gives two different potential reasons for the findings: The first might be "that learners will not transfer (or are reluctant to transfer) L1 features which they consider marked" (104). In this case, he explains, learners tend to

> avoid transferring the modal meaning of Dutch past tenses to English past tenses even though there is positive evidence for this in the input. Instead the modal meaning is reallocated to the explicitly hypothetical morpheme *would*. So instead of transferring the form from their L1, they apply an explicit morphological marking of the probability as a form of reacting against ambiguity in the verb forms of conditional sentences (Kellerman 1989:88).

A second tendency is that of "creating morphological symmetry in verb forms of the two clauses that make up these [conditional] sentences" (Kellerman 1989:88). So the use of *would* might be a form of alignment of the two parts of the sentences. Kellerman does not explain, however, what might cause the use. For example, processing might be easier thanks to the synchronised morphology.

This explanation might also hold for the conditionals in C4. Speakers in the corpus do not align the verb forms in conditional sentences per se, because only 3 out of 58 conditionals (not counting the politeness conditionals in C5) actually have this form. However, example 58 as well as examples 42 to 53 use *would* or *could* plus the infinitive in the apodosis (C2). So the use of this form is differentiated in the corpus. The use of *would* in both parts of the sentence is neither random nor a form of alignment. Examples 59 to 64, however, which also use *would* in both the protasis and the apodosis, are listed under a separate category, C5, as politeness conditionals, aka speech act conditionals.

9.6 Conditionals and politeness

9.6.1 C5: speech act conditionals

The last category, C5, consists of sentences that are so-called *speech-act conditionals* (Cowan 2008:458 f.). They are marked and pragmatically motivated: The main motivation is politeness. Politeness is a pragmatic principle based on cultural perceptions of language use. Although politeness in the general sense is a judgement of socially acceptable behaviour, in the following, only linguistic phenomena will be discussed.

Leech (2014) differentiates between pragmalinguistic and sociopragmatic politeness. The first refers to the linguistic form and pragmatics, the latter to pragmatics and society (Leech 2014:IX). Crystal (1980:358) defines politeness as the "linguistic features mediating norms of social behaviour." And although a detailed analysis the politeness requires an analysis of the social context, there are some linguistic forms and principles that can be regarded as *polite* in Western cultures in general.

Brown/Levinson (1978) presented one of the first models of politeness, which – despite some criticism – remains a classic in the field. It is built on Grice's theory of *implicature* (Grice 1975), the assumption that there are parts of an utterance that the speaker assumes the hearer to recognise without making them explicit. Brown/Levinson focussed on the redressing and mitigation of *face-threatening acts* (cf. Leech 2014:33). *Face* serves as a psychological explanation of comity (in Western cultures). It is seen as the "positive self-image or self-esteem that a person enjoys as a reflection of that person's estimation by others" (Leech 2014:25). Consequently, the speaker threatens the hearer's *face* with every request. The hearer's self-image is at stake because he needs to decide whether or not to fulfil the request. Every request is therefore at the hearer's cost and thus a *face-threatening act*. According to Leech (2014:11), polite requests are polite in the sense that the speaker tries to lessen a potential offence by seemingly offering different outcomes. Politeness strategies in English are, e.g. questions, modal auxiliaries and hypothetical past tense forms (Leech 2014:13).

Grammars also explain the use of conditional sentences as a politeness strategy for different speech acts. Biber et al. (1999:821) explain that "[t]he conditional clause mitigates the force of the suggestion or command, making it the hearer's choice." Eastwood (1994) states that the 'type 2' conditional, i.e. the hypothetical conditional, can be used as a means of politeness (Eastwood 1994:336). Similarly, Swan (2016) elaborates that it "can make suggestions sound less definite, and so more polite" (entry 239). Leech/Svartvik observe the same (2002:175), so does Cowan (2008:458). Swan (1995) lists conditionals and negatives (162) as well as the modal verbs *would, could* and *might* (161) as means of making questions, request and suggestions less direct. All grammars see the function of the modals *would, could; should* (Alexander 1988:275) as well as the use of conditionals (either 'type 2', i.e. the hypothetical conditional, or 'type 1' with *should* in the protasis) as means of politeness. They make the face-threatening act weaker since the request is less direct.

In the BusinessELF corpus, 6 conditionals are used for politeness purposes. They are categorised as C5. S1mGr is the only speaker who uses this politeness form. It is not the only form that is used to express explicit politeness, though. However, it is one that is characterised – in formal language as well as in the corpus – by its explicit pragmatic function. Even though 6 out of 64 utterances are not a statistically reliable category, it indicates that the speaker felt the necessity to mark the utterance as polite. And that this need is fulfilled with the help of this specific form of conditionals, just as it is in inner circle use.

S1mGr uses 6 such speech act conditionals for formulating his requests (examples 59–64). On the propositional level, the sentence expresses the speaker's gratitude for a future action by the hearer, while on the illocutionary level, the sentence is a request. This request is made in a very formal and indirect way because the requested action is at the hearer's costs. So the speaker is being very polite by "distancing the request from the here-and-now and from direct imposition" (Leech 2014:13 f.).

And even though examples 59 to 64 are all uttered by S1mGr, he is not the only speaker who uses politeness forms. However, he is the only one who uses this explicitly polite form. In the six examples that form category C5, he uses a formulaic conditional starting with *I would appreciate* ..., albeit without the neutral pronoun *it*, which usually serves as an object in the formula in standard English. He reinforces the politeness formula in 5 out of the 6 examples (59 to 63) with the adverb *really*, as in the example (59) below:

59	if you could • keep me updated on things.	I really would appreciate it	MARK S1mGr 670

In example 59, the predicate in the protasis is *could*, the modal that is sometimes used instead of *would* in hypothetical conditionals (cf. e.g. Alexander 1988:275). That makes his request even less direct and thereby more polite since the meaning of the utterance includes the notion of capability. So it gives the hearer even more 'room' for denying the request and is therefore more polite. *Could* is used in 5 out of the 6 requests (examples 59; 61–64). SımGr is explicitly indirect and polite. Yet not all his requests use this form (*would/could* in both the protasis and the apodosis); he sometimes uses the present tense for polite requests and combines it with *would* as well, i. e. he uses C3 conditionals as politeness forms.

9.6.2 *C3 conditionals as forms of politeness*

Although politeness is a guiding principle in requests in the corpus, not all requests belong in C5. Some polite conditionals use a combination of the present tense in the protasis and *would* in the apodosis and are thus listed in C3. However, as the example below shows, their function differs with regard to the level of indirectness – and is therefore considered forms of politeness – as well as with reference to time. Most of the sentences in C3 refer to conditions and consequences, the original function of conditionals. Examples 42 and 52, however, are conditionals used to express a request. They are less formal than the requests in C5. Example 42 is SımGr's indirect request to his hearer to introduce him to his colleagues:

42	if they are at the Norwegian stand	I wouldn't mind to • yeah just introduce myself	DIS SımGr 82

In example 42, the SımGr combines a present tense in the protasis with *would* + infinitive in the apodosis, making use of a politeness strategy, i. e. a C3 conditional. Even though the sentences are not standard, they are grammatical in English. *Will* and *would* can be used in the *if-clause* to "emphasize willingness and unwillingness" (Alexander 1988:283), e. g. in polite formulae, particularly in formal contexts. Biber et al. (1999:495) explain that "*[w]ould* is used particularly to mark both volition and prediction; *will* is also common with both meanings (and is often ambiguous)."

And it is an expression of politeness because the protasis refers to a realistic condition in the present (or in Declerck/Reed's (2001) terminology, it is a *factual-P conditional* because it refers to a situation that forms part of the actual world (62)). Yet the apodosis contains a polite request. This request is marked by *would*. The combination is used because, firstly, the speaker does not know if it will come true, i. e. if he will actually meet the person he wants to meet. Secondly, he needs to be polite and use a form that mitigates the face-threatening act. Requests are therefore usually expressed with the help of *would*, since *would* sounds less definite (Alexander 1988:239) and therefore more polite. However, SımGr combines the use of *would* with a present tense predicate in the protasis because he knows the proposition of the condition to be real.

Another possible explanation, according to Declerck/Reed (2001), is that the protasis (or *P*-clause) does not form part of the clause that is seemingly the *Q-clause* (Declerck/Reed 2001:171) or apodosis. That is, the speaker might have combined two clauses here, maybe due to incomplete planning. One option might have been: "If they are at the Norwegian stand, I can meet them/introduce myself …", which would have been rather direct, though. Therefore, it might have been perceived as impolite. The apodosis, however, could be a strategy to avoid a pragmatic failure, i. e. avoid impoliteness. The sentence could, therefore, also be the apodosis to a different, covert, protasis.

From a pragmatic point of view, however, the sentence fulfils different functions: It carries the intended meaning ("I want to meet these people; I can meet them while they are at the stand"), it carries the illocution, i. e. a request ("Please take me to the stand"), and it expresses the illocution in an indirect, and therefore polite way. It gives the hearer a chance to either fulfil the request or find an excuse not to (e.g. "They are busy."). If it violates a grammar rule, it does so because it puts pragmatic principles over grammatical norms. And pragmatics is principle-governed (Leech 2014:35), unlike grammar, which is rule-governed. And principles are regulative, i. e. politeness is more important than grammar rules because they regulate social needs. Therefore, speakers sometimes 'break' grammar rules – or rather, they 'bend' them – in order to achieve a social goal.

The same principle applies to example 52 below. S3mNr has offered S1mGr a promotion t-shirt. He asks S1mGr to choose his size, and S1mGr expresses his preference in a conditional sentence:

52	If you have one.	I would prefer large actually.	BACK S1mGr 1634/35

Here, S1mGr uses the present tense in the protasis since he is referring to a present situation. In the apodosis, however, he uses *would.* He combines it with the adverb *actually* in order to make his request indirect and thus less demanding because "*would* can be used to make a request even more polite" (Swan 1995:246). He also chooses a very polite verb (i.e. *prefer*) for his request.

9.6.3 C1 conditionals as forms of politeness

Polite requests in the corpus can also take the form of C1 conditionals, as in examples 5 and 6:

5	if I have a cigarette?	Do you mind	MARK S2fFr 47
6	if I • take these two?	Do you mind	MARK S1mGr 371

In both examples, the speakers use the combination of a question that contains the formula *Do you mind* with a conditional to make their request indirect and thereby polite. Yet in both cases, the 'object' of the decision is right in front the hearer. In example 5, S2fFr knows her intention of having a cigarette might bother S1mGr. So she leaves him the choice of whether or not the action (having a cigarette) will be fulfilled. Theoretically, he has the option of answering, for example, *Actually, I do mind*, or by giving her permission to go ahead with her intention (as he actually did in the following utterances).

In example 6, S1mGr refers to sample CDs that S2fFr brought to the trade fair. In the actual order of clauses in the utterance, the apodosis preceded the protasis. In both examples, 5 and 6, the decision is left to the hearer, hence the question. Yet the speakers' behaviour influences the situation in which they find themselves, hence the present tense in the protasis.

All in all, the complexity of conditional clauses lies in the variety of aspects that influence their form. These are pragmatic functions like politeness strategies, but also the probability of the proposition as well as the speakers' attitude towards the proposition. Some of the non-standard forms of conditionals in the BusinessELF corpus can be explained as forms of politeness. That applies not only to the speech act conditionals in C5, but to some of the non-standard forms. Politeness seems to play an important role since this is the first meeting of the participants. And since speakers adapt their utterances to their social needs, they use explicitly or implicitly polite forms. However, these forms are not always standard forms, even though they are grammatical. So speakers put their communicative needs – being socially agreeable, being polite etc. – over grammatical forms. And what is more: None of the conditionals in the corpus causes a misunderstanding due to the choice of grammatical forms. All conditionals are interpreted by the hearer in a way that the discourse – even though not always with the desired outcome – was socially agreeable and could go on without interruptions.

9.7 BusinessELF conditionals and reference to time

By definition, conditionals indicate the likelihood or probability of an event or situation. Furthermore, as we have seen above, they can express the speaker's attitude towards the content. At the same time, conditionals have to indicate the location in time – past, present or future – of the situation or event expressed by the predicate.

In the BusinessELF corpus, conditionals only refer to present or future events. None of the conditionals in the corpus uses the past perfect tense in the protasis, which is the marker of events and situations that did not happen in the past (cf. e. g. Alexander 1988:280, Cowan 2008:456).

The majority of conditionals in the corpus refers to future events and situations. Out of the 64 conditionals, 16 refer to present situations or events (examples 1, 2, 3, 5, 6, 11, 13, 23, 24, 29, 32, 33, 44, 52, 55, 56), while 47 refer to future situations. For all of these, different combinations of tenses (and modals) are used. And conditionals that refer to the future are found in all categories. Most utterances with conditionals refer somehow to business related topics, e. g. procedures, contracts etc. When talking about more personal topics, speakers focussed mostly on their taste in music, working conditions, motivation or sometimes holidays. Topics of the past did come up, yet no conditionals were used.

Conditionals that refer to the present and to the future are distributed unevenly across the categories. Out of the 31 conditionals in C1, 10 refer to present situations, while 21 refer to future situations or events. In C2, only two conditionals refer to the present, i. e. example 32 and 33 (see above). In example 33, S4mGr talks about the price drop for musical articles with the example of Madonna. He refers to the present. In 32, he refers to the reliability of one of the employees of a label. Both examples were discussed above. The other 8 examples refer to future events or situations. And even in C3, which consists of 12 examples, 8 conditionals refer to future situations, while 4 examples express present situations. These are examples 42, 44, 40 and 52. And out of these, examples 44 and 52 are forms of politeness (cf. chapter 9.6, above). In C4, which combines the past tense in the protasis with either the past tense or *would*, two examples, i. e. 55 and 56, refer to a present situation. The other 3 conditionals refer to the future. C5, however, is made up of constructions that are requests for future actions.

All in all, in the BusinessELF corpus, the vast majority of conditionals refer to the future, only a small minority to the present and none to the past. Conditionals that are used to refer to present situations spread – even though not evenly – across all categories of conditionals.

However, there seems to be a tendency to express present situations with the combination of present tenses, i. e. with C1 conditionals. So there is a preference for what might loosely be called a 'clear grammatical form' for a specific location in time. It seems that present conditionals are used for present situations. This tendency makes communication clearer and less equivocal. However, the location in time is not the determining factor for forms of conditionals since the correlation of tense and time is not straightforward. So the use of conditionals is – among other aspects such as likelihood and the speaker's stance – guided by the time in which the proposition occurs or might occur.

9.8 Expression of probability and preference

The original function of conditionals is the expression of probability. So the combination of tenses is supposed to express the likelihood or certainty the speaker assumes for a situation. And although further functions come in, e.g. politeness, the speaker's stance on the likelihood of an action is usually the decisive criterion for the choice of tenses. This criterion also shows in the choice of tenses in the BusinessELF corpus.

Speakers in the BusinessELF corpus make use of very different forms of conditionals to express different attitudes towards the likelihood of the fulfilment of the situation. According to most grammars, the standard combination of tenses to express certainty is the combination of the present tense with the *will*-future. However, with 31 out of 64 conditionals, the most frequent combination of tenses in the corpus is the present tense in both parts of the sentence, either as a full verb or a modal (C1).

Cowan (2008:451) defines the combination of present tense in both the protasis and the apodosis as an *inference conditional*, a conditional in which the "proposition of the result clause is inferred from the proposition of the *if* clause." In an inference conditional, the result clause can state a "certainty or merely a possibility, with different degrees of likelihood" (ibid.). Other grammarians, like Alexander (1988), do not list this form of a conditional at all. Alexander only mentions the variation of the present tense in the protasis in combination with a modal in the apodosis (he calls it "if + present + modal" (Alexander 1988:275)).

He explains that "if we do not feel 'certain' enough to use *will*, or if we want to express the idea of e.g. necessity, we can use another modal instead" (ibid.). Eastwood (1994) calls this combination, present in both protasis and apodosis, the "type 0 conditional" (Eastwood 1994:335). According to his definition, it can be used to express the "automatic result of a possible future action" (ibid.). He defines it as a marked form expressing an absolute certainty. The *will*-future, on the other hand, is used if the speaker *expects* the proposition to occur.

Speakers in the BusinessELF corpus, however, use the combination of present tense indicative in both parts of the conditional (or present tense and modal in the present) as an unmarked form, not necessarily implying a specific likelihood or logical consequence. Numerically speaking, speakers use the *will*-future in combination with the present tense in 10 cases (examples 32 to 41 in Table 6). So when speakers in the corpus want to express a realistic condition, they prefer the combination of present tense + present tense (C1) over present tense + *will*-future (C2).

C3 is a form of the conditional that is not described as a standard form of the conditional. However, as mentioned above, some grammars list the combination of present tense + *would* (or *could*) as a means to be more polite (Alexander 1988:283, see also Swan 1995:246). In the BusinessELF corpus, the combination is used in 12 sentences. Two of these examples are requests, i. e. examples 42 and 52, so they are in line with standard grammar. The others fulfil different communicative functions. Example 43 is a speculation about a future arrangement, i. e. it uses *would* to express a different degree of likelihood:

43	if one day (they) go to Vital	I guess it would be • • easy for you to do it	DIS S3mNr 79

In example 43, the band S3mNr refers to has already talked to him about the option of establishing a new distribution contract. He expresses their willingness to change contracts and be published under a new label. Under the new label, they could be distributed by S1mGr, the addressee of the utterance. So the condition is likely. However, whether S1mGr will distribute the band or not is S3mNr's decision, and the speaker is only expressing an option, hence the hypothetical form with *would*.

Example 44 (which was discussed above) also has a rupture between the protasis and the apodosis:

44	if it's only the uh commercial aspect which uh decides about taking a certain label on or not	would be very boring	DIS S1mGr 1053

The example has been discussed above since the protasis refers to a realistic situation, expressed in the present tense, just like in standard English. Yet the speaker uses a hypothetical form for the apodosis, expressing an attitude rather than the likelihood of the proposition. He is also distancing himself from the proposition with the form of *would*. He does not regard the proposition as real, or, more likely, he does not want it to be the necessary consequence of the protasis. He thus mixes degrees of hypotheticality through the use of different grammatical forms.

The remaining 7 utterances in C3 are all used in the core negotiation. They use a similar principle for the discussion of options of business deals (see chapter 10.2 below). The smallest category of conditionals in the corpus is C4, which consists of 5 conditionals using a past tense or *would* in the protasis. Although the smallest, it is also the category with the highest variation in tense combination.

Forms of conditionals in C4 include the combination of past tense/past tense (example 54), past tense + *would* + infinitive (the standard hypothetical conditional; (example 55)) and the combination of *would* + infinitive in both parts of the sentence (examples 56 to 58). All 5 conditionals refer to unlikely or impossible situations that the speakers either speculate about (e.g. example 55; see above) or that they wish for, as in example 56 (see above).

Conditionals of C3 are either used as markers of politeness, just like in inner circle usage, or to express a possibility, yet one that is not likely. Furthermore, they are used to express if the speaker wishes for the proposition to happen or not to happen. Since the majority of these forms (8 out of 12) is used in the core negotiation, their communicative function seems to be related to the type of discourse. So the use of different conditionals is influenced by both, the probability of the proposition and the communicative function in the discourse. Therefore, the 8 conditionals in this category will be discussed in more detail below (chapter 10).

All in all, the use of conditionals in the BusinessELF corpus differs from inner circle use in that

- forms that have a marked function in inner circle Englishes are used for unmarked functions
- conditionals with present tenses in the apodosis refer to very likely or certain outcomes
- conditionals that use the past tense or *would* in the protasis refer not only to unlikely, but also to unwanted outcomes
- present tense combinations are used to express propositions that are likely, yet not as certain as in standard usage

and

- speakers use a form of conditionals that combines the present tense in the protasis with *would* + infinitive in the apodosis (C3) not only as a marker of politeness, but to indicate a critical or unwanted outcome.

10. Conditionals and discourse phases

10.1 Conditionals in homeleic discourse

The distribution of conditionals varies across different discourse phases. And although all categories are used across the different phases, their number and function varies according to the phase of discourse. There is a rough tendency to use C3 and C4 conditionals in the core negotiation and C1 and C2 conditionals more in the homeleic phases. These phases are business related, yet not part of the core negotiation. What is more relevant, however, is the fact that conditionals of the same category sometimes fulfil different functions in different discourse phases.

Homeleic discourse, aka *phatic communication*, is used in Functional Pragmatics to refer to the parts of the discourse that are not part of the pattern of action as such. Roughly speaking, these parts deal with 'lighter' or more personal topics or so-called 'small talk'. Out of the 64 complete conditionals, the majority, i. e. 44, is used in the homiletic parts of the discourse.

Maaß-Sagolla (2010) studied phases of discourse of engineers and students of engineering with a pedagogical aim. She stresses the importance of phases with a social function for the overall communicative success. They enable what she considers the more 'serious' parts of the discourse, or what would be considered the *patterns of action* in Functional Pragmatics (cf. e. g. Grießhaber 1987, Rehbein 1995).

Phatic communication is part of the so-called *small talk*. It is the part of discourse that fulfils social functions. Little (1970; 1978:236; quoted in Maaß-Sagolla 2010:101) explains that

> [p]hatic communion can build an emotional bridge between two strangers, or two men who have to do business together but are a little suspicious of each other, across which genuine communication can take place which would not have been possible without the early meaningless exchanges that produced a more friendly and relaxed atmosphere.

In Functional Pragmatics, the non-institutionalised phases of discourse are called 'homeleic' discourse. They are the phases of discourse that fulfil other functions than the institutionalised patterns of action. Rehbein/Fienemann (2004) define homileic discourse as follows:

> In functional pragmatics a certain type of non-institutional linguistic action with a high degree of social pleasantry is called a 'homileic discourse' (cf. Ehlich and Rehbein 1980,

> Fienemann, Oldörp and Olhus 2001; s. also Kotthoff 2002). Characteristics of homileic discourse are e.g.: a circle of people talking while doing something enjoyable, i.e. eating (homileic discourse space); no clear rules about turns exist; often people 'talk all at once'; topics are often changed due to association; in particular relationships with people are subjects of conversation; ex[p]eriences are dealt with [in] a communicative manner, whether made together or embedded in a prior common knowledge to which the speakers allude; there is an unusually large number of linguistic procedures involving the toning field and the prompting field together with frequent use of exclamations etc. (Quoted from Fienemann 2006:11).

These phases of the discourse are not part of the negotiation as such, but are, as Little points out, none the less important. Especially in field of business with only a limited number of providers or potential business partners, it is important for negotiators to appeal to others, as SimGr pointed out on the second day of the recordings.

Basically, the recordings can all be subdivided into the phases of homeleic discourse, parts that affect the negotiation (e.g. arranging for further steps) and that are part either of the pattern of buying and selling or of other patterns and the core negotiation. Conditionals from all categories except C5 are used in both the homileic parts as well as the core negotiation. However, they are used with different tendencies and to different extents:

1) All categories of conditionals but C5 are used in all phases of the discourse.
2) C5 is not used in the core negotiation.
3) C1 and C2 sentences are used most extensively in the homileic phases of discourse.
4) C3 and C4 sentences are used more extensively in the core negotiation.

Out of the 31 conditionals in C1 that make use of the present tense and modals both in the protasis and the apodosis (including the *going to*-construction in example 18), 23 are used in the homileic parts of the discourse, while 8 form part of the core negotiation. Examples 4, 7, 8, 9, 12, 20, 21 and 25 are used in the core negotiation, which equals almost 1/3.

Out of the 8 conditionals in C2, i.e. conditionals that make use of the more 'standard' combination of simple present in the protasis and *will*-future in the apodosis, only one, i.e. example 34, is used in the core negotiation. So combined, the categories of the 'realistic' conditionals, i.e. C1 and C2, are used primarily in the homileic phases. In C3, in which the present tense in the protasis is combined with *would* or *could* in the apodosis, 8 out of 12 conditionals are used in the core negotiation. In C4, which only consists of 5 utterances, 3 conditionals, i.e. 54, 55, 56, are used in the phatic parts of the discourse. And only two, i.e. 57 and 58, which belong to the subcategory of *would/would* conditionals, are used in the core negotiation.

Even though there is no absolute relation between form and phase, a tendency can be noticed in the BusinessELF corpus to use conditionals from C1 + C2 in the phatic part of the discourse, while the majority of those constructions that use *would* or *could* (without the requests in C5) are used in the core negotiation. And out of the 20 conditionals in the core negotiation, 10 make use of the modal *would* or *could* (sometimes more than one in the complete utterance). Out of the 17 conditionals in C3 and C4 combined, 16 conditionals contain a form (or two forms) of *would* and *could;* and 10 out of these are used in the core negotiation.

So the share of conditionals with *would* or *could* is higher in the core negotiation, while in the phatic parts significantly more realistic conditionals are used than conditionals with *could* and *would*. And although the data base is too small to be statistically relevant and there is an uneven distribution of forms of conditionals, speakers show a tendency to use conditionals with *would* in the core negotiation. So hypothetical forms, and thereby the differentiation between reality and hypothetical actions or situations, seems to be more relevant in the core negotiation.

10.2 Conditionals in the core negotiation

Forms of conditionals from all categories but C5, the politeness conditionals, are used in the core negotiation. In the conditionals of C5, however, further actions are requested as to what the hearer does as the next step. So they do form part of the negotiation in the wider sense because they deal with the continuation of the cooperation. However, they do not form part of the discussion of the terms and forms of the business deal(s) in question and are therefore not considered part of the core negotiation.

The focus here is mainly, although not exclusively, on the recording *Marketingcooperation*. As opposed to the other two recordings, no deal has been closed yet. The major part of the discourse is a negotiation with S1mGr as the potential buyer and S2fFr as the seller. Both parties negotiate the terms and conditions of a potential business deal. S2fFr is at the trade fair to see different companies and offer them her products for distribution in different European countries. She wants to get into the German market with her products and contacted S1mGr beforehand. S1mGr is at the trade fair meeting representatives of different record companies from different countries. He wants to learn which products and business terms they offer that might be suitable for the German market and his company's range of products.

S1mGr and S2fFr discuss different 'deals': a *label deal,* i.e. an arrangement according to which S1mGr's company would distribute all artists that publish their music under the same label, or the distribution of 'the whole catalogue', i.e. the entire product range of S2fFr's company, or the distribution of only one artist. The last option comes up in the negotiation. It is problematic, however, since it is not profitable for either party. S2fFr aims at a label deal for the label *Double Moon* she represents.

S1mGr agreed to the meeting to find out more about the company, especially about details of a potential cooperation. He did not know before the meeting if he wanted to take on one of the labels, the whole catalogue or probably nothing at all. However, in case of a deal, his company's main interests are the exclusive distribution rights for the German market and the effort and resources the company is willing to invest in promoting and selling their products in Germany, especially the marketing budget.[31] He is in a position to decide about a deal. However, he does not show this in the negotiation and occasionally claims he has to discuss aspects of the deal with his boss, who was not at the trade fair.

As the language use shows, for S2fFr, the stakes are higher: She wants to use S1mGr's company to enter the German market, while S1mGr is less eager to close a deal. He is in a more powerful position representing the German market leader. So S1mGr is the negotiator who is less willing to make a commitment at this point, a fact that shows in his language use. One of the main linguistic features, especially of S1mGr's language use, in the core negotiation is the use of conditionals. Especially the use of conditionals formed with *would* stands out quantitatively as well as qualitatively (see below).

Out of the 15 conditionals used in the core negotiation in the recording Marketingcooperation, S1mGr uses 10. And out of these, two belong in C4. 3 out of his 10 conditional sentences belong in C1, and 5 belong in C3. C3 conditionals are formed with present tense + *would.*

S1mGr is not the only speaker who uses this form of conditionals. 6 conditionals from C3 are used by S1mGr; and 2 are used by S2fFr. S2fFr uses this form in examples 46 and 48. S3mNr also uses this form of conditionals in example 43. The example was discussed above, but does not form part of the core negotiation. However, S1mGr is the speaker who uses more subjunctives because he is the one who is less eager than the others, especially than S2fFr, to make a commitment in the negotiation.

Since 8 out of 12 conditionals in C3 are used in the core negotiation, the question is: What is the communicative function of the different categories, especially C3, in the core negotiation? And since none of the other categories is used so

31 This was explained to me by Sm1Gr prior to the recording.

intensively – in relation to the overall quantity of the category – I will also discuss two passages of discourse which are crucial points in the negotiation. In these passages, speakers make more intensive use of conditionals than in the rest of the negotiation. I will show that there is a difference in function to conditionals from C1 and C2. This function is avoiding commitment or, linguistically speaking, avoiding commissives. For some of the examples, instead of only the utterances listed in Table 6, I will provide a short passage of the discourse in question. So the content will be more accessible, and I will be able to show the effect on the hearer as well as the communicative behaviour that triggered the forms.

10.2.1 C1 conditionals as expressions of likelihood

C1 and C2 are the categories of 'realistic' conditionals in the corpus. Out of the 31 conditionals that fall in this classification, 8 are used in the core negotiation. Some of the realistic conditionals in the core negotiation – as by definition – express the likely consequences of a scenario under discussion.

In example 21, S2fFr expresses her fear of a potential deal going wrong, putting her company in danger if they should not be able to react to changes:

21	if we are not able to give/ you know to be flexible	I think we can easily die	MARK S2fFr 643

She starts out with a conditional in the present tense using a modal *be able to* in connection with the pronoun *we*. She seems to have a concrete scenario in mind since the first part is uttered fluently and the verb *give* as well as the personal pronoun *we* are rather concrete. However, she changes her plan halfway through the utterance into the more neutral form *to be flexible*, without a concrete action verb and with *you know* as a filler. In the apodosis, she also uses the pronoun *we*. In the first part, *we* is used as opposed to *you*, excluding the hearer. But in the changed version, it might be including the hearer. She tries to form common ground through a situation with which he can identify. She points out a shared interest. After that, she concludes that *we*, i.e. the companies in their field, *can easily die* (example 21). She thereby includes her company as well as S1mGr's in the utterance, i.e. in the group that is affected. With the utterance, she paints a pessimistic scenario, should they not be able to react to changed conditions. So instead of confrontation, she uses the – even though pessimistic – scenario to establish common ground with her hearer. She assumes that shared interests will result from this common ground, i.e. from the situation that affects to both of them. So she uses shared objectives in her conditional to show cooperation with her hearer.

This assertion is uttered at the end of the core negotiation, after she has not been able to convince S1mGr of the deal she wanted to get. The conclusion – having to stay flexible in order to be safe, i. e. to survive as a business – refers to the fact that they have not agreed on a specific deal and that S1mGr made her agree to different proposals out of which he can pick.

As the example shows, the present tense conditionals are used to express not only a realistic situation, but one with which the speaker can identify. There is no barrier between the time of speaking and the time and situation expressed in the conditional. The situation feels 'close' to the speaking situation, i. e. the speaker does not feel any distance between the two. So the – even though non-standard – form of the conditional expresses a proposition that is likely and that the speaker can identify with.

10.2.2 C1 conditionals as expression of attitude

Not all conditionals in the corpus express the likelihood of scenarios. Some conditionals in C1 to C4 express an attitude towards future actions. C1 conditionals are used for scenarios that speakers do not only consider likely, but that they would actually appreciate or prefer over other options. C4 conditionals, which form the other extreme, are conditionals that refer to scenarios that speakers are concerned or sceptical about (cf. 10.2.5).

In the examples 12 and 25, which are both C1 conditionals, the speakers express an attitude towards the proposition: Example 12 expresses S1mGr's agreement to different release dates for some smaller European countries. And example 25 expresses S3mNr's opinion (or wish) that the companies involved in the deal ought to stick to the agreed release date. In both cases, the speaker identifies with the proposition or finds it preferable:

12	if Portugal releases it three months after us	that's fine with me	BACK S1mGr 1084
25	And if it says „out now"	it should really be out now	BACK S3mNr 1099

Both examples do not really express the likelihood of the proposition in the apodosis, but the speaker's attitude towards it. Example 12 does so with the explicit agreement to a scenario (Portugal, i. e. the company's subsidiary in Portugal, using a different release date than the subsidiaries in the other European countries). Example 25 expresses the attitude with the help of the modal *should*. Here, *should* means that it would be the right thing to do (cf. Hornby 2015:1436).

In the other examples from C1 that are used in the core negotiation, S1mGr and S2fFr discuss potential deals. However, S1mGr does not really close a deal or agree to S2fFr's suggestions. In some of the conditionals, e.g in examples 7 and 8 below, he merely points out potential consequences of the deal under discussion.

All of the examples below are from the end of the core negotiation, ranging from se (519) to se (565); all were uttered before S2fFr's agreeing to 'stay flexible', i. e. to give S1mGr the option to pick different titles as long as she closes no deal with any other company (in se (643)). In the examples, S1mGr raises the topic of not being willing to publish as many of her products as she wishes. He points out the consequence for her: selling less in Germany. He expresses that with realistic conditionals in examples 7 and 8:

7	if we decide only to make • like ten percent of your catalogue available	then there are still ninety percent which, you know, which are not available in Germany	MARK S1mGr 527
8	if you only work with us	then we only make • • a few titles available	MARK S1mGr 565

Regarding the content, examples 7 and 8 are very similar to each other: They express the consequences of the deal under discussion, which S1mGr regards as critical for S2fFr's company. In example 7, S1mGr points out a potential problem on S2fFr's side: After having clarified the matters of exclusivity and discussed different options with S2fFr, he informs her that he is only interested in distributing certain artists in Germany, but not a whole label or her entire catalogue (the other two options discussed in the negotiation). Although she is willing to give him the exclusive distribution rights, he only wants to purchase few of her products to distribute them in Germany – if at all. He points out the problem of her losing business. He makes the negative consequence explicit. This way, he builds and attunes their discourse knowledge in order to avoid misunderstandings. He 'puts his cards on the table' and lets her know that, if he purchases any products from her company, he will only buy and distribute a small part of her product range. So he gives her the opportunity to make an informed decision about the potential agreement.

In order to do so, he uses a present tense form in both the protasis of the conditional sentence (*if we decide*) and the apodosis (*there are still ninety per cent*) and forms a complete realistic, yet non-standard conditional sentence. The present tense in both parts of the sentence indicates that for him, there is no temporal or other boundary between the discourse situation and the consequential future situation (ninety percent of her catalogue, i. e. product range, not being available in the intended market, Germany). Thereby, he ascribes a realistic quality to the proposition of his sentence. Using present tenses, he does not separate what he says from a future scenario. For him, this is a realistic scenario which will come about as a consequence of his decision.

He verbally indicates that the situation and the consequences are realistic to him, i.e. he is ready to commit to the proposition. This choice of tenses is also an indicator that he has already made up his mind: He is not going to sell the label she originally offered in Germany. Yet, he does not say so in a direct way and keeps his options open. Instead, he uses the conditional as an indirect and hence polite form to present the scenario playing in his mind. However, he does not directly express his rejection of the deal, which makes him appear more likeable and kind. So he considers the social aspect of the business encounter while informing his hearer, indirectly, of his business choices and uses indirect forms of rejection.

A similar function can be seen in example 20. In the original passage of discourse, a misunderstanding, precedes the utterance: S2fFr offers S1mGr to choose certain *titles;* he assumes that that would mean different companies could distribute publications by the same artist. That way, he, i.e. his company, would receive the exclusive distribution rights only for the titles, yet not for the publications by the artist in question. So he points out the problem of competition over certain artists using the example of Precious Sousa. He starts the discussion of the scenario with the help of a conditional in example 20:

20	If you deal with like three companies and everybody says: Well, I would like the Precious Sousa	and then you have to, you know	MARK S1mGr 538

In the example, Sm1Gr does not make the problem explicit, but uses an incomplete utterance in the form of the conditional. Thus, he hints at the problem rather than explicitly describing the situation. In the protasis, he uses the present tense and the personal pronoun *you.* In this utterance, *you* can refer to S2fFr as a person as well as to her company.

So S1mGr verbally creates a scenario in which her company deals with other companies as well. In the scenario, these companies all aim at selling different musical publication by the same band, Precious Sousa. He uses a fictional quotation with the pronoun *I* and the modal *would.* This might indicate a difference between the likelihood of the scenario (S2fFr's company dealing with different companies; his concrete concern) and the scenario of the artist in question, the less relevant and therefore less threatening proposition. The apodosis, however, is not completed. He leaves it to the hearer to draw on her professional knowledge to fill the gap. The hearer will finish the utterance mentally, i.e. she will, in her mind, create her own scenario of the consequences. Due to their professional knowledge, they both know what the consequences are. So he can rely on the hearer to assume the same consequences as he does and therefore understand his concerns. The predicate, in this case the modal verb *have to*, is in the present tense and expresses an obligation or necessity. The present tense makes the scenario appear 'closer', i. e. at one with the speaking situation. It therefore appears more concrete.

The assumed problem that underlies this utterance was caused by a misunderstanding. As soon as this becomes apparent in the discourse (in se (538)), S2fFr rushes to clarify the misunderstanding. She assures S1mGr in se (539 ff.) that the scenario (different companies competing over one artist) will not obtain. The following passage of the discourse shows how the misunderstanding comes about by her offer. At the end (se (540 ff.)) she understands his concern and clarifies the misunderstanding:

(531)	S2fFr	I mean, uhm • would you be/would you agree maybe to make uh, uh, you know, exclusivity, but on/• only on some titles?
(532)	S2fFr	That you pick up?
(533)	S1mGr	Uhm¯·
(534)	S2fFr	((2s)) Would it be possible?
(535)	S2fFr	Or is that something you • cannot consider for various reasons?
(536)	S1mGr	I mean then you could have competition, you know.
(537)	S2fFr	Yeah.
(538)	S1mGr	If you deal with like three companies and everybody says: Well, I would like the Precious Sousa, and then you have to, you know …
(539)	S2fFr	Oh, no.
(540)	S2fFr	No, no, no.
(541)	S2fFr	What I wanna say is, for example, okay you sound very interested in Precious Sousa and would like to release it in Germany.
(542)	S1mGr	Yeah·
(543)	S2fFr	I give you the exclusivity on Precious Sousa.
(544)	S1mGr	Yeah, alright·
(545)	S1mGr	Okay.
(546)	S2fFr	I won't give it to anybody else.

Excerpt: Exclusivity on some titles (MARK)

The trigger of the misunderstanding is her question if he could consider exclusive distribution rights for some titles (se (531)f.). As an answer, S1mGr raises the issue of competition in utterance (536). The question tag *you know* is used here to directly address and involve the hearer. By the question tag, he refers to their shared discourse and professional knowledge: If the scenario in question, i. e. the proposition of utterance (531) and (532), exclusive rights for titles, is put into practice, competition will be the consequence. Her augment *Yeah* (se (537)) can be interpreted as agreement, but is more likely an indicator of attention. It shows the speaker that she is processing what he is saying. It makes him utter the issue in a more explicit form in a conditional in se (538). And the conditional makes the problem more explicit through the concrete example, as explained above.

She then realises the problem: He assumes he will only receive the exclusive rights for the titles in question, not the artists. She quickly jumps in in se (539) and se (540) to clarify the misunderstanding. The repetition of *no* indicates her eagerness to contradict his assumption. She starts the next utterance (541) with a matrix construction *What I wanna say is ...* to guide the hearer's attention to the clarification.

Matrix constructions (also known as *complement constructions*) are, from a syntactic point of view, sentences that take subordinate clauses. Rehbein (2003) discusses matrix constructions from a pragmatic point of view. According to his argumentation, they help guide the hearer's understanding of the speaker's attitude (or *stance* in the terminology of Halliday 1994). So they add to the propositional content of an utterance. In this case, S2fFr adds to the function of the following utterance. She uses a meta-discourse strategy indicated through the matrix construction *What I wanna say.* This construction announces the following clarification. She then clarifies her intended proposition in steps: She indicates agreement so far with the augment *okay*, then uses a concrete example, Precious Sousa, to demonstrate her point. She puts the hearer in the centre with the help of the personal pronoun *you* (*you sound very interested and would like to release it*). He indicates with the help of the augment *Yeah* that he is following her argumentation. This way, she includes him in the construction of shared discourse knowledge.

Her next utterance (se (543)) looks like a promise. It is, however, part of the scenario she is constructing. She is referring to the scenario in se (541) of him being interested in Precious Sousa. And although the utterance looks like a speech act, i. e. the promise of the exclusive rights, it really is a hidden conditional. The protasis of the intended conditional is *If you would like to release Precious Sousa in Germany, I give you the exclusivity on it.* So she breaks the conditional down into different utterances to make sure the hearer follows her step by step. This way, the two can clarify the misunderstanding.

At the same time she indicates the potential promise of exclusive rights on the basis that he is interested in the artist in question. However, the conditional uses a present tense in the (intended) apodosis, yet not in the protasis (*If you would like to release ...*). The protasis contains two verbs: *you said,* which initiates a quotation, and *you would like*, the proposition quoted after *you said. You said* is also a *verbum dicendi.* So she refers back to what S1mGr said and uses both the *verbum dicendi* and the subjunctive.

A *verbum dicendi* is a verb from the semantic field of 'uttering'. Its function is to change or shift the illocutionary force of the sentence (cf. ten Thije 2007). It has a similar function as a matrix construction and is used to shift the illocution to a different, in this case unbinding, level. Since S1mGr's actual interest is something she can only speculate about, she uses the modal *would*. It is a scenario that she would appreciate. The commissive that would follow from it, however, is something she can commit to: giving S1mGr the exclusive rights. So she expresses it in the present tense. She does not avoid the commissive, i. e. a promise. On the contrary, she makes the proposition sound very 'present' and connected to the speaking situation. It is something she is ready to commit to. And although the construction is not a 'grammatical' conditional, the situation in question is 'real' and 'present' to her. This is reflected in her use of the present tense. So the underlying construction is a C1 conditional.

In another example of a realistic conditional from C1, S2fFr's actually promises S1mGr the exclusive distribution rights. This utterance (example 9) occurs earlier in the discourse. She acknowledges her willingness to give S1mGr an exclusive deal for her company's products if he offers to distribute them in Germany:

9	if you make an offer	we give you exclusivity (for this).	MARK S2fFr 519

S2fFr uses a C1 conditional, i. e. one with the present tense in both the protasis and the apodosis. She addresses the hearer, S1mGr, directly using the pronoun *you* and the active verbal construction *make an offer*. Then she follows it up with the assertion *we give you exclusivity*. She refers to his wish to receive the exclusive distribution rights. Using the pronoun you, she affirms that he – or his company – will receive exclusivity (for the distribution). At the same time, she uses *we*, i. e. the first person plural, as the subject of the apodosis. She thereby expresses her 'role' as the representative of the company. So she makes the assertion more binding since it is the whole business for whom she is affirming the effects of the offer. This combination turns her conditional into a promise. She affirms that, as a consequence of his offer, the exclusivity will follow, i. e. her company will give his company the exclusive distribution rights. Since she uses a present tense in both parts of the sentence, there is no temporal or other difference between the speaking situation and the utterance. So the consequence expressed in her utterance is binding, and she is committing the company she represents to a future action. Therefore, the C1 conditional here actually expresses a commissive.

10.2.3 C2 conditionals as expression of attitude

Conditionals from C2 are the conditionals in the 'standard' form. S2fFr uses one conditional from the category in the core negotiation, towards the end of the core negotiation in *Marketingcooperation.* S1mGr just acknowledged that his company is not interested in distributing her whole catalogue. He points out that problems might occur if S2fFr closes distribution deals with different companies and they all want to distribute the same titles. Before that, the two discussed the exclusivity of the deal, and she assured him the exclusive distribution rights (cf. se (519), example 9 above). Then he lets her know that he is not interested in distributing her whole product range, referred to as the *whole catalogue.* She realises that if he receives the exclusive distribution rights yet only uses it for single artists (or labels), this will lead to problems on her side. She expresses that with a conditional in example 34:

34	if you tell me: Uh okay, I am only interested in re-leasing Precious Sousa	it will be a problem for me to give you this exclusivity on our whole catalogue.	MARK S2fFr 548

In example 34, S2fFr starts the conditional with a matrix construction and the focus on the hearer: *If you tell me.* So she puts herself in his position and utters an affirmation that she ascribes to him. She uses the personal pronoun *I* in place of S1mGr. She chooses the example of Precious Sousa and expresses, on the level of the proposition, that he select Precious Sousa for distribution in Germany. In the apodosis, she uses the neutral pronoun *it* announcing that a problem will occur as a consequence. Here, she uses the *will*-future in the apodosis. This construction does not only express a realistic condition, *if you only publish Precious Sousa,* and the likely consequence, *I will have a problem to give you the exclusive rights.* Moreover, the consequence is something that she wants to avoid. She makes this clear with the help of a matrix construction and her choice of pronouns as well as the conditional: The choice of tenses, although a standard from, is not a regular choice in the BusinessELF corpus. It is likely that she uses it to express that, on the one hand, the consequences are likely, i. e. realistic. But on the other hand, she also uses it to distance herself from these consequences, e. g. by avoiding a more personal construction like *I will have a problem.* She also uses the neutral pronoun *it* and the vague verb *be* to indicate a certain 'neutrality'. So she avoids indicating who is responsible for the action in question by using a neutral, i. e. impersonal, construction.

The overall form of the conditionals indicates that she distances herself from the proposition of the apodosis and avoids explicitly blaming anyone. This might be explained by S2fFr's concerns about this potential – albeit realistic – outcome of the scenario in question. The construction of a conditional with the *will*-future, although it is an unmarked form in standard Englishes, is a rare construction in the BusinessELF corpus. It is used in 1 out of 19 conditionals in the core negotiation and in 10 out of 64 conditionals in the whole corpus. Its combination with other linguistic means like neutral pronouns and matrix constructions suggests a caesura between the speaking situation and the situation expressed in the utterance. So in the core negotiation, it is used to express likely scenarios that the speaker wants to 'get away from' because they feel critical or sceptical about them.

10.2.4 C3 conditionals as expression of attitude

The largest number of conditionals in the core negotiation is from category C3, the category that combines the present tense in the protasis with *would* in the apodosis. It is the least 'grammatical' form of a conditional, one that is not listed in traditional grammars. It was not mentioned by Swan, for example, neither under 'ordinary tense-use' nor under 'special tense-use' (Swan 1995:246 ff.), nor Cowan 2008 or Eastwood 1994. Greenbaum/Nelson 1996:341 state that "the modal in all three types of conditions is usually *would*", but list only examples of hypothetical conditionals in the past tense.

Alexander (1988) lists variations of what he refers to as the 'type 1 conditionals'. 'Type 1 conditionals' are formed with the present tense in the protasis and express realistic conditions. They are conditional sentences in which *if*, combined with the present tense, can be followed by a modal, e. g. *could, may, should* (Alexander 1988:275). However, he does not list *would* in this context. His argument is that the other modal [instead of *will*, B. D.] can be used "[i]f we don't feel 'certain' enough to use *will*" (Alexander 1988:275). *Would*, however, is only listed as a marker of politeness. Biber et al. (1999:495) list *would* explicitly as a marker of prediction (and volition) even if *will* is more common.

In a paper on the *Konjunktiv II*, the equivalent of the conditional mood in German, Redder (1992) argues that the function of the *Konjunktiv II* is to set apart what is being said from what is real (see chapter 9). She uses the framework of Functional Pragmatics (Ehlich/Rehbein 1972) to argue that the German modal *würde* is used to ascribe a purely mental quality to a proposition because knowledge (π) is set apart from reality (P) and from verbalised knowledge (p): $\pi \leftrightarrow$ p/P. This function is fulfilled in many conditional sentences in English by the modal *would*. It is a function that is used in categories C3 and C4 in the corpus.

C3 conditionals fulfil basically four different functions in the core negotiation: They are used to make suggestions about potential cooperation or offers (e.g. example 46, 51), to evaluate suggestions and offers (examples 45, 47, 49), to make inquiries (48), and to summarise aspects that have been negotiated so far.

Summaries are an important function in negotiations because they clarify what negotiators have agreed upon. They are an opportunity for speakers to verbalise their take-away from the negotiation and to have the hearers compare it to their understanding. This way they 'synchronise' their discourse knowledge and avoid misunderstandings. The function might be even more important in lingua franca discourse because speakers run a higher risk of being misinterpreted. So some extra effort might be required, and lingua franca speakers need to compare and attune their understanding of the ongoing discourse more than speakers from the same language background.

So lingua franca speakers need room to inquire about the hearer's opinion on certain options. Example 48 is a conditional in the form of a question. By this question, S2fFr inquires about S1mGr's approach to their cooperation:

48	if you decide to release an album/I mean to distribute an album	would you ask also for the European territories?	MARK S2fFr 470

She uses a present tense in the protasis because she finds the proposition of the protasis likely. Moreover, she is also hoping for S1mGr to agree to said offer. The apodosis, however, is formed with *would.* By *would,* she separates the proposition from the speaking situation (cf. Redder 1992). So she marks the proposition of the apodosis as unlikely. It is an option that she would not be happy about. So *would* in this construction functions as a marker of the distance between the speaking situation and the described situation, i. e. the proposition of the clause. It sets S2fFr's knowledge as well as her hearer's knowledge apart from reality and from what is being said.

Examples 45, 47, and 49 are used to evaluate different suggestions made earlier in the discourse:

45	provided the label uhm, you know, does proper promotion if there's like a marketing budget	This could be, could be a good thing for us	MARK S1mGr 81

Example 45 is the first evaluation of an offer by S2fFr and is used early in the discourse *Marketingcooperation.* S2fFr offered S1mGr a label for distribution in Germany. He uses a conditional beginning with the conjunction *provided* instead of *if.* He expresses the condition in a present tense, referring directly to the label as the agent. He uses the adjective *proper* to classify the action (promotion) he expects from the label. In this clause, there is no difference between the speaking situation and the proposition concerning time. In the apodosis, however, he uses *could*. He repeats it, which indicates a hesitation. *Could* is an indicator, like *would*, of hypotheticality. It is used in this case to show that he does not consider the consequence as real or existing yet. He also tries to keep the options open since he is only just starting the negotiation. He uses this form to mark the utterance as a verbalisation of a hypothetical situation. So far, he is only negotiating, i. e. discussing options, and does not want to be understood as accepting S2fFr's offer.

The same function lies behind examples 47 and 49, which both evaluate suggestions. Example 47 is uttered much later in the negotiation, after S1mGr has been offered different forms of cooperations. He evaluates S2fFr's suggestion to offer only some titles in Germany (see above):

47	if we uh make, make certain titles available	I think that, that could be a way	MARK S1mGr 336

In the original utterance of example 47 (se (336)), the apodosis precedes the protasis. After the matrix construction *I think,* which embeds the sentence and lifts it to a different, more hypothetical level, the modal verb *could* supports the hypothetical quality. So the first part of the utterance guides the hearer's understanding of what is to come in the protasis. The protasis, in second position, is formed with a present tense and the personal pronoun *we*. The proposition, *making 'certain titles' available*, refers to S2fFr's last offer for S1mGr to select titles from the catalogue. She makes the offer because she has not been able to convince him to distribute her whole catalogue, nor a complete label. In this utterance, S1mGr uses the apodosis to embed his potential future actions. He thus ascribes a hypothetical quality to them although he uses a present tense in the protasis. Distributing only some titles in Germany is the one option he can commit to. So he expresses it in the present tense because for him it is realistic. At the same time he uses the conditional to mark the utterance as part of the negotiation process, i. e. of the discussion, and not as the acceptance as an offer. The different tenses and moods in the two parts of the sentence reflect different degrees of commitment: a high commitment to the proposition of the protasis, yet a low degree of commitment to the apodosis, indicated by the mood of the verb.

The same tenses, yet uttered in a different order, are used in example 49 (se (522)) in the same discourse. They verbalise a potential consequence of the suggestion discussed in example 47 above. It is the utterance that precedes example 20 (above) and causes the misunderstanding between S1mGr and S2fFr about the exclusive distribution rights:

49	if we only take certain titles	then it probably would make sense for you to deal with other territories	MARK S1mGr 522

In the utterance, S1mGr takes the proposition of the apodosis in example 47 (see above) and uses it as the protasis. The tense is the same, the present tense, because it is the deal that he can commit to. In this utterance, the consequence is expressed not only with the modal *would*, which gives it a hypothetical quality. This hypothetical quality is supported by the adverb *then*, putting a further mental distance between the first part of the utterance and what is to come next. (The noun t*erritories* at the end is a slip of the tongue which he corrects into *companies;* (se (525)); see excerpt below).

S1mGr adds the adverb *probably* and uses the neutral construction *would make sense* as well as the infinitive. These are all linguistic means that take the focus away from the agent of the sentence. So the quality of the utterance becomes more theoretical and thereby hypothetical. All these linguistic features are included because the proposition of the apodosis is a consequence S1mGr wants to avoid; or wants for his hearer, S2fFr, to avoid.

He goes to a lot of effort to separate the consequences in the apodosis from the realistic condition(s) in the protasis. Again, the hypothetical construction is used to ascribe a mental quality to the proposition (cf. Redder 1992) separating it from the speaking situation. The syntactic means and the mood of the predicate mark the contrast between the realistic protasis and the explicitly hypothetical apodosis. So the speaker ascribes two different qualitics to the different parts of the sentence: a realistic quality to the protasis and a hypothetical quality to the apodosis. And the 'ungrammatical' use of tenses fulfils a communicative function: It reflects his stance towards the two different propositions.

The following passage of the discourse shows S1mGr's four connected utterances (se (522) to (525)) in which he points out the issue of competition to S2fFr:

(522)	S1mGr	I mean, the thing is if, if we only take certain titles, then it probably would make sense for you to deal with other territories.
(523)	S1mGr	((1s)) Uh, not territories, with other companies in Germany.
(524)	S1mGr	Maybe they think uhm • that other titles could do ((1s)) good as well.
(525)	S1mGr	Know what I mean?

Excerpt: Preparing the hearer for unwanted utterances (MARK)

S1mGr prepares and follows up the conditional in se (522). He does not address the issue directly and prepares the hearer for the critical issue. Even though he does not want to address it directly, he finds it so important that he chooses to discuss it. S1mGr uses both *I mean* and *the thing is* as matrix constructions and 'double-embeds' the following conditional sentence. *I mean* is an idiom that is usually used to add information or clarify a meaning.[32] It is used here to guide the hearer's attention towards the issue in the conditional. S1mGr uses these strategies to mitigate the impact of his utterance. Using two matrix constructions, he puts a barrier between the speaking situation thus far and what is to come next. This strategy is described with the metaphor of *hedging* in Conversation Analysis.

A further function of matrix constructions, according to Rehbein (2003:4), is that they put the speaker in a position to not actually fulfil a speech act, but to refer to it. The speaker thus takes the speech act out of the speaking situation and transposes it to a different level. This way, a partial meta-discourse becomes possible (Rehbein 2003:4) and the characterisation of the illocutionary act becomes *p*-related (i.e. referring to the proposition, B. D.) as opposed to being related to the hearer or speaker.

In the example at hand, the first matrix construction is followed by the chunk *the thing is*. According to Delahunty (2012:41) the phrase *the thing is* signals "an unexpected development of the current topic, leading to a change in its trajectory". S1mGr's intention is to 'open a room' for a discussion of his concerns. So he uses two matrix constructions here to lift the second part of the utterance out of the speaking situation. He transfers it to a level on which it can be discussed without any consequences of action or obligations. He therefore transposes the proposition onto a different – in this case hypothetical – level. This way matrix constructions, according to Rehbein (2003:4), enable 'meta-discussions' about a speech act without the speaker committing the act.

Another function that this type of conditional has in the discourse is to enable summaries of parts of the negotiation. Examples 50 and 53 are summaries of such aspects of the discourse. Both conditionals are used in the passage of discourse; example 50 in se (632), and example 53 in se (634). They are the core part of S1mGr's summary of the options he and S2fFr discuss. S1mGr summarises the take-away from a passage of discourse. To show his utterance in connection with other utterances and the organisation of his summary, the passage of discourse as well as S2fFr's reaction in se (631) to se (636) are given. The modals *could* and *would* are underlined to demonstrate the high density of markers of hypotheticality:

32 cf. http://dictionary.cambridge.org/dictionary/english/i-mean?q=I+mean; (13/10/2015).

(631)	S1mGr	So that means that we could do, uhm we could do both.
(632)	S1mGr	We could do a label deal if I say: Well, Déja-vu is a great label, we would like to • • make the whole catalogue available.
(633)	S1mGr	We could do that.
(634)	S1mGr	Or I could say: Well, as long as no other company decides to • uh ((1s)) take on a certain • label • • exclusively, then I could say: Okay, ((1,5s)) through, through the whole catalogue I would/• • or from the whole catalogue I would, would pick like ((1s)) ten, twenty titles, whatever, and make them available.
(635)	S2fFr	Yeah.
(636)	S1mGr	That's alright.

Excerpt: Would/could in C3 conditionals (MARK)

In se (631), S1mGr announces his summary with the augment *So*. He thereby guides the hearer's attention to the following utterances and indicates the conclusion that is to follow. He then uses the matrix construction *that means*, indicating that his focus is on the shared discourse knowledge, i. e. on understanding. After a short hesitation, which might be caused by planning processes, he summarises *we could do both*. He uses *we* to form an in-group with his hearer, S2fFr, and the modal *could* to lift the following statement to a hypothetical level.

He then breaks down the options into two different conditionals, which both have the same set of tenses and moods: indicative of the present tense for the protasis, hypothetical *would* in the apodosis. In utterance (632) (example 50), he repeats the deictic form *we* and stresses the connection with the hearer. He uses the modal *would* in the apodosis in front position. The front position stresses his taking up both the grammatical and deictic form of the construction before, i. e. in se (631). In the protasis, however, he switches to *I* and uses the present tense. He uses a *verbum dicendi* to set the proposition apart from the rest (cf. ten Thije 2007). With the help of the *verbum dicendi* and the simulated quotation *Déja-vu is a great label ...*, the speaker puts a distance between the speaking situation and the assumed situation. That way he 'disables' or 'diactivates' the illocutionary force. He indicates to his hearer, S2fFr, that he is not really promising or suggesting the proposition in question, but merely summarising it and putting it up for discussion.

Ehlich (1979) discusses 'quoting' as a similar language function. He calls the function "Suspendierung", i. e. suspending, of the illocutionary force. According to Ehlich (1979), quoting is a means of talking about the proposition of utterances, although a past utterance in his paper, without performing the speech act of the original utterance. He argues that speakers 'suspend' the illocutionary force of the original utterance by quoting it. And although Ehlich focuses on past utterances whose proposition is transferred without the original illocution, the principle seems to apply here too: The speaker suspends the illocution, i. e. the commissive, albeit not of a past utterance, but of a current utterance. Here, it is used with reference to something the speaker speculates about, but that the hearer has not actually uttered. The speaker only assumes it could be part of an unfolding discourse. Hence the 'simulated' quoting. It is a means speakers apply in order to suspend the illocution of an utterance.

This is the function SɪmGr uses after verbalising the option of the label deal (se (632)), in order not to come under any legal obligation. SɪmGr repeats the assertion *we could do …*, this time with the deictic form *that.* With its help, he refers back to the utterance before and concludes the first aspect for his hearer. In the following part, he announces the alternative with the conjunction *Or* at the beginning and a matrix construction with *could.* Again, this is a form of a simulated quotation.

In se (634), the matrix construction of the utterance is not a complete conditional. However, it is connected to the first conditional *If I say … we could …* (se (632)). The speaker seems to shorten the construction. He still makes sure to use the modal *could* together with the original verb *say* from the protasis and thereby stresses the hypothetical form.

In following sentence, the SɪmGr starts a further conditional in which he separates the speaking situation from the content of the discussion. It begins with the conjunction *as long as*, which replaces *if.* It is a marked subordinating conjunction that refers to time on the one hand; i. e. in this case, the period of time during which S2fFr has not established a contract with another distribution company. However, it also means 'provided that' or 'on condition that' (English Grammar Today).[33] It is the protasis of the next conditional and is subordinated to the matrix construction *Or I could say*, which is the main clause. At the same time, it is subordinated to the assertion *We could do a label deal*, the apodosis of the earlier conditional and the first option in the summary (se (632); example 50). The apodosis of this conditional is again *then I could say*. The actual second option follows in the next sentence. It is a simulated quotation again. It is introduced by *Okay*, which suggests a conclusion. The actual proposition, however, is *from the whole catalogue I would pick …* In this conditional, the prepositional phrase *from the whole catalogue* precedes the actual predicate, which is expressed with the modal *would* again. The construction not only reflects SɪmGr's complex mental processes – summarising and differentiating different options –, but also his eagerness to suspend the illocution in order to keep his suggestions on a hypothetical level and up for discussion, i. e. negotiation.

---

33 https://dictionary.cambridge.org/grammar/british-grammar (19/01/2020)

At this point, the speaker, S1mGr, uses very complex syntactic constructions and explicit subjunctive forms. He uses *could* 6 times within the 4 utterances, and *would* 4 times. He summarises his understanding of the two options discussed before and implicitly requests his hearer to evaluate his summary. She does so in se (635). He, in turn, acknowledges their discourse knowledge with the assertion *That's alright* in se (636). In the summary, however, he uses a high quantity of conditionals, matrix constructions and the modals *could* and *would* as well as the *verbum dicendi* 'say'.

'Say' is used to make the hypothetical quality of his utterances very clear. With its help, S1mGr makes sure the hearer interprets his utterances as options. He avoids commissives and stresses the purely mental quality of his summary. This way, he ensures that S2fFr understands the intention behind the summary (comparing discourse knowledge; cf. Rehbein 1995) and does not interpret the utterances as his taking up any of her offers. With the combination of linguistic means, he avoids coming under any legal obligation. He is not ready to commit to the deal yet and shows it in the explicit marking of hypothetical scenarios. She, on the other hand, does not need to go to so much effort because she, as opposed to S1mGr, actually wants the deal and is ready to commit to it.

All the C3 conditional constructions in the core negotiation are used when the speaker is not yet willing to commit to the offer 'on the table'. For example, S1mGr does not want to accept the offer made by S2fFr. In all the conditional constructions from C3 discussed above, there is one part that the speaker finds acceptable or is ready to commit to. However, there is another part – the proposition of the apodosis – that the speaker is not ready to commit to. The ruptures between the different levels of acceptance or commitment are indicated by different linguistic means such as neutral forms, augments, matrix constructions, and by switching from the indicative mood, here in the present tense, to the hypothetical verb forms indicated by *would* or *could*, the forms that replace the subjunctive in English. This function is taken one step further in the conditionals of C4.

10.2.5 Explicit hypotheticality: C4 conditional in the core negotiation

C4 is the category that is closest to hypothetical conditionals in Standard English. Conditionals in C4 use forms of the past tense in the protasis (or modals that can also be used as the past tense) and forms of the subjunctive (or in one case the past tense) in the apodosis.

In C4, 3 out of 5 sentences contain a form of *would* or *could*, but they are not politeness strategies. Two of these conditionals, 57 and 58, are used in the core negotiation. Both are used at crucial points, i. e. when details of a potential deal are discussed, yet the speaker does not want to commit to the action or situation under discussion.

In utterance 57, S1mGr inquires about the exclusivity of a deal that S2fFr suggested after he did not accept her first attempt at a label deal. The deal in question is the one discussed in the examples above, the one that would allow S1mGr to choose various titles from the catalogue and distribute them in Germany without committing to distributing a whole label:

57	If, if I would say: Well I would like to make certain titles available in Germany	would that • then be an exclusive ((1s)) deal?	MARK S1mGr 517

Example 57 is used before the constructions in examples 50 and 53. It is an inquiry about the aspect that matters most to S1mGr: exclusive distribution rights. He uses a similar double embedding technique as in the examples above: starting the conditional with the *verbum discendi* 'say'. He combines the conditional with a matrix construction. By these means, he stresses the purely mental, i. e. hypothetical, quality to the following proposition. He puts a difference between the constructed situation 'would say' and his actually saying it. So on a mental level, he creates a difference between his action (uttering the option) and the possibility of doing so. He stresses the hypothetical quality with the help of the if-clause with *would*. This clause functions as a matrix construction embedding (and changing the quality of) the following utterance.

He goes to a lot of effort, linguistically and mentally, to express the difference between the speaking intention and the actual situation. And he uses the embedding strategy as well as the markers of probability to make his hearer, S2fFr, mentally follow the steps away from the speaking situation and onto the hypothetical level. In the discourse, he follows it up with the question if she would deal with other companies in Germany as well (se (518)), a situation he finds problematic and therefore wants to avoid:

(517)	S1mGr	((1s)) If, if I would say: Well I would like to make certain titles available in Germany, would that • then be an exclusive ((1s)) deal?
(518)	S1mGr	_Or would you offer your titles to other distribution companies in Germany as well?

Example: Or would you offer your titles (MARK)

In se (517) and (518), the speaker combines two utterances – indicated by a missing pause between both complete sentences – that are opposites to one another regarding the proposition (exclusive deal vs. her offering the titles elsewhere). However, from a grammatical point of view, they form two apodoses to the same protasis. The speaker, S1mGr, combines the contradicting propositions of the two sentences (*would that then be an exclusive deal* vs. *would you offer your titles to other distribution companies …*). The question urges his hearer, S2fFr, to take a stance and explicitly commit to one of the two options in question.

He starts his utterance after a pause in the discourse with the repetition of the conjunction *if*, which starts the matrix construction *If I would say*. The repetition might indicate planning difficulties, which are likely to indicate increased mental activity. This point of the negotiation is especially important because he needs to examine different options and to make his hearer aware that he is not committing to the deal.

He therefore embeds an assertion that he ascribes to himself and that takes the form of a simulated quotation in a conditional sentence. And he uses a conditional within the embedded sentence. He even sets the embedded clause apart by starting in with *Well*. *Well* is used in English to indicate that something different is about to be uttered. In this case he sets the utterance apart by the scenario of him accepting the offer.

So he uses two conditionals and a matrix construction to lift the scenario away from the speaking situation. He indicates the difference between the speaking situation, i. e. reality, and the hypothetical scenario on his (and on his hearer's) mind with the help of syntactic features. He indicates the difference between the discourse situation and the hypothetical scenario he is discussing with his hearer by using a subjunctive for the verb, again to set the proposition apart from the speaking situation and to allow for a meta-discourse. He then asks about a potential consequence of the scenario with the question *would that then be an exclusive deal*? The question forms the apodosis of conditional sentence he started with *if I would say*. The direct question puts the hearer in a position where she has to evaluate the scenario in a direct answer. The direct answer creates shared discourse knowledge. It makes explicit, to both participants, where they stand and which consequences would come from the scenario in question. This co-constructed discourse knowledge is the very basis of the decisions S1mGr needs to take. They therefore form the essence of the negotiation. This co-construction of knowledge through negotiation is the basis on which negotiators take their decisions. It forms the very feature that Grießhaber (2000) defines as the characteristic of the language of business and business discourse.

Se (517) is the utterance with the most explicit use of conditional forms. It is a complete conditional sentence as well as an indirect utterance embedded in a conditional. The speaker, S1mGr, marks the probability of his utterance in various steps in order to explicitly set the proposition apart from the speaking situation. Again, he ascribes a purely mental quality to the unfolding meta-discourse (cf. Redder 1992). He keeps this up in the attached utterance *Or would you offer your titles to other distribution companies in Germany as well?* (se (518)), the scenario he tries to exclude. The forms help him mark the proposition as hypothetical and thereby as unbinding.

Similarly, he uses the modal verbs *would* and *could* in example 58, which was uttered earlier in the same discourse. S2fFr just offered him the distribution of certain labels for whose publications her company has the exclusive European distribution rights. She is looking for a partner who would distribute the products in Germany:

58	((1s)) provided, you know, we would do like a distribution agreement	So you could give, give those titles to us and we would …	MARK S1mGr 275

Example 58 is an indirect request. S1mGr's asks S2fFr to confirm that his understanding of the offer she made is correct. The utterance stands out in the discourse because the *So* interrupts the ongoing discourse and focusses the hearer's attention on the utterance. The utterance, in turn, is the conclusion, i. e. summary, of the preceding discourse. He verbalises his understanding of her suggestion by summarising it: *So you could give those titles to us.* It is the first part of her offer. With the help of the *So,* he indicates the conclusion that is about to follow: That her company holds the rights for those 'titles', i. e. musical publications. They are therefore in a position to offer his company the products in question for sale in Germany. He is double-checking his understanding of the discourse so far. He verbalises it to give S2fFr the opportunity to correct him if need be or to fill in potential gaps. He makes sure they share the same discourse knowledge in order to avoid misunderstandings at this crucial part of the negotiation.

The second part of the apodosis starts with his company's actions in the deal, *and we would …*. However, that part is incomplete. At this point, he is not interrupted, but breaks off his utterance. There is a break of 1 second before he continues with the protasis. In the original discourse, the protasis is in second position. It is very likely an addition to the conclusion, and probably the speaker did not plan for the sentence to be a conditional. But during the utterance of the first part, he became aware that his hearer, S2fFr, might interpret the utterance as a request to actually give him the titles for sale. So she might interpret his indirect question as a sign of willingness to close a deal. He probably felt a need to avoid this misunderstanding. And so he added the protasis, spontaneously forming a conditional. The protasis starts with *provided,* a rare and strong subordinating conjunction, which stresses that a condition needs to be fulfilled beforehand. So here, the complex utterance might indicate his increased mental activity and his strong intention to avoid any misunderstandings.

Before he actually verbalises the condition, he uses the augment *you know*, referring to their shared discourse knowledge. He reminds his hearer that there is something else to be accomplished before the proposition of the apodosis can be realised. So he activates their shared knowledge before uttering the actual condition. The condition (*we do like a …)* is then verbalised with the pronoun *we*, a deictic element that is used to stress their shared interests.

He uses the modal verb *would* in *we would do like a distribution agreement*. In this case, not only *would* and the sentence structure set the utterance apart from the discourse, i. e. realistic level. The effect is also supported by his choice of words: The noun *distribution agreement*, although a technical term, is weaker than the legal term 'contract'. The verb 'do' is not specific, which makes it less concrete (and although it is not idiomatic, it is easy for the hearer to understand). And the insertion of *like* as a preposition removes the concrete action – agreeing to a contract – further from the speaking situation. S1mGr also removes it farther from the pronoun *we*, and thereby from the agent of the action. On a mental level, the proposition becomes less concrete and the mood of the verb, the substitution for the subjunctive in English, changes its quality. All these linguistic means, and especially the use of the conditional, indicate that the speaker avoids commissives.

S1mGr is very determined not to cause any misunderstanding when it comes to commissives and to commitment. He avoids making S2fFr believe that he is offering or promising to distribute her products in Germany. He sets the potential form of cooperation and the conditions for that to happen apart from the speaking situation.

During the whole core negotiation, S1mGr seems to be very eager to suspend the illocution. He indicates that very clearly to his hearer. Therefore, he uses a variety of linguistic means, at whose core is the conditional. He avoids any legal obligation at the crucial points in the core negotiation. Not only does he use explicit hypothetical conditionals, but also a variety of linguistic means like matrix constructions, augments, and 'neutral' constructions in order to avoid commissives. The combination of these linguistic means sets the speaking situation apart from the scenarios to which he is not ready to commit. So he linguistically differentiates between two functions: aspects he is ready to commit to and aspects he wants to mark as hypothetical and set apart from reality.

10.3 Modal verbs and conditionals: avoiding commitment

Setting the proposition apart from the speaking situation is a function used at various points in the negotiation. Not only S1mGr uses this function, but other speakers as well. Sometimes speakers use the modal verbs *would* and *could*, although not in a complete conditional sentence. The modal marks hypotheticality also outside conditional sentences and is frequently used in the core negotiation. It is an efficient linguistic means that marks a non-committal utterance. Most of all, the modals are easy to integrate in the sentence and easy to understand for the hearer. They require little mental and linguistic effort. It is especially important in oral communication because oral communication is fast and can usually not be repeated. So speakers make extensive use of these forms at crucial points in the negotiation.

The following excerpt (se (522) to se (562)) is part of the core negotiation. The part that is discussed above (cf. chapter 10.2.5). The forms of *would* and *could* have been underlined to emphasis their quantity. They indicate at which crucial points in the negotiation speakers suspend the illocution:

(522)	S1mGr	I mean, the thing is if, if we only take certain titles, then it probably would make sense for you to deal with other territories.
(523)	S1mGr	((1s)) Uh, not territories, with other companies in Germany.
(524)	S1mGr	Maybe they think uhm • that other titles could do ((1s)) good as well.
(525)	S1mGr	Know what I mean?
(526)	S1mGr	I mean, I mean I would like to have the exc, the exclu/to have an exclusive deal.
(527)	S1mGr	But uhm if we decide only to make • like ten percent of your catalogue available, then there are still ninety percent which, you know, which are not available in Germany.
(528)	S1mGr	And maybe other • • distribution companies ((1s)) would like to make that available, so ...
(529)	S2fFr	Yeah.
(530)	S2fFr	((2s)) Uhm yeah uh, uh it, ((1s)) it would be a problem.
(531)	S2fFr	I mean, uhm • would you be/would you agree maybe to make uh, uh, you know, exclusivity, but on/• only on some titles?
(532)	S2fFr	That you pick up?
(533)	S1mGr	Uhm¯·
(534)	S2fFr	((2s)) Would it be possible?
(535)	S2fFr	Or is that something you • cannot consider for various reasons?
(536)	S1mGr	I mean then you could have competition, you know.
(537)	S2fFr	Yeah.
(538)	S1mGr	If you deal with like three companies and everybody says: Well, I would like the Precious Sousa, and then you have to, you know ...
(539)	S2fFr	Oh, no.
(540)	S2fFr	No, no, no.
(541)	S2fFr	What I wanna say is, for example, okay you sound very interested in Precious Sousa and would like to release it in Germany.
(542)	S1mGr	Yeah·
(543)	S2fFr	I give you the exclusivity on Precious Sousa.
(544)	S1mGr	Yeah, alright·
(545)	S1mGr	Okay.

(546)	S2fFr	I won't give it to anybody else.
(547)	S1mGr	Yeah, that makes sense.
(548)	S2fFr	Uh now if you, if you tell me: Uh okay, I am only interested in releasing Precious Sousa, uhm I/it will be a problem for me to give you this exclusivity on our whole catalogue.
(549)	S1mGr	Yeah·
(550)	S1mGr	Sure.
(551)	S1mGr	Sure.
(552)	S2fFr	You know?
(553)	S1mGr	I understand.
(554)	S2fFr	Uhm but I think it's fair to give the exclusivity when someone wants/ you know, takes the decision of working on, on, on a product.
(555)	S1mGr	Right.
(556)	S1mGr	Yeah.
(557)	S2fFr	I mean, I, I cannot imagine to propose the same album somewhere else.
(558)	S1mGr	I think, I think for a certain title it's, it's, it's easy to give an [exclusi]/exclusivity, whatever.
(559)	S2fFr	I mean, (in France) would ( ). [*hesitating*
(560)	S1mGr	Uhm ((3s)) what I could see …
(561)	S1mGr	We, ((1s)) we really would have to find a way ho/to work together.
(562)	S1mGr	Because I'm pretty sure we won't make the whole • • catalogue available.

Excerpt: Would and could in the core negotiation (MARK)

The passage shows an important part of the core negotiation. It is the part where S1mGr lets S2fFr know that he will only distribute certain titles in Germany (cf. above). He is not interested in the whole label, her original offer. He anticipates that the deal will not be satisfactory for her and raises the issue in se (522). She sees the problem and reacts after a 2-second-pause in se (530). She first agrees to the assumption (*that would be a problem),* then makes a modified offer in se (531). By doing so, she starts another circle of negotiation (cf. Rehbein 1995). He raises the issue of her losing money (see discussion above). The two clarify the misunderstanding about different companies distributing the same artists in Germany. In the end, no agreement is reached although S2fFr offers S1mGr different options. The importance of the exclusivity of the distribution rights becomes obvious further down in the discourse (se (536 ff.)). He explicitly negotiates this aspect, but lets her know in se (561) and se (562) that he will not distribute her company's whole range of products, i.e. her 'whole catalogue', in Germany.

In the passage, *would* is used 11 times, and *could* 3 times; S2fFr uses *would* 6 times; S1mGr uses *would* 5 times and *could* 3 times. So in the overall use of conditional forms, there is no significant difference between the two. However, looking at the phases of the discourse, there are two rounds in which S2fFr offers S1mGr the deals. And there is a more intensive use of conditionals and the conditional modals in the first part, where SımGr discusses the exclusive rights as well as the problem of competition, i.e. in se (522) to se (530) and in se (530) to se (559). In se (531), S2fFr makes the second offer. Between se (538) and se (558), the two use *would* only twice and mainly use indicatives in the present tense and in the *will*-future.

S2fFr, who is making the new offer, uses verbs in the present tense and the *will*-future (*I give you the exclusivity ...; I won't give it to anybody else ....; If you tell me .../it will be a problem; I think it's fair to ..., I cannot imagine to propose the same album somewhere else*). She thereby indicates her commitment to the options. SımGr, on the other hand, reacts in very short utterances, mostly with augments. He closes this round in se (560 ff.), also with two conditional forms: *what I could see*, which he does not complete, and *we really would have to find a way ...* The verb forms indicate that he does not commit to or accept her preceding suggestions.

In the following segment, se (562), he turns down her offer for the whole catalogue, using the *will*-future. He puts his rejection in a future tense. Thereby, he puts a distance between the speaking situation and the assertion. He thus makes the rejection less direct. He also uses *I'm pretty sure* for the same purpose. So he remains cooperative and polite when turning down her offer. Being polite is important for their cooperation because the discourse does not end here, but the two start another round of negotiation when she offers him a different label. And as Knapp (2002:241f.) points out, diverging goals are accepted in business negotiation.

In this passage of discourse, both speakers guide the hearer's attention and understanding with the help of augments. *I mean* is used 7 times in the excerpt, *you know* 6 times. 7 matrix constructions guide the hearer's perception and support the suspension of the illocution with the 14 subjunctive modals.

All in all, a lot of linguistic work is done by both speakers to ensure their communicative intention is interpreted accordingly by the hearer, i.e. misunderstandings are avoided. They especially use a very high amount of subjunctive forms to mark the parts of their utterances that are negotiated, i.e. that are still under discussion. So commitment, and especially commissives, are avoided with the help of different linguistic means, especially with the conditional.

10.4 Personal pronouns across conditionals

One of the grammatical forms that also varies, even though to a weaker degree, is the use of personal pronouns. There is a difference in the use of personal pronouns indicating a human agent of the action e.g. the speaker or hearer, or their organisation, and neutral pronouns such as *it* or other constructions that make the agent less identifiable.

Most conditionals in the corpus contain a personal pronoun; some conditionals contain the name or the noun describing a person's function or role, such as 'my colleague'. Constructions such as the passive voice or neutral pronouns like *it* can shift the focus away from the agent. These grammatical means can express to which degree the speaker either commits to an utterance or holds certain agents responsible.

Table 7 below lists the use of the different personal pronouns or noun-phrases in the different parts of the conditional sentences in different categories (C1–C5). It indicates how the use of personal pronouns correlates with the different types of conditionals:

Tab. 7: Pronouns in different categories of conditionals

	I		**You**		**We**		**They**		**personalized pronoun/noun**		**it or other non-personal pronoun**	
	Protasis	*apodosis*	*protasis*	*apodosis*	*protasis*	*apodosis*	*protasis*	*apodosis*	*protasis*	*apodosis*	protasis	apodosis
C 1	8	5	12	9*	4	5	3	1	-	2	4	9
C 2	3	3	4	1	-	2	2	1	1	-	-	3
C 3	1	4	2	1	4	1	2	-	-	-	3	6
C 4	3	2	-	1	1	-	-	-	-	-	1	2
C 5	-	5	4	—	2	-	-	-	-	-	-	1
total	15	19	22	12	11	8	7	2	1	2	8	21

**Example 19 does not contain a subject pronoun because it is an imperative; however, it was added to this category because it refers to the second person.*

Table 7 indicates the correlation between the personal pronouns and non-personalised pronouns in the different parts of the conditional sentences and across the different categories of conditional sentences in the BusinessELF corpus. It differentiates between pronouns of the 1st and 2nd person in the singular and plural and other personalised pronouns such as *he* when referring to a work colleague etc. on the one hand, and *it* or other expressions indicating a 'neutral' form on the other hand. With these forms and constructions, speakers can avoid explicitly mentioning the agent of the action in question. And by taking the focus off the agent, they can make the construction more 'neutral'.

The most frequently used personal pronoun in the protases in the Business-ELF corpus is *you*. It is used in 22 out of 64 examples, which equals almost one third of all conditionals. The, quantitatively speaking, second strongest pronoun is *I*. It is used in 15 clauses, followed by *we* with 11 occurrences. Between the different categories, there are different tendencies: While in C1, the largest category, almost all pronouns are used, C3, C4 and C5 have a tendency to use the singular pronouns. In C2, the pronoun *we* is not used at all; the mostly used pronoun is *you*. In C3, however, the most frequently used pronoun is *we*, whereas in C4, the category with the most hypothetical conditionals, the focus is on *I*. The pronoun *you* is not used at all in C4 conditionals, and it is scarcely used in C3.

Despite the fact that the corpus is too small for a statistical analysis, there seems to be a tendency to use the pronoun of the second person singular in C1 and C2 conditionals. So in these – more realistic – conditionals, the focus is mostly on the hearer. In C3 and C4, generally speaking, the focus seems to shift to the first person.

In C3, the category that is not described as a category in standard grammar but makes up 12 out of 64 conditionals in the corpus, the focus is more on neutral or non-personalised subjects as well as on the first person plural, *we*.

Out of the 21 apodoses with the inanimate, i.e non-personal, subjects such as *it* or *that*, 9 are used in C1, and 6 are used in C3. In C3, the non-standard category which contains 12 conditionals, 6 sentences have an inanimate subject in the apodosis, while 4 sentences use *we* in the protasis. So inside this category, there is a tendency to combine the form of *would* or *could* in the apodosis with an inanimate form of subject or agent, while in the protasis the main subjects are *we*, *you* and *they*.

The animate, i. e. identifiable, subjects in the protasis are often combined with neutral or inanimate subjects in the apodosis. That supports the effect of a distance between the realistic actions in the protasis, fulfilled by identifiable agents, and the hypothetical actions in the apodosis, which are carried out by inanimate agents. So in some constructions, the combination of tenses and pronouns make the agents of the sentences less concrete. This way, they support the distance between the speaking situation and the hypothetical situation under discussion. However, the tendency is rather weak and the corpus small. So this would have to be studied with the help of a lager data base.

11. Discussion

11.1 Conditionals as features of BusinessELF

The aim of this dissertation project was to see if there are features of LFE in business contexts that are different to the Englishes used in other lingua franca contexts. The first part of the analysis showed that the data base for this project, the BusinessELF corpus (cf. chapter 7.2), had almost all the features of LFE that were described for the general, academic and business use of LFE. The only exception was the use of topic changes to overcome misunderstandings (cf. House 2002, Meierkord 1996) and the preference for 'here-and-now'-topics (cf. Meierkord 2002). Since in business negotiations, non-linguistic goals determine the topics of the discourse, changing or avoiding topics is simply not an option. The question that remained then was if there are any features of LFE in the BusinessELF corpus that have not been described before.

My hypotheses were that speakers in business negotiations would avoid commissives in order not to come under any legal obligation as long as they are not ready to form a contract. I further assumed that, as long as negotiators find themselves short of reaching their goal in a negotiation, they indicate, linguistically, that their contributions are part of a discussion, not of an agreement. Therefore, they choose linguistic forms that mark an utterance as a proposal, question, summary etc. rather than a promise.

My hypothesis regarding the language forms that differ in the BusinessELF corpus was that the linguistic forms in the corpus, especially the conditionals, as well as matrix-constructions, inversions etc., are used to indicate the degree to which the speaker commits to the proposition of an utterance.

Speakers in the BusinessELF corpus are competent English speakers using mostly standard forms. However, at crucial points in the negotiation, they use more complex sentences with less standard forms. Forms vary, especially in the core negotiation, when speakers are not ready to commit to a proposal. Speakers use more non-standard forms than in the rest of the discourse. They set the proposition apart from the speaking situation using a variety of conditional sentences and forms, as described in chapter 9.5. The most important feature of LFE in the BusinessELF corpus was the combination of present tense in the protasis and *would* in the apodosis to differentiate two levels of 'reality', the use present tenses in both the protasis and apodosis in unmarked conditionals and the use of *would* in both parts of a conditional sentence when they were not used as politeness forms. In combination with other language features like matrix constructions, *verba discendi,* etc., the different conditionals fulfil communicative functions that do not exist in most other contexts, mainly weakening or suspending the illocutionary force of utterances (cf. chapter 10.2).

The share of conditionals in the BusinessELF corpus is very high: 64 out of the 3,784 utterances were complete conditional sentences, which equals 1.69%. And their forms also vary. All together, there are 5 categories of conditional sentences in the BusinessELF corpus (cf. chapter 9), out of which only C5, the speech act conditionals, i.e. politeness forms, are the same as in inner circle usage in form and function. Most other categories seem to fulfil a function that they do not have in many other contexts:

- C1 conditionals, i.e. conditionals with a present tense predicate in both the protasis and the apodosis, are used in inner circle contexts to mark scientific truths (Cowan 2008:459). In the BusinessELF corpus, however, they express unmarked conditions. So speakers in the BusinessELF corpus use a form of conditional sentences that exists in standard language use, but apply it in contexts that differ from inner circle usage.

The form could be an indicator of simplification or incomplete learning, i.e. it could be a simple mistake or error (cf. Corder 1967). However, the advantage of this present tense/present tense form, especially in oral communication, is that it is clear and direct. So another explanation could be that the form is attractive to lingua franca speakers because it is easy to process – for both the speaker and the hearer – and clear in its reference. Thus it prevents misunderstandings.

- C2 conditionals, i.e. conditionals with a present tense predicate in the protasis and a form of the *will*-future in the apodosis, are the standard form of realistic conditionals. In the BusinessELF corpus, however, they are used – as opposed to C1 conditionals – in very few contexts. In these contexts, a difference is made between the desirability of the proposition of the protasis or the speaker's commitment to it and their commitment to the proposition of the apodosis. So the form is the same as in standard, i.e. inner circle usage, but its function is different in the BusinessELF corpus.

A question for further research could be if this form – the standard realistic conditional – is used more frequently in other corpora or whether it is 'outnumbered' by different forms of conditional sentences in other LFE constellations.

- C3 conditionals are a form of conditionals that is not listed in standard English grammars.

The category is, however, a productive form in oral language use.

Some examples from the spoken part of the British sub-corpus of the International Corpus of English (ICE-GB) (http://ice-corpora.net) show that the form of the conditional is used – at least orally – in the inner circle as well:

1) <ICE-GB:S1A-006 #301:1:B> If it's a really nice day we could walk
2) <ICE-GB:S1A-010 #107:1:B> Or if you put it here you could give it a a W
3) <ICE-GB:S1A-015 #14:1:A> I'm sure you would love it if that is well I mean
4) <ICE-GB:S1A-018 #330:1:B> Well you could have it if you're lecturing couldn't you
5) <ICE-GB:S1A-020 #68:1:C> I mean if she's a student at Saint Martin's she would would presumably be covered.

Examples 1) to 4) indicate suggestions, so they might be interpreted as forms of politeness. While the protasis is in the present tense, indicating a realistic option, the modal *would* in the apodosis leaves room for the hearer make different suggestions. Example 3) also uses *would* in order for the speaker to come across as less direct and to leave the hearer a choice.

Example 5), however, indicates different degrees of certainty in the two parts of the sentence. While the speaker is more certain about the proposition of the protasis, i. e. the person in question being a student at a specific institution, they are not so sure about the consequence: the person in question being covered. So the function of the form of the conditional in oral British English use is similar to the functions in the BusinessELF corpus: The use of *would* in the apodosis functions either as a means to leave more options for the hearer or to indicate different degrees of certainty about the proportion of the clause.

However, the function of expressing non-preferred options might be specific to LFE or at least to the BusinessELF corpus. And this category of conditionals fills a gap here between C4 conditionals, which express hypothetical situations, and the realistic situations in C1 and C2 conditionals. Presumably, speakers felt a necessity to express a specific type of situations: situations in which the condition was realistic, yet the consequences could be expressed as markedly hypothetical. Therefore, the consequences, i. e. apodoses, are expressed with a form of *would* or *could*. These modal verbs mark the verb as different from the speaking situation and as having a theoretical, i. e. hypothetical, quality just like they do in oral inner circle use. C3 conditionals therefore are more hypothetical than C1 and C2 conditionals, yet not as hypothetical as C4 conditionals.

One of the questions for further research could be if the form fulfils the same functions in other contexts as it does in the BusinessELF corpus and if it is used more frequently in some contexts than in others.

- C4 conditionals, i.e. conditionals with a past tense or *would* or *could* in the apodosis and in the protasis, are conditionals that exist in different varieties of English even though they are not standard forms.

The use of *would* and *could* in the protasis of conditional sentences is a feature of oral language use; in American English even more than, e.g., in British English (cf. Ranta 2010). So the use of these forms might also – at first sight – be explained as a form of oral language use (see 11.2 below).

11.2 Conditionals in spoken language (L1 + L2)

The use of *would/would* in conditionals can often be explained as a language mistake or a form of learner language. However, the construction is not only found in learner language, but also in oral language use.

Ranta (2010), as mentioned above, compares the use of conditionals by LFE speakers and inner circle (American) English speakers. She compares both groups with the help of the ELFA corpus and the MICASE corpus. She refers to realistic conditionals as *1st conditionals*, to conditionals "based on an unreal condition" and constructed with *would* + past tense (for the condition) as *2nd conditionals* and to conditionals "constructed with *would have* + the past perfect" as *3rd conditionals* (Ranta 2010:94), in accordance with a widely used categorisation of conditionals. She describes her findings regarding the quantitative use of conditional sentences as follows:

> Overall, the rate for using *would/would have* in hypothetical *if*-clauses for ELFA is 29% and for MICASE only 2%, but the difference is largely explained by the fact that in ELFA, *would* occurs much more frequently in 2nd conditional *if*-clauses (26% of all 2nd conditionals) compared to MICASE, in which the percentage is 1.3%. However, in the case of 3rd conditionals, the non-standard use becomes clearly more frequent in MICASE, too: ELFA speakers use *would have* in 3rd conditionals if-clauses 75% of the time, and MICASE speakers in 24% of the instances. (Ranta 2010:96).

According to Ranta's (2010) findings, lingua franca speakers, as well as inner circle speakers, use *would* in both the protasis and the apodosis of conditional sentences. However, speakers in the ELFA corpus, i.e. lingua franca speakers, use *would* in the protasis almost 20 times more often than inner circle speakers, i.e. American English speakers, and *would have* 3 times more often.

Unfortunately, Ranta (2010) does not give the topics or contexts in which these forms were used. So it cannot be seen which communicative intentions may have triggered the forms and why they appear significantly more often than in inner circle contexts. However, the finding that even inner circle speakers frequently use what she refers to as a non-standard form of 3rd condition makes her – rightfully – question the hypothesis that the usage is only a form of imperfect learning. Drawing on the *Handbook of Varieties of English* (Kortmann/Schneider 2004), she stresses that the forms in question are used by native speakers of standard English and of varieties of the inner and outer circle (Ranta 2010:96). That makes her rightfully hypothesise that the non-standard forms of the *if*-clauses cannot be explained as mere interferences or "imperfect learning" (Ranta 2010:97), but rather as a structure "typical of spoken English grammar" (Ranta 2010:102).

The use of the explicit marker of probability in the protasis of conditional sentences that refer to unrealistic conditions in the past is, according to Kellerman (1989:107 f.), "common in both British and American English". The so-called "intrusive have" (Filmore 1985; quoted in Kellerman 1989:108) is used in both varieties "combined with *'d* in sentences like *If I'd've known you were coming, I'd've baked a cake.*" (Kellerman 1989:108). And Kellerman concludes that "[i]n the spoken language, it does not seem stigmatized" (1989:108).

The use of *would have* in both parts of the conditional sentence in American English is also mentioned by Cowan (2008:8), although he does not refer to the phenomenon as the *intrusive have*. He gives the following example: **If I would have seen her, I would have said hello* and explains that "[s]trictly speaking, the grammatical version" of the sentence is with the past perfect form *had seen* (Cowan 2008:8). He goes on to observe that "[h]owever, the version [above; *would have* + past participle in the protasis and *would* + infinitive in the apodosis, B. D.] is becoming more common in spoken American English." So, basically, Cowan's (2008) finding echoes Kellerman's (1989) and explains the form as a phenomenon of oral language use.

The same explanation is given by Swan (2016). In the 2016 edition of *Practical English Usage*, Swan observes that "[c]onditional *would* is sometimes used in both clauses of an *if*-sentence. This is very informal, and quite common in speech. It is not usually written, and is incorrect in formal writing" (entry 244). In the earlier edition, he further added that it was "common in spoken American English" (Swan 1995:251), an observation he left out in the later edition (Swan 2016).

However, since the percentage Ranta (2010) finds is rather small, compared to the use of the standard forms, the attribute 'typical' might be a bit too strong. But it is definitely a feature of the English language that is used also in the inner circle.

Ranta (2010) further argues that these forms of the conditionals might be typical features of spoken Englishes around the world, so-called 'vernacular universals' (Chambers 2004; quoted in Ranta 2010:102) or 'angloversals' (Mair 2003; quoted in Ranta 2010:102). As a reason, she assumes that ELF speakers have "less 'obligation' to be norm-oriented and/or monitor their speech for standardness even in academic contexts than native speakers have" (Ranta 2010:102 f.). This supposed independence of lingua franca speakers might be one reason for them not to use standard forms. Since Ranta (2010) does not give the context of the utterances, however, it is not possible to see whether there are other conditions that would explain the forms.

The use of *would* in both parts of the conditional sentence therefore is a phenomenon of oral language use. And inner circle speakers use it less frequently than expanding circle, i. e. lingua franca, speakers (only 1.3% in MICASE; Ranta (2010:96)). The use of *would* + past participle, on the other hand, becomes more frequent in oral language use among inner circle speakers too. So the phenomenon can be considered as a marked form of language use. And although it is not the form of choice for the majority of speakers, it fulfils a communicative function for some speakers or perhaps only in some situations.

Taking Kellerman's (1989) and Ranta's (2010) findings on the use of *would/would* in conditional sentences into consideration, two explanations of the form are available that support and complement each other:

1) The tendency to use *would* in both the protasis and the apodosis in oral language use (although it is not (yet) accepted in written language use). This tendency, however, is stronger in lingua franca English discourse than in inner circle discourse (cf. Ranta 2010).
6) The need felt by lingua franca speakers to stress the subjunctive function in order to avoid misunderstandings. So the forms might be used more intensively by ELF speakers due to their communicative need for clarity.

So the categories C3 and C4 are not mistakes caused by incomplete learning or slips of the tongue. They are, more likely, categories of conditionals that lingua franca speakers use, at least in business negotiations. Here, they can be used to indicate different levels of commitment. So LFE speakers use a marked form, yet one that is fast to produce and easy to process, to ensure successful communication. They mark the probability explicitly and thereby avoid misunderstandings.

11.3 Combination of tenses and degrees of commitment

The different combinations of tenses in the conditional sentences in the BusinessELF corpus not only indicate the probability which the speaker assumes for the proposition of a sentence; in the BusinessELF corpus, they also indicate to what degree a speaker is willing to commit to the proposition of an utterance and, most of all, to the consequences of that utterance. Consequences are further actions that would be required outside the communicative situation and the developing – legal, financial and other – obligations that arise from an agreement.

Table 8 below indicates how the combination of tenses in the different conditional sentences C1–C4 is related to the speaker's commitment to the proposition of the utterance (C5 was left out because it reflects politeness functions). Along a continuum of commitment from a high commitment on the left side to low commitment on the right, there are different combinations of tenses, moods and modals. A high commitment equals a commissive, while a low commitment equals a hypothetical quality of an utterance:

Tab. 8: Forms of conditionals and levels of commitment

high commitment			**low commitment**
←			→
C1 conditionals	C2 conditionals	C3 conditionals	C4 conditionals
present/present	present/*will*-future	present/*would*	*would/would (could)*
If you only work with us, […] we only make a few titles available (example 8)	if you tell me: Uh okay, I am only interested in releasing Precious Sousa, it will be a problem for me to give you this exclusivity on our whole catalogue (example 34)	If you decide … would you ask for .the European territories? (example 48)	If I would say …, would that be an exclusive deal? (example 57)
If you make an offer, we give you exclusivity (example 9)	Uhm it will be a problem for me if you ask me to give you the exclusivity on the whole catalogue and you don't do anything … (example 35)	If we only take certain titles, then it probably would make sense for you to deal with other … (example 49)	Provided …. We would do like a distribution agreement, … you could give those titles to us …(example 58)

Standard grammars usually only differentiate between the present tense conditionals on the left hand-side (C1 and C2) and the hypothetical conditionals on the right hand-side (C4; usually with a past tense in the protasis). Conditionals from C1 and C4, however, widen the spectre of conditional sentences in the BusinessELF corpus (as well as, for C3 conditionals) in oral language use.

LFE speakers in the corpus obviously felt the necessity for further categories: C1 conditionals, which have a marked function in standard English, are used as unmarked, realistic conditionals. They express a strong commitment or realistic situation, i. e. one that is expressed with the help of C2 conditionals in inner circle usage.

C2 conditionals, the standard form of realistic conditions in the inner circle, move to the right as far as commitment is concerned. They form the second strongest category regarding the level of commitment. So they express a lower commitment than C1 conditionals, yet a higher one than C3 conditionals.

C3 conditionals fill the gap between the realistic conditionals of category C1 and category C2 on the left and what is purely hypothetical, i. e. C4 conditionals, on the right. C3 conditionals indicate a low commitment to the proposition of the apodosis, i. e. a critical attitude. The proposition of the protasis, on the other hand, is considered a realistic or desired situation, i. e. one to which the speaker is willing to commit.

On the far right, *would* or *could* are used in both parts of the conditional sentence. The level of commitment is the lowest because the proposition is considered unrealistic or dis-preferred. C4 is a category only used as a politeness form or in oral language use in inner circles. In the BusinessELF corpus, however, the form is used to mark the far end of the continuum, i. e. the lowest degree of commitment. Those are the conditionals that indicate the suspension of the illocution (cf. Ehlich 1979) and the avoidance of commissives.

So the distribution of conditional forms, i. e. of what is marked by the subjunctive or conditional in other languages, is not as two- or threefold as most grammars describe it. Rather, the degree of probability varies in different forms of conditionals. In the BusinessELF corpus, there are more than just the 2 'standard' categories 'real' vs. 'unreal' (Cowan 2008:450/454): Speakers apply 4 different types of conditionals (plus one polite category that is in line with standard language use) to express different degrees of certainty/hypotheticality and of commitment.

The degree of commitment can also be varied in smaller degrees with the help of different linguistic means such as *verba discendi*, matrix constructions, augments and other deictic procedures, lexical choices etc. All these linguistic means help the respective hearer interpret the speaker's attitude toward the proposition of the utterance. The scenario in question can thus be discussed without the speaker having to commit to the consequences. And as speakers, LFE speakers in high stakes encounters try to be as clear about their commitment as possible in order to avoid misunderstandings. At the same time, they have to be efficient in their use of language and time. So they use various linguistic devices to mark communicative functions clearly.

Table 9 below indicates the different language means that speakers combine in their conditional sentences and how they relate to the illocutionary force of an utterance through the grammatical category (realistic – hypothetical) they express:

Tab. 9: Grammatical forms and illocutionary force

	Verb forms and tenses		**grammatical category**	**illocutionary force**
	protasis	apodosis	hypothetical	statement
C4 + further linguistic means	verba dicendi *would* *could*	matrix constructions – *would/could* neutral pronouns as subject		
C4	*would/could*	*would/could*		
C3	present tense	*would/could* + infinitive		
C2	present tense	*will*-future present tense 1st pers pronouns		
C1	present tense	present tense		
Conditional	combination of forms		realistic	commissive

As Table 9 indicates, C1 conditionals and C2 conditionals form the realistic conditionals that indicate a strong illocutionary force of an utterance. The illocutionary force decreases in the C3 conditionals and, even more so, in the C4 conditionals. Using conditionals, especially C4 conditionals, speakers add further linguistic means to their utterance to ensure that hearers interpret their utterances as hypothetical. So they suspend the illocution (Ehlich 1979) and mark this in multiple ways. Utterances with these linguistic forms are used in the discussion of options, but are not offers. The degree to which the indicative mood is replaced by conditional forms increases the degree of hypotheticality of the conditional sentence. This, in turn, indicates a weaker illocutionary force of an utterance or its complete suspension.

So all in all, speakers in the ELF corpus use different grammatical forms – especially of conditional sentences – to indicate whether or not they are ready to commit to the proposition of an utterance. Different forms of conditionals indicate different degrees of commitment (cf. Table 8). And non-standard forms are not used randomly in the BusinessELF but fulfil communicative functions.

Unfortunately, the data base for this study is quite small so that no statistically relevant conclusions are possible. However, out of the different categories of conditionals that are used as communicative means in the corpus (cf. Table 6), C3 conditionals, i.e conditionals with a present tense in the protasis and the modal *would* or *could* in the apodosis, are the most productive category. Further research could look into the question if they fulfil a similar function as in the BusinessELF corpus in other contexts too. If it can be defined, with the help of different corpora, in which contexts they are used and for which purposes, they could be defined as a feature of a LFE for specific purposes, e. g. LFE for business.

In the BusinessELF corpus, however, they proved to be a valuable and effective communicative strategy. This strategic use was enabled by the high productive as well as receptive communicative competence of the different speakers in the corpus.

12. Conclusion and outlook

The aim of this study was to contribute to the description of different forms of LFE, with a focus on ELF in business negotiations. The aim in the wider research context is to see what defines LFE – in general as well as in specific contexts.

Lingua franca speakers, by definition, were not raised in the language, in this case English, and do not use it as their first and everyday means of communication. They use it for restricted purposes. It is therefore likely that they do not understand all notions the way inner circle speakers are supposed to do. And they are likely to assume that their hearers do not do so either. So speakers in lingua franca situations take this issue into consideration and use linguistic means to facilitate understanding – not only on the lexical, but primarily on the pragmatic level. The forms they use are not always standard forms. However, these forms have to be easy to produce and easy to process for the hearer. So some of the language forms used in the data for this dissertation, especially the conditionals, fulfil communicative purposes and ensure understanding. They ought not to be ascribed to incomplete learning. They are, more likely, linguistic choices competent speakers make to facilitate communication.

The data used for the dissertation project was LFE in the conservative sense, i. e. speakers in the corpus were from the expanding circle and do not use English as their first language. All speakers use English for their professional goals, i. e. the pursue aims outside the communicative situation. The data base, the BusinessELF corpus, consisted of authentic language data recorded at an international music trade fair.

The first, i. e. structural, part of the dissertation was a comparison of the forms of LFE in the BusinessELF corpus to those found in other research projects. It showed that the BusinessELF corpus had what can be called "typical features" of LFE even though the data were recorded in a specific context, namely in business negotiations.

Communication in general was successful, i. e. understanding was achieved and no serious communicative problems or disturbances were detected. Few instances occurred when communication became problematic. And when problems occurred, speakers overcame them through cooperative linguistic behaviour. Explanations or negotiations of meaning were used to ensure understanding. However, the goal of the negotiations, a business deal, was not achieved in all cases. Still, the encounters were successful, because diverging goals and not reaching an agreement are acceptable – and a regular occurrence – in business encounters. On the social and language level, however, participants in the study reached all their goals: Speakers were cooperative, friendly and agreeable. Communication was mostly smooth, clear and efficient. On the legal level, no misunderstandings occurred that needed to be settled or clarified.

All participants were successful in that they reached their communicative goals, even though not their business goals. Their language use was typical of LFE when it came to strategies and structure. And although many of the structural features are the same as in other data and corpora, the use of conditionals stood out. What set the data for this dissertation apart from most other studies was the high number of conditionals used in the corpus. Although, due to the small data base, I could not prove that the number of conditionals was statistically higher than in other forms of discourse, the functional use of conditionals was proven with the help of a qualitative-interpretative approach, i. e. Functional Pragmatics.

The analysis showed that speakers used different forms of conditionals systematically. Therefore, a correlation, if not causal relation, between forms and communicative intentions could be shown. As the analyses have also shown, conditionals in the BusinessELF corpus are used to encode not only speakers' assumptions about the likelihood of linguistic content to be realised, but mainly to express *stance*. In the case of the BusinessELF data, the conditional sentences show to which degree the speaker *would like* the proposition of the conditional sentence to be realised.

Language usually leaves room for speakers to decide whether or not to apply standard forms or to divert from these forms. Sometimes, competent speakers put other goals over grammatical correctness, e. g. to attune their utterances to their own communicative needs or to what they assume to be the hearer's needs. Since lingua franca communication is very much about being polite and cooperative and – especially in professional contexts – about being efficient, speakers are likely to adapt the language to their needs. Avoiding misunderstandings was one of the crucial objectives in the corpus for this dissertation. So speakers used forms that are not always grammatical but that helped them fulfil communicative aims. One of these aims was to avoid commissives and not come under any (legal) obligation.

The function of separating the proposition and illocution in order to avoid commissives makes the use of conditionals noteworthy for a linguistic discussion. However, the issue might appear primarily in high stakes discourses. In business negotiations the consequences are usually different to many other contexts. It would be interesting to see if similar features appear in other lingua franca encounters in different or similar contexts. So it would be interesting to gather more data in lingua franca business English encounters to see if similar linguistic forms are used and at which points. More data would also allow for statistically relevant observations.

If larger data bases show a similar use of conditionals, they could be defined as one of the features setting LFE in professional contexts apart from other forms of LFE. So far, however, the use of conditionals can be seen as a communicative strategy enabling speakers and hearers in the BusinessELF corpus to communicate successfully and efficiently in LFE.

In a different research project, the assessment of speakers' competence, e. g. through standardised and anchored tests, could help compare the use of forms across different levels of competence. It will still not answer the question if speakers use a specific form because they do not know another, e. g. standard, form or because they want to facilitate comprehension for the hearer, though. So future research into the field might consider not only the assumed communicative intention, but perhaps the speakers' competence and language awareness as well. This in turn might help to see which forms are really used due to the speakers' mastery of the language and which are used because of their communicative competence – or lack of it.

Furthermore, future research could offer larger corpora and perhaps examine grammatical forms such as conditionals across different domains of language use. They might be able to answer the question if they can be a defining criteria of LFE usage in business contexts.

So far, however, it remains to be said that English is an attractive language for lingua franca speakers because it offers a variety of linguistic forms that are easy to use. Forms like conditionals are quick and simple to add to an utterance. More importantly perhaps, they are easy for hearers to interpret. That way, English enables communication across different levels of competence and is a handy and attractive lingua franca for different domains.

13. Tables and signs

HIAT conventions: Signs used in the transcripts

Sign	**Meaning**
S1mGr	speaker' acronym (=Speaker 1, male, German)
• • /• • •	pauses shorter than 1 second
((1s))	pause of 1 second
_Or would you offer your titles to other distribution companies in Germany as well?	Missing pause before the utterance
...	unfinished utterance
Uhm¯.	constant intonation
Uh`	falling intonation
Uh´	rising intonation
[	begin of comment (additional actions during the discourse or utterance)
]	end of comment
se (13)	segment (13) (=element in list of utterances)

Literature

Ahvenainen, T. 2005: Problem-solving mechanisms in information exchange dialogues with English as a lingua franca. Unpublished PhD thesis. University of Jyväskylän.

Alexander, L. G. 1998: Longman English Grammar. Harlow: Pearson Education.

Ammon, U. 1994: The present dominance of English in Europe. With an outlook on possible solutions to the European language problems. Sociolinguistica 8/1994. 1–14.

Austin, J. L. 1962: How to do things with words. J. O. Urmson/M. Sbisa (eds.). Cambridge, MA: Harvard University Press.

Baumeister, D./B. Dresemann/O. Traxel/R. Zahn 2005: Multiple Cs: What might the C in C-Test stand for twenty-four years down the line? M. Ó Dúill/R. Zahn/K. D. C. Höppner (eds.): Zusammenarbeiten: Eine Festschrift für Bernd Voss [Fremdsprachen in Lehre und Forschung 37]. Bochum: AKS-Verlag. 21–41.

Beerkens, R. 2008: Let's keep it simple. Cölfen, H., J. tenThije/C. Spiegel (eds.): Multilingualism – Applied Linguistics Approaches. Duisburg: Universitätsverlag Rhein-Ruhr. 9–17.

Beneke, J. 1991: Englisch als Lingua franca oder als Medium interkultureller Kommunikation? R. Grebing (ed.): Grenzenloses Sprachenlernen. Festschrift für Reinhold Freudenstein. Cornelsen and Oxford University Press: Berlin. 54–66.

Berns, M. 2005: Expanding on the Expanding Circle: where do WE go from here? World Englishes, Vol. 24, no. 1. 85–93.

Biber, D./S. Johansson/G. Leech/S. Conrad/E. Finegan 1999: Longman Grammar of Spoken and Written English. Harlow: Pearson Education Limited. 3rd impression 2000.

Björkman, B. 2008: 'So where we are?' Spoken lingua franca English at a technical university in Sweden. English Today 94, Vol. 4, No. 2 (June 2008). 35–41.

Björkman, B. 2010: From code to discourse in spoken ELF. A. Mauranen/E. Ranta (eds.): English as a lingua franca. Studies and findings. Newcastle upon Tyne: Cambridge Scholars Publishing. 225–251.

Bolton, K. 2004: World Englishes. A. Davies/C. Elder (eds.): The Handbook of applied linguistics. London: Blackwell. 369–396.

Breiteneder, A. 2005: The naturalness of English as a European lingua franca: a case fo the 'third person -s'. VIEWS 14 (2). 3–26.

Brown, P./S. Levinson (1978): Universals in Language Usage: Politeness Phenomena. E. Goody (ed.): Questions and Politeness: Strategies in Social Interaction. Cambridge: Cambridge University Press. 56–310.

Brutt-Griffler, J. 1998: Conceptual questions in English as a world language: Taking up an issue. (Reply to Widdowson 1997). World Englishes 17/3. 381–392.

Brutt-Griffler, J. 2002: World English. A study of its development. Clevedon et al.: Multilingual Matters.

Bühler, K. 1934: Sprachtheorie. Oxford: Fischer.

Bußmann, H. 1990: Lexikon der Sprachwissenschaft. Stuttgart: Kröner.

Clyne, M. 1994: Inter-cultural communication at work. Cambridge et al.: Cambridge University Press.
Clyne, M. 1997: Multilingualism. J. Coulmas (ed.): The Handbook of Sociolinguistics. Oxford: Blackwell. 301–14.
Cogo, A./M. Dewey. 2006: Efficiency in ELF communication: from pragmatic motives to lexico-grammatical innovation. Nordic Journal of English Studies 5.2. 59–93.
Corder, S. P. 1967: The significance of learners' errors. International Review of Applied Linguistics 5. 161–169.
Cowan, R. 2008: The Teacher's Grammar of English. Cambridge: Cambridge University Press.
Crystal, D. 1980: A dictionary of linguistics and phonetics. Malden, MA: Blackwell. 5th ed. 2003.
Crystal, D. 1995: The Cambridge Encyclopedia of the English language. Cambridge: Cambridge University Press.
Crystal, D, 1997: English as a global language. 2nd ed. 2003. Cambridge: Cambridge University Press.
Crystal, D. 2003: English as a global language. Cambridge et al.: Cambridge University Press. 2nd ed.
Davies, A./C. Elder 2004: The Handbook of Applied Linguisitcs. Maiden, MA et al.: Blackwell.
De Bruyne, J. 1993: Spanische Grammatik. Tübingen: Niemeyer.
Declerck, R./S. Reed 2001: Conditionals. A comprehensive empirical analysis. Berlin/New York: Mouton de Gruyter.
Delahunty, G. 2012: An analysis of The thing is S sentences. Pragmatics 22:1. 41–78.
Dewey, M. 2007: English as a lingua franca and globalization: an interconnected perspective. International Journal of Applied Linguistics 17:3. 332–354.
Dewey, M. 2010: English as a lingua franca: Heightened variability and theoretical implications. A. Mauranen,/E. Ranta (eds.): English as a lingua franca. Studies and findings. Newcastle upon Tyne: Cambridge Scholars Publishing. 60–83.
Dresemann, B. 2007: Receptive multilingualism in business discourses. J. D. ten Thije/L. Zeevaert (eds.): Receptive Multilingualism [Hamburg Studies on Multilingualism 6]. Amsterdam/Philadelphia: John Benjamins. 179–193.
Eastwood, J. 1994: Oxford Guide to English Grammar. Oxford: Oxford University Press.
Edmondson, W./J. House 1981: Let's talk and talk about it. A pedagogical interactional grammar of English. München: Urban/Schwarzenberg.
Ehlich, K. 1979: Verwendungen der Deixis beim sprachlichen Handeln; linguistisch-philologische Untersuchungen zum hebräischen deiktischen System. Frankfurt am Main: Lang.
Ehlich, K. 1992: HIAT – a Transcription System for Discourse Data. J. Edwards/M. Lampert (eds.): Talking Data – Transcription and Coding in Discourse Research. Hillsdale: Erlbaum. 123–148.
Ehlich, K./J. Rehbein 1972: Zur Konstitution pragmatischer Einheiten in einer Institution: Das Speiserestaurant. D. Wunderlich (ed.): Linguistische Pragmatik. Frankfurt/M.: Athenäum. 209–254.

Ehlich, K./J. Rehbein 1976: Halbinterpretative Arbeitstranskriptionen (HIAT). Linguistische Berichte 45/76. 21–46
Ehlich, K./J. Rehbein 1977: Wissen, kommunikatives Handeln und die Schule. H.C. Goeppert (ed.): Sprachverhalten im Unterricht. München: Fink. 36–114.
Ehlich, K./J. Rehbein 1979: Erweiterte Halbinterpretative Arbeitstranskriptionen (HIAT 2): Intonation. Linguistische Berichte 59. 51–75.
Ehlich, K./J. Wagner 1995: Introduction. K. Ehlich/J. Wagner (eds.): The Discourse of Business Negotiation. Berlin/New York: Mouton de Gruyter. 1–6.
Ehrenreich, S. 2010: English as a business lingua franca in a German multinational corporation. International Journal of Business Communication 47/4. 408–431.
Ellis, R. 1994: The study of second language acquisition. Oxford: Oxford University Press. 4th impression 1996.
Ellis, R. 1997: Second language acquisition. Oxford: Oxford University Press.
Ertel, D. 2000: Turning negotiation into a corporate capability. Harvard Business Review on negotiation and conflict resolution. Boston, MA: Harvard Business School Press. 101–128.
Everitt, B.S./A. Skrondal 1998: The Cambridge Dictionary of Statistics. Cambridge: Cambridge University Press. 4th edition 2002.
Fienemann, J. 2006: Erzählen in zwei Sprachen. Diskursanalytische Untersuchungen von Erzählungen auf Deutsch und Französisch. Münster et al.: Waxmann.
Firth, A. 1990: Lingua franca negotiations: towards an interactional approach. World Englishes 9. 269–280.
Firth, A. 1996: The discursive accomplishment of normality: On 'lingua franca' English and conversation analysis. Journal of Pragmatics 26. 237–259.
Fisher, R./W. Ury 1981: Getting to Yes. Negotiating an agreement without giving in. Glenfield: Random House. 2nd ed. 1991.
Friedman, J. 1998: Dictionary of business terms. Hauppauge, NY: Barrons; 4th edition 2007.
Giles, H./J. Coupland/N. Coupland 1991: Accommodation Theory: Communication, Context, and Consequence. H. Giles/J. Coupland/N. Coupland (eds.): Contexts of Accommodation. New York, NY: Cambridge University Press. 1–68.
Gnutzmann, C. 1999: English as a global language. Perspectives for English language teaching and for teacher education in Germany. C. Gnutzmann (ed.): Teaching and learning English as a global language: native and non-native perspecitves. Tübingen: Stauffenburg. 157–169.
Gnutzmann, C. 2004: Lingua franca and international language. U. Ammon et al. (eds.): Sociolinguistics. An international handbook of the Science of Language and Society. Berlin, New York: de Gruyter. 328–359.
Goffman, E. 1974: Frame analysis: An essay on the organization of experience. Harvard University Press. Reprint 1981.
Graddol, D. 2003: The decline of the native speaker. G. Aderman/M. Rogers, (eds.): Translation today. Trends and Perspectives. Clevedon et al.: Multilingual Matters. 152–167.

Graddol, D. 2006: English next. Why global English may mean the end of 'English as a foreign language'. London: British Council.
Green, M. 2007: Speech acts (revised version 2020). *The Stanford Encyclopaedia of Philosophy.* (https://plato.stanford.edu/entries/speech acts/).
Greenbaum, S./G. Nelson 1996: The International Corpus of English (ICE) project. World Englishes 15/1. 3–15.
Grice, H. P. 1975: Logic and Conversation. H. P. Grice: Studies in the way of words. Reprinted 1989. Cambridge, Mass.: Harvard University Press. 22–40.
Grießhaber, W. 1987: Authentisches und zitierendes Handeln. Band I: Einstellungsgespräche. Tübigen: Narr. Band II: Rollenspiele im Sprachunterricht. Tübingen: Narr.
Grießhaber, W. 2000: Zum Begriff 'Wirtschaftssprache'. Überlegungen und Vorschläge zur Analyse der Fachsprache der Wirtschaft. S. Beckmann/König, P. P./G. Wolf (eds.): Sprachspiel und Bedeutung. Tübingen: Niemeyer. 403–413.
Grießhaber, W. 2001: Verfahren und Tendenzen der functional-pragmatischen Diskursanalyse. Vom Speiserestaurant zum Cybercafé. In: Ivanyi, Z./A. Kertész (eds.) Gesprächsforschung: Tendenzen und Perspektiven. Frankfurt/M. et al.: Lang. 75–95.
Halliday, M. A. K. 1994: An Introduction to Functional Grammar (2nd ed.). London: Arnold.
Halliday, M. A. K., McIntosh, A./P. Strevens 1964: The linguistic sciences and language teaching. London: Longman.
Harvard Business School Press 2000: Harvard Business Review on negotiation and conflict resolution. Boston: Harvard Business School. 77.
Hellyer-Jones, R./P. Lampater, with P. Aston and G. Schindler, 1996: Grammar in Profile. Grammatisches Übungsbuch für die Sekundarstufe II. Stuttgart: Klett. 3rd ed. 2014.
Hidalgo, R. 2002: Establishing topic in conversation: A contrastive study of left-dislocation in English and Spanish. A. Downing/Moya, J./J. I. Albentosa (coordinators): Talk and text. Studies on spoken and written discourse, Cuenca: Ediciones de la Universidad de Castilla-La Mancha. 31–50. (http://www.ucm.es/info/circulo/no11/hidalgo.htm).
Holmes, J./M. Stubbe 2004: Strategic code switching in New Zealand workplaces: Scaffolding, solidarity and identity construction. J. House/J. Rehbein (eds). Multilingual communication. Amsterdam: John Benjamins. 155–78.
Hornby, A. S. 1995: Oxford advanced learner's dictionary of current English. 5th edition. Oxford: Oxford University Press.
Hornby, A. S. 2015: Oxford advanced learner's dictionary of current English. 9th edition. Oxford: Oxford University Press.
House, J. 1999: Misunderstanding in intercultural communication: Interactions in English as lingua franca and the myth of mutual intelligibility. C. Gnutzmann (ed.): Teaching and learning English as a global language: native and non-native perspectives. Tübingen: Stauffenburg. 73–89.
House, J. 2002: Communicating in English as a lingua franca. Eurosla yearbook 2, Amsterdam: Benjamins. 243–261.

House, J. 2002a: Developing pragmatic competence in English as a lingua franca. K. Knapp/C. Meierkord (eds.): Lingua franca communication. Frankfurt/M.: Peter Lang. 245–267.

House, J. 2003: English as a lingua franca: A threat to multilingualism? Journal of Sociolinguistics 7/4 2003. 556–578.

House, J./J. Rehbein 2004: What is multilingual communication? J. House/J. Rehbein: Multilingual communication. Amsterdam: John Benjamins. 1–17.

Hüllen, W. 1992: Identifikationssprachen und Kommunikationssprachen. Über Probleme der Mehrsprachigkeit. Zeitschrift für Germanistische Linguistik 20 (3). 298–317.

Hülmbauer, C. 2007: 'You moved, aren't?' – The relationship between lexicogrammatical correctness and communicative effectiveness in English as a lingua franca. VIEWS (Vienna English Working Papers) 16/2. 3–35. (www.univie.ac.at/Anglistik/views.html).

Intemann, F. 2005: Taipei ground, confirm your last transmission was in English...? - an analysis of aviation English as a world language. C. Gnutzmann/F. Intemann (eds.): The globalisation of English and the English language classroom. Tübingen: Narr. 71–88.

Jackson, F. (ed.) 1998: Mind, Method and Conditionals. Selected Essays. London: Routledge.

Jenkins, J. 1998: Rethinking phonology in teacher education. VIEWS (Vienna International English Working Papers) 7(1). 40–46.

Jenkins, J. 2000: The phonology of English as an international language. Oxford: Oxford University Press.

Jenkins, J. 2003: World Englishes. New York: Routledge.

Jenkins, J. 2006: Current Perspectives on Teaching World Englishes and English as a Lingua Franca. TESOL Quaterly 40, Vol. 1, 2006. 157–181.

Jenkins, J./Modiano, M./B. Seidlhofer. 2001: Euro-English. English Today 68, 17/4. 13–19.

Kachru, B. 1985: Teaching World Englishes. Indian Journal of Applied Linguistics 15/1. 85–95.

Kachru, B. 1989: Teaching World Englishes. Indian Journal of Applied Linguistics. Vol. 15/1. 85–95.

Kachru, B. 1991: Liberation linguistics and the Quirk concern. English Today 7 Vol. 1. 3–13.

Kachru, B. 1996: English as lingua franca. U. Ammon et al.: Sociolinguistics. An international handbook of the science of language and society. Berlin: M. de Gruyter, Vol. 2. 906–913.

Kahane, H./R. Kahane 1976: Lingua Franca: The story of a term. Romance Philology 30:1. 25–41.

Kellerman, E. 1989: The imperfect conditional. K. Hyltenstam/L. Obler (eds.): Bilingualism across the lifespan: aspects of acquisition, maturity and loss. Cambridge: Cambridge University Press. Reprint 1994. 87–115.

Klein-Brayley, C./U. Raatz 1984: A survey of research on the C-Test. Language Testing 1, Issue 2. 134–146.

Klimpfinger, T. 2007: 'Mind you, sometimes you have to mix' – The role of code-switching in English as a lingua franca. VIEWS (Vienna International English Working Papers) 16(2). 36–61.

Knapp, K. 1998: English als Fachsprache in internationalen Institutionen des 20. Jahrhunderts. L. Hofmann/Kalverkämper, H./H. E. Wiegand with C. Galinski and W. Hüllen (eds.): Fachsprachen – languages for specific purposes. Ein Handbuch zur Fachsprachenforschung und Terminologiewissenschaft. Vol. 1. Berlin: de Gruyter. 840–849.

Knapp, K. 2002: The fading out of the non-native speaker: A case study of unco-operative lingua franca communication. K. Knapp/C. Meierkord (eds.): Lingua franca communication. Frankfurt: Lang. 217–244.

Kortmann, B./E. W. Schneider 2004: Handbook of Varieties of English, Berlin: Mouton de Gruyter.

Krashen, S. D. 1981: Second Language Acquisition and Second Language Learning. Oxford: Pergamon.

Kratzer, A. 2012: Modals and Conditionals. Oxford: Oxford University Press.

Leech, G. 2014: The pragmatics of politeness. Jericho: Oxford University Press.

Leech, G./J. Svartvik 2002: A Communicative Grammar of English. Harlow/London: Pearson Education Ltd. 3rd edition.

Lesznyák, A. 2004: Communication in English as an international lingua franca. An exploratory case study. Norderstedt: Books on Demand.

Levelt, W. J. M. 1989: Speaking – from intention to articulation. Cambridge, MASS: Massachusetts Institute of Technology Press.

Levinson, S.C. 1979: Activity Types and Language. Linguistics, 17, 365–399.

Lewicki, R./A. Hiam 2006: Mastering business negotiation. A working guide to making deals and resolving conflict. Hoboken, N. J.: Jossey-Bass.

Liberman, A. 2007: Do it real quick, or: the death of the adverb. Oxford Ethymologist (http://blog.oup.com/2007/08/adverb).

Little, P. 1970: Communication in business. London: Longman. 3rd ed. 1978.

Loos, E. 2000: Language choice, linguistic capital and symbolic domination in the European Union. Language problems and language planning, 24/1, Spring 2000, 37–53.

Maaß-Sagolla, S. 2010: Small, middle and professional talk. Frankfurt/Main: Peter Lang.

Mair, C. 2013: The World System of Englishes. Accounting for the transnational importance of mobile and mediated vernaculars. English World-Wide, 34(3), 253–278. (https://doi.org/10.1075/eww.34.3.01mai)

Marlos, E. 1981: Why answer? A goal-based analysis of a speech event. D. Sankoff/H. Cedergren (eds.): Variation Omnibus. Carbondale, Ill.: Linguistic Research Inc.

Mauranen, A. 2003: The corpus of English as lingua franca in academic settings. TESOL Quarterly 37/3. 515–527.

Mauranen, A. 2006: Signaling and preventing misunderstanding in English as lingua franca communication. International Journal of the Sociology of English 177. 123–150.
Mauranen, A. 2006a: Discourse Reflexivity – A Discourse Universal? The Nordic Journal of English Studies 5 (2). 13–40.
Mauranen, A. 2012: Exploring ELF. Cambridge: Cambridge University Press.
McArthur, T. 1992: Oxford concise companion to the English language. 3rd ed 2005. Oxford: Oxford University Press.
McArthur, T. 2002: The Oxford Guide to World English. Re-published 2003. Oxford: Oxford University Press.
McArthur, T. 2003: Oxford Guide to World English. Oxford: Oxford University Press.
Meeuwis, M. 1994: Nonnative-nonnative intercultural communication: An analysis of instruction sessions for foreign engineers in a Belgian company. Multilingua 13 (1/2). 59–82.
Meierkord, C. 1996: Englisch als Medium der interkulturellen Kommunikation. Frankfurt: Lang.
Meierkord, C. 1998: Lingua Franca English: Characteristics of successful non-native-/non-native-speaker discourse. EESE (Erfurt Electronic Studies of English) 7/98. (http://www.uni-erfurt.de/eestudies/eese/artic98/meierk/7_98.html).
Meierkord, C. 2002: 'Language stripped bare' or 'linguistic masala'? Culture in lingua franca communication. In Knapp, K./C. Meierkord 2002: Lingua franca communication. Frankfurt et al.: Lang. 109–133.
Meierkord, C. 2005: Interactions across Englishes and their lexicon. C. Gnutzmann/F. Intemann (eds.): The globalization of English and the English language classroom. Tübingen: Narr. 89–104.
Meierkord, C. 2012: Interactions across Englishes. Linguistic choices in local and international contact situations. Cambridge: Cambridge University Press.
Meierkord, C. 2019: Attitudes towards exogenous and endogenous uses of English: Uganda's judgement of English structures in varieties of English. International Journal of English Linguistics 10:1. (https://doi.org/10.5539/ijel.v10n1p1).
Meierkord, C./B. Dresemann 2009: Handreichung zum Modul *Lingua Franca Kommunikation in der Entwicklungszusammenarbeit*. Bad Honnef: InWent.
Meierkord, C./K. Knapp 2002: Approaching lingua franca communication. K. Knapp/C. Meierkord (eds.): Lingua franca communication. Frankfurt/M.: Lang. 9–28.
Ministerium für Schule und Weiterbildung des Landes Nordrhein-Westfalen 2007: Kernlehrplan für den verkürzten Bildungsgang des Gymnasium – Sekundarstufe I (G 8) – in Nordrhein-Westfalen Englisch. Frechen: Ritterbach. (https://www.schulentwicklung.nrw.de/lehrplaene/lehrplan/18/gym8_englisch.pdf).
Modiano, M. 2006: Euro Englishes. B. Kachru/Kachru, Y./C. L. Nelson (eds.): The handbook of world Englishes. Malden et al.: Blackwell. 223–239.
Mollin, S. 2005: The Institutionalization of Euro-English? Form and Function of an Emerging Non-Native Variety of English in Europe. PhD-Thesis, University of Freiburg.

Mollin, S. 2007: New variety or learner English? Criteria for variety status and the case of Euro-English. English World-Wide 28:2. 167–185.
Murphy, R. 1985: English grammar in use. Cambridge et al.: Cambridge University Press. 2nd edition 1994.
Neeley, T. 2012: Global business speaks English. Harvard Business Review May 2012. (https://hbr.org/2012/05/global-business-speaks-english).
Noll, V. 1999: Die mediterrane lingua franca. N. Greiner/Kornelius, J./G. Rovere (eds.): Texte und Kontexte in Sprachen und Kulturen. Festschrift für Jörn Albrecht. Trier: Wissenschaftlicher Verlag Trier. 219–227.
Oaksford, M./N. Chater 2010: Cognition and conditionals. Probability and logic in human thinking. Oxford: Oxford University Press.
Pennycook, A. 2000: English, politics, ideology: From colonial celebration to post-colonial performativity. T. Ricento (ed.): Ideology, politics and language policies: Focus on English. Philadelphia: Benjamins. 107–119.
Phillipson, R. 1992: Linguistic imperialism. Oxford: Oxford University Press.
Pienemann, M. 1998: Language processing and second language development: Processability Theory. Amsterdam: John Benjamins.
Pitzl, M.-L. 2005: Non-understanding in English as a lingua franca: examples form a business context. VIEWS (Vienna International English Working Papers) 14(2). 50–71.
Pölzl, U./B. Seidlhofer 2006: In and on their own terms: the habitat factor in English as a lingua franca interactions. In: International Journal of the Sociology of Language 177 (2006). 151–176.
Pons 2010: Das große Handbuch Spanisch. Stuttgart: Pons.
Prince, E. 1981: Topicalisation, focus-movement and Yiddish-movement: A pragmatic differentiation. Proceedings of the 7th Annual Meeting of the Berkeley Linguistics Society. 249–264.
Prodromou, L. 2007: Is ELF a variety of English? English Today 90, Vol. 23:2. 47–53.
Proshina, Z. G. 2005: Intermediary translation from English as a lingua franca. World Englishes 24 (4). 517–522.
Quirk, R. 1990: Language varieties and standard language. English Today 6, Issue 1. 3–10.
Ranta, E. 2006: The 'attractive' progressive – why use the –ing form in English as a lingua franca? Nordic Journal of English studies 5 (2). 95–116.
Ranta, E. 2010: Syntactic features of spoken ELF – learner language or spoken grammar? A. Mauranen/E. Ranta (eds.): English as a lingua franca. Studies and findings. Newcastle upon Tyne: Cambridge Scholars Publishing. 84–106.
Ranta, E. 2013: Universals in a universal language? Exploring verb-syntactic features in English as a lingua franca. Academic Dissertation. Tampere: University of Tampere.
Redder, A. 1992: Funktional-grammatischer Aufbau des Verb-Systems im Deutschen. L. Hoffmann (ed.): Deutsche Syntax. Ansichten und Aussichten. (IdS-Jahrestagung 1991) Berlin: de Gruyter. 128–154.
Rehbein, J. 1977: Komplexes Handeln. Elemente zur Handlungstheorie der Sprache. Stuttgart: Metzler.

Rehbein, J. 1995: International sales talk. K. Ehlich/J. Wagner (eds): The discourse of business negotiation. Berlin/New York: Mouton de Gruyter. 67–102.

Rehbein, J. 2003: Matrix-Konstruktionen in Diskurs und Text. N. Baumgarten/C. Böttger/ M. Motz/J. Probst (eds.): Übersetzen, Interkulturelle Kommunikation, Spracherwerb und Sprachvermittlung – das Leben mit mehreren Sprachen. Festschrift für Juliane House zum 60. Geburtstag. Zeitschrift für Interkulturellen Fremdsprachenunterricht [Online], 8(2/3). 1–24. (http://www.ualberta.ca/~german/ejournal/Rehbein1.htm).

Rehbein, J./J. Fienemann 2004: Introductions. Being polite in multilingual settings. J. House/J. Rehbein (eds.): Multilingual Communication. Amsterdam, Philadelphia: Benjamins. 223–278.

Schneider, E. 2007: Postcolonial English. Varieties of English Around the World. Cambridge: Cambridge University Press. (https://doi.org/10.1017/CBO9780511618901).

Schuchardt, H. 1909: Die Lingua franca. Zeitschrift für Romanische Philologie 33. 441–461.

Searle, J. 1969: Speech Acts. Cambridge: Cambridge University Press.

Seidlhofer, B. 2001: Closing a Conceptual Gap: The Case for a Description of English as a Lingua Franca. International Journal of Applied Linguistics 11. 133–158.

Seidlhofer, B. 2004: Research Perspectives on teaching English as a lingua franca. Annual Review of Applied Linguistics 24. 209–239.

Seidlhofer, B. 2005: Englisch als Lingua Franca und seine Rolle in der internationalen Wissensvermittlung. Ein Aufruf zur Selbstbehauptung. S. Braun/K. Kohn (eds.): Sprache(n) in der Wissensgesellschaft. Proceedings der 34. Jahrestagung der Gesellschaft für Angewandte Linguistik. (forum Angewandte Linguistik 46). Frankfurt et al.: Peter Lang. 27–45.

Seidlhofer, B. 2005a: Standard future or half-baked quackery? Descriptive and pedagogic bearings on the globalization of English. C. Gnutzmann/F. Intemann (eds.): The Globalization of English and the English language classroom. 159–173.

Seidlhofer, B. 2005b: Englisch als Lingua Franca und seine Rolle in der internationalen Wissensvermittlung. Ein Aufruf zur Selbstbehauptung. S. Braun/K. Kuhn (eds.): Sprache[n] in der Wissensgesellschaft. Proceedings der 34. Jahrestagung der Gesellschaft für angewandte Linguistik. Frankfurt/M. et al.: Lang. 27–45.

Seidlhofer, B. (ed.) 2006: Controversies in applied linguistics. Berlin: Cornelsen.

Seidlhofer, B./A. Breiteneder/M.-L. Pitzl 2006: English as a lingua franca in Europe: challenges for applied linguistics. Annual Review of Applied Linguistics 26. 3–34.

Smith, L. E. 1983: English as an international language. No room for linguistic chauvinism. L. E. Smith (ed.): Readings in English as an international language. Oxford/New York: Pergamon.

Svartvik, J./G. Leech 2006: English: One Tongue, many voices. New York: Palgrave Macmillan.

Swan, M. 1995: Practical English Usage. Oxford: Oxford University Press.

Swan, M. 2016: Practical English Usage. 4th, fully revised edition. Oxford: Oxford University Press.

Swan, M./B. Smith 2001: Learner English. Cambridge University Press.

Tannen, D. 1979: What's in a frame? Surface evidence for underlying expectations. R. Freed (ed.): New directions in discourse processing. Norwood, NJ. Ablex. 137–181.

ten Thije, J. D. 2007: De verbo dicendi zeggen. A. Redder (ed): Diskurse und Texte. Festschrift für Konrad Ehlich zum 65. Geburtstag. Tübingen: Stauffenburg. 305–319.

Thomas, J. 1983: Cross-cultural pragmatic failure: Applied Linguistics 4. 91.112.

Tracy, B. 2013: Negotiation in business. New York: Amacom.

Traxel, O./B. Dresemann 2010: Collect, calibrate, compare: A practical approach to estimating the difficulty of C-Test items. R. Grotjahn (ed.): Der C-Test: Beiträge aus der aktuellen Forschung/The C-Test: Contributions from current research. Frankfurt/Main: Lang. 57–69.

Varonis, E. M./S. Gass 1985: Non-native/non-native conversations: A model for negotiation of meaning. Applied Linguistics 6 (1). 71–90.

Wagner, J. 1995: What makes a discourse a negotiation? K. Ehlich/J. Wagner (eds.): The discourse of business negotiation. Berlin/New York: Mouton de Gruyter. 9–36.

Wagner, J./A. Firth 1997: On discourse, communication and (some) fundamental concepts in SLA research. The Modern Language Journal 81/3. 285–300.

Whinnom, K. 1977: Lingua Franca: Historical Problems. A. Valdman (ed.): Pidgin and Creole linguistics. Indiana: Indiana University Press. 295–310.

Widdowson, H. 1997: EIL, ESL, EFL: global issues and local interests. World Englishes 16/1. 135–146.

Wittgenstein, L. 1958: Philosophical Investigations. Oxford: Basil Blackwell.

Zeevaert, L./J. ten Thije 2007: Introduction. Receptive Multilingualism. Linguistic analyses, language policies and didactic concepts. J. ten Thije/L. Zeevaert (eds.): Receptive Multilingualism: Linguistic analyses, language policies and didactic concepts. 3–21.

MEHRSPRACHIGKEIT

HERAUSGEGEBEN VON WILHELM GRIESSHABER UND JOCHEN REHBEIN

BAND 1

Katharina Meng, Jochen Rehbein (Hrsg.)
KINDLICHE KOMMUNIKATION – EINSPRACHIG UND MEHRSPRACHIG
2007, 480 S., br., 29,90 €, ISBN 978-3-8309-1188-3

BAND 9

Karen Schramm
L2-LESER IN AKTION
2001, 560 Seiten, 35,90 €, E-Book 978-3-8309-6082-9

BAND 11

Petr Bednarský
DEUTSCHE UND TSCHECHISCHE PRÄPOSITIONEN KONTRASTIV – AM BEISPIEL VON *AN*, *AUF* UND *NA*
1999, 220 Seiten, 22,90 €, E-Book 978-3-8309-6102-4

BAND 12

Larysa Tarasevich
DIMENSIONALE PRÄPOSITIONEN
2003, 174 Seiten, 22,90 €, E-Book 978-3-8309-6277-9

BAND 13

Bernd Meyer
DOLMETSCHEN IM MEDIZINISCHEN AUFKLÄRUNGSGESPRÄCH
2004, 250 Seiten, 22,90 €, E-Book 978-3-8309-6297-7

BAND 14

Shinichi Kameyama
VERSTÄNDNISSICHERNDES HANDELN
2004, 244 Seiten, 26,90 €, E-Book 978-3-8309-6366-0

BAND 16

Waltraut Timmermann
TEMPUSVERWENDUNG IN CHINESISCH-DEUTSCHER LERNERSPRACHE
2005, 304 Seiten, 26,90 €, E-Book 978-3-8309-6485-8

BAND 17

S. Cigdem Sagin Simsek
THIRD LANGUAGE ACQUISITION
2006, 166 Seiten, 22,40 €, E-Book 978-3-8309-6604-3

BAND 18

Jutta Fienemann
ERZÄHLEN IN ZWEI SPRACHEN
2006, 312 Seiten, 26,90 €, E-Book 978-3-8309-6576-3

BAND 19

Edgardis Garlin
BILINGUALER ERSTSPRACHERWERB
2008, 518 Seiten, br., 39,90 €, ISBN 978-3-8309-1730-4

BAND 20

Konrad Ehlich, Antonie Hornung (Hrsg.)
PRAXEN DER MEHRSPRACHIGKEIT
2006, 196 Seiten, 22,40 €, E-Book 978-3-8309-6731-6

BAND 21

Alexandra Eberhardt
DIE SPRACHLICHE UMSETZUNG NEUER TECHNOLOGIEN IM FRANZÖSISCHEN
2007, 240 Seiten, 22,40 €, E-Book 978-3-8309-6854-2

BAND 22

Katharina Böttger
DIE HÄUFIGSTEN FEHLER RUSSISCHER DEUTSCHLERNER
2008, 230 Seiten, br., 29,90 €, ISBN 978-3-8309-1979-7

BAND 23

Karen Schramm, Christoph Schroeder (Hrsg.)
EMPIRISCHE ZUGÄNGE ZU SPRACHERWERB UND SPRACHFÖRDERUNG IN DEUTSCH ALS ZWEITSPRACHE
2009, 219 Seiten, br., 27,90 €, ISBN 978-3-8309-2220-9

BAND 24

Erkan Özdil
CODESWITCHING IM ZWEISPRACHIGEN HANDELN
2010, 236 Seiten, 22,30 €, E-Book 978-3-8309-7287-7

BAND 25

Pere Comellas, Conxita Lleó (Hrsg.)
RECERCA I GESTIÓ DEL MULTILINGÜISME / MEHRSPRACHIGKEITSFORSCHUNG UND MEHRSPRACHIGKEITSMANAGEMENT
2010, 314 Seiten, 23,90 €, dt. u. katal.
E-Book 978-3-8309-7325-6

BAND 26

Claudia Benholz, Gabriele Kniffka, Elmar Winters-Ohle (Hrsg.)
FACHLICHE UND SPRACHLICHE FÖRDERUNG VON SCHÜLERN MIT MIGRATIONSGESCHICHTE
2010, 204 Seiten, br., 24,90 €, ISBN 978-3-8309-2323-7

BAND 27

Michael de Jong

DAS KONZEPT DER MENTALITÄT IM SPRACHLICHEN HANDELN

2010, 246 Seiten, 26,90 €, E-Book 978-3-8309-7361-4

BAND 28

Susanne Lippert

SPRACHUMSTELLUNG IN BILINGUALEN FAMILIEN

2010, 352 Seiten, 26,90 €, E-Book 978-3-8309-7338-6

BAND 29

Alexandra Wojnesitz

„DREI SPRACHEN SIND MEHR ALS ZWEI"

2010, 244 Seiten, 22,40 €, E-Book 978-3-8309-7411-6

BAND 30

Lirim Selmani

DIE GRAMMATIK VON *UND*

2012, 278 Seiten, 26,90 €, E-Book 978-3-8309-7550-2

BAND 31

Galia Datcheva

***MAL*, *WOHL* UND IHRE BULGARISCHEN ENTSPRECHUNGEN**

2011, 274 Seiten, 40,40 €, E-Book 978-3-8309-7551-9

BAND 32

Susanne Prediger, Erkan Özdil (Hrsg.)

MATHEMATIKLERNEN UNTER BEDINGUNGEN DER MEHRSPRACHIGKEIT

2011, 240 Seiten, br., 32,90 €, ISBN 978-3-8309-2602-3

BAND 33

Yazgül Şimşek

SEQUENZIELLE UND PROSODISCHE ASPEKTE DER SPRECHER-HÖRER-INTERAKTION IM TÜRKISCHDEUTSCHEN

2012, 328 Seiten, 26,90 €, E-Book 978-3-8309-7633-2

BAND 34

Catherine Nanjala Agoya-Wotsuna

DIE SPRACHSITUATION KENIAS ALS VORAUSSETZUNG FÜR DIE VERMITTLUNG DES DEUTSCHEN ALS FREMDSPRACHE

2012, 336 Seiten, 31,99 €, E-Book 978-3-8309-6488-9

BAND 35

Elmar Winters-Ohle, Bettina Seipp, Bernd Ralle (Hrsg.)

LEHRER FÜR SCHÜLER MIT MIGRATIONSGESCHICHTE

2012, 336 Seiten, br., 29,90 €, ISBN 978-3-8309-2733-4

BAND 36

Marine Lalayan

DEUTSCHSPRACHIGE HOCHSCHULKOMMUNIKATION IN ARMENIEN

2013, 312 Seiten, 39,90 €, E-Book 978-3-8309-7917-3

BAND 37

Angelika Redder, Julia Pauli, Roland Kießling, Kristin Bührig, Bernhard Brehmer, Ingrid Breckner, Jannis Androutsopoulos

MEHRSPRACHIGE KOMMUNIKATION IN DER STADT

2013, 242 Seiten, br., 34,90 €, ISBN 978-3-8309-2965-9

BAND 38

Gulsum Massakowa

REZEPTIVE MEHRSPRACHIGKEIT IN DER INTERTÜRKISCHEN KOMMUNIKATION

2014, 392 Seiten, 35,99 €, E-Book 978-3-8309-8185-5

BAND 39

Jule Böhmer

BILITERALITÄT

2015, 392 Seiten, br., 34,90 €, ISBN 978-3-8309-3253-6

BAND 40

Daniela Rotter

DER FOCUS-ON-FORM-ANSATZ IN DER SPRACHFÖRDERUNG

2015, 234 Seiten, br., 34,90 €, ISBN 978-3-8309-3253-6

BAND 41

Michaela Kuchenreuther

EIN ZWEISPRACHIGES WÖRTERBUCH KONSULTIEREN

2015, 242 Seiten, 29,90 €, E-Book 978-3-8309-8317-0

BAND 42

Olga Fekete

KOMPLEXITÄT UND GRAMMATIKALITÄT IN DER LERNERSPRACHE

2016, 256 Seiten, br., 34,90 €, ISBN 978-3-8309-3391-5

BAND 43

Erkan Gürsoy

KOHÄSION UND KOHÄRENZ IN MATHEMATISCHEN PRÜFUNGSTEXTEN TÜRKISCH-DEUTSCHSPRACHIGER SCHÜLERINNEN UND SCHÜLER

2016, 242 Seiten, br., 34,90 €, ISBN 978-3-8309-3394-6

BAND 44

Philip Bracker

DIE ENTSTEHUNG ETHNISCHER IDENTITÄT BEI ‚MENSCHEN MIT TÜRKISCHEM MIGRATIONSHINTERGRUND'

2017, 288 Seiten, br., 39,90 €, ISBN 978-3-8309-3580-3

BAND 45

Gülşah Mavruk

MICROTEACHING IN DER UNIVERSITÄREN LEHRERAUSBILDUNG

2018, 328 Seiten, br., 39,90 €, ISBN 978-3-8309-3653-4

BAND 46

Diana Maak, Julia Ricart Brede

WISSEN, KÖNNEN, WOLLEN – SOLLEN?!

2019, 326 Seiten, br., 39,90 €, ISBN 978-3-8309-3088-4

BAND 47

Angelika Redder, Meryem Çelikkol, Jonas Wagner, Jochen Rehbein

MEHRSPRACHIGES HANDELN IM MATHEMATIKUNTERRICHT

2018, 436 Seiten, br., 44,90 €, ISBN 978-3-8309-3849-1

BAND 48

Heike Roll, Heike Roll, Markus Bernhardt, Christine Enzenbach, Hans E. Fischer, Erkan Gürsoy, Heiko Krabbe, Martin Lang, Sabine Manzel, Işıl Uluçam-Wegmann

SCHREIBEN IM FACHUNTERRICHT DER SEKUNDARSTUFE I UNTER EINBEZIEHUNG DES TÜRKISCHEN

2019, 238 Seiten, br., 29,90 €, ISBN 978-3-8309-4088-3

BAND 49

Tanja Sterling

BILITERALITÄT IM SPANNUNGSFELD VON PERSÖNLICHER IDENTITÄTSBILDUNG UND INSTITUTIONELLER SPRACHENFÖRDERPOLITIK

2021, 306 Seiten, br., 34,90 €, ISBN 978-3-8309-4258-0

BAND 50

Esin Işıl Gülbeyaz

SCHRIFTSPRACHERWERB UND MEHRSPRACHIGKEIT

2020, 378 Seiten, br., 44,90 €, ISBN 978-3-8309-4610-6

BAND 51

Tülay Altun

DAS OSMANISCHE REICH IN SCHÜLERVORSTELLUNGEN UND IM GESCHICHTSUNTERRICHT DER SEKUNDARSTUFE I UND II

2021, 566 Seiten, br., 49,90 €, ISBN 978-3-8309-4328-0

BAND 52

Heike Roll, Markus Bernhardt, Christine Enzenbach, Hans E. Fischer, Claudia Forkarth, Erkan Gürsoy, Heiko Krabbe, Martin Lang, Sabine Manzel, Işıl Uluçam-Wegmann (Hrsg.)

SCHREIBFÖRDERUNG IM FACHUNTERRICHT DER SEKUNDARSTUFE I

2022, 352 Seiten, br., 39,90 €, ISBN 978-3-8309-4328-0

BAND 53

Seda Yilmaz Wörfel

ADVERBIAL RELATIONS IN TURKISH-GERMAN BILINGUALISM

2022, 268 Seiten, br., 34,90 €, ISBN 978-3-8309-4542-0

BAND 54

Christiane Hohenstein, Antonie Hornung (Hrsg.)

SPRACHE UND SPRACHEN IN INSTITUTIONEN UND MEHRSPRACHIGEN GESELLSCHAFTEN

2022, 416 Seiten, br., 49,90 €, ISBN 978-3-8309-4589-5

BAND 55

Zeynep Kalkavan-Aydın (Hrsg.)

SCHRIFTSPRACHERWERB UND SCHRIFTVERMITTLUNG BEI MEHRSPRACHIGKEIT

2022, 250 Seiten, br., 34,90 €, ISBN 978-3-8309-4439-3

BAND 56

Stefan Sudhoff, Jan D. ten Thije (Hrsg.)

MULTILINGUALISM IN ACADEMIC AND EDUCATIONAL CONSTELLATIONS

2024, 424 Seiten, br., 44,90 €, ISBN 978-3-8309-4788-2